Tourism Administration

TOURISM ADMINISTRATION

Vivek Verma

CENTRUM PRESS
NEW DELHI-110002 (INDIA)

CENTRUM PRESS
H.O.: 4360/4, Ansari Road, Daryaganj,
New Delhi-110002 (India)
Tel: 23278000, 23261597, 23255577, 23286875
B.O.: No. 1015, Ist Main Road, BSK IIIrd Stage,
IIIrd Phase, IIIrd Block, Bengaluru-560085 (INDIA)
Tel: 080-41723429
Email: centrumpress@gmail.com
Visit us at: www.centrumpress.com

Tourism Administration

First Edition, 2012

ISBN 978-93-81293-88-1

PRINTED IN INDIA

Printed at Tarun Offset, Delhi

Contents

Preface

Tourism in real sense is visiting different places by an individual for search of knowledge, to know culture of the various places or it may be business tour. Since the dawn of civilization man in his primitive age began touring.

Today tourism has flourished as a full fledged industry. It is one of the fastest growing and foreign currencies earning industry. Administration is also required for this industry. In the present book we have endeavored to bring everything related to tourism. This book looks at the issues related to tourism administration.

It discusses the purposes of tourism administration and examines the concepts of absorptive capacity and cultural compatibility. It goes on to explore issues about strengthening the capacity of the public sector and problems of malpractice on the part of government officials. The role and scope of tourism administration and the various forms of organization found, are discussed as are questions of decentralization and private sector organizations.

The importance and influence of government and business relationships are also discussed. This book goes on to consider the legal framework for tourism and concludes by describing various international organizations.

Author

1

Introduction

INTRODUCTION

GENERAL CONSIDERATIONS

In most of the countries in the region, tourism is a sector that is not very well defined and whose activities are often included under other sectors in national accounts. However, in Mexico, Central America, and the Caribbean, which are frequently affected by disasters, tourism is a significant sector of the economy because of the foreign currency earnings and employment it generates.

Tourism activities may be grouped together under the following headings:

- Coastal tourism, typical of most of the islands and seafront areas in the Caribbean, Mexico, and Central America, although also found in South American countries;
- Tourism based on natural and historic heritage, commonly found in Mexico, America Central and South America;
- Marine tourism, including yachting, diving, touring on relatively small sail or motor-powered vessels, sport fishing and the like;
- Cruise tourism, traditionally very popular in the Caribbean but also extending to South and Central America in recent years;
- Winter tourism;
- Business travel;

- Family trips to visit friends and relatives; and
- Restaurant operations and activities.

Impact assessment can be dealt with similarly for all tourism activities except for cruise tourism, which generally does not require installations other than port facilities for their operation. In contrast to business travel, which takes place year round, tourism in the region is essentially seasonal as international tourists seek a break from the cold weather prevailing in their countries of origin. Therefore, typical tourism seasons are different for countries in the northern and southern hemispheres.

Another characteristic of tourism is that damage to infrastructure or operations caused by disasters has repercussions on other sectors. Services such as restaurants and taxis that cater to visitors are also affected. The tourist industry attends to the needs of visitors either in their country of origin (domestic tourism) or in other countries (international inbound/outbound tourism).

In general terms, domestic and inbound tourism are normally more affected by a disaster, although residents of the affected country who are planning to travel abroad (outbound tourism) may also be affected. In general, international inbound tourism has increased markedly in Latin America and the Caribbean in recent years in tandem with the industry's sustained growth worldwide. Caribbean economies depend to a high degree on tourism, while Central American economies have experienced tourism growth greater than 5% a year in recent years. Moreover, both the World Tourism Organization and the World Travel and Tourism Council foresee growth rates for the sector of 5% in the Caribbean and between 2% and 10% for the rest of the region.

International inbound tourism generates sizable foreign currency earnings, domestic and foreign investment, male and female employment and tax revenues. The sector is also linked to a wide variety of production chains for both local and imported goods and services, including ground, marine, and air transportation; communications and informatics; financial and business services; commerce; construction; and productive services in general. The sector can also lead to significant imports of goods and services not produced locally. In short, the impact of a disaster on the sector has ramifications for other sectors. Tourism must be sustainable over time, meaning it needs a range of attitudes, behaviours, strategies, plans, laws and regulations in response to economic, social and environmental needs. A comprehensive tourism policy is required to enable an improvement in the country's economic opportunities, which benefit communities and enterprises, and to contribute to personal, social and economic growth for men and women.

TOURISM AND VULNERABILITY

Throughout the region, tourism facilities have sprung up in many destinations without proper planning for ecological and vulnerability concerns. The resulting facilities are often located in hazardous areas due to the absence of environmental management and natural resource land-use regulation, as well as a lack of adequate construction standards or regulatory compliance in hotel infrastructure and related human settlements. To a large degree, tourism depends on the preservation of the environment and of cultural, social, and historical heritage.

Therefore, the effects of disasters can be aggravated if the aspects are not strictly addressed. It is well known that in some areas or regions –such as the Caribbean or Central America– the tourism developments most frequented by international vacationers are highly exposed to natural phenomena with significant hazard risk. The best tourism destinations in the region are frequented by tropical storms and hurricanes, as well as floods and earthquakes.

Although vulnerability varies from one country to another, the fragile nature of the land and marine ecosystems in the region is obvious, as is the lack of suitable environmental management, disaster-aware land-use planning and building standards. Other long-lasting natural phenomena, such as droughts and prolonged eruptions of volcanic ash, can indirectly affect tourism through the national supply chain –

farming and agribusiness, or even access to water for human consumption– or by reducing the comfort foreign tourists experience. When supplies are stressed, the industry may suffer from resentment among a local population denied basic services while foreigners receive privileged treatment. The sector is also exposed to another type of vulnerability related to the volatility of demand. News of a real or potential disaster can prompt immediate cancellation of reservations by foreign tourists and diminish future tourism flows and income for a long time.

SOURCES OF INFORMATION

The tourism sector specialist can use various domestic and international sources to obtain reliable information both on the pre-disaster situation and on the damage caused by the action of the underlying phenomenon.

Domestic information sources includen the following:

- Recent censuses or surveys on tourism spending and stays;
- National statistics offices;
- Information provided by national tourism sector authorities;
- Hotel and tourism associations;
- Tour operators;
- Central banks;
- Port and airport authorities; and
- Insurance companies.

Useful international sources include, among others, the following:

- Central American Tourism Integration Secretariat;
- Caribbean Hotel Association;
- Caribbean Tourism Association;
- International reinsurance companies; and
- World Tourism Organization.

Reviews of the information published by these international bodies and field visits to the aforementioned local institutions will allow the specialist to gather information on the situation both before and after the event.

ESTIMATION OF DAMAGE AND LOSSES

As in other sectors, it is necessary to estimate direct damage to assets and indirect losses in economic flows derived from tourism. Afterwards, it will be necessary to calculate the impact on the main macroeconomic variables (*e.g.*, gross domestic product, foreign accounts and public finances), employment and the differential effect on women.

DIRECT DAMAGES

As a first step in estimating the direct damage to the sector, it is necessary to establish the baseline. This refers to tourism-specific assets that are not included in any other sector, and it requires detailed information on items such as the number and capacity characteristics of several types of stablishments:

- Hotels, by category;
- Guest houses or family-run establishments;
- Cultural and historical attractions;
- Docks and jetties;
- Vessels or transportation vehicles;
- Winter tourism facilities; and
- Restaurants.

The tourism specialist may use such data as a basis for comparison when assessing direct damage to the infrastructure and equipment of the sector. The area affected by a disaster may be superimposed on this baseline as the first step in damage assessment.

Estimating direct damage for the tourism sector is essentially the same as for the housing sector, and what was indicated in that stage will not be repeated here. In the case of tourism facilities, equipment might include water collection and purification works, wastewater collection and treatment plants, electricity generators and large-scale air conditioners. Likewise, any damage to the sector's transportation infrastructure and equipment should be included –docks, leisure vessels and other works– so the tourism specialist must work closely with the transport and communications specialist to make his/her work easier and to avoid double accounting. Moreover, the tourism specialist must make estimates –once again, in close cooperation with the environmental specialist– on the impact on natural resources that make up the tourism environment, such as erosion or silting of beaches. Undoubtedly, these estimates will be specific to the sector in some cases, whereas in other cases cooperation with other sector specialists will be essential. It should be noted that beach erosion is common in the case of tropical storms and hurricanes in the Caribbean and Central America. Nature tends to return the beaches to their pre-disaster condition, but the process may be a lengthy one.

INDIRECT LOSSES

As in the case of direct damage, the tourism specialist must obtain basic information on the pre-disaster conditions for making comparisons against the post-disaster situation.

In this regard, the specialist should obtain the following information for each of the categories of establishments or recreation and tourism transportation equipment:

- Number of rooms, listed by capacity;
- The occupancy rate of each type of room and changes over time (the demand curve);
- Number of restaurants and their capacity;
- Capacity of vessels and average occupancy during the tourism season;
- Employment –by type of job or trade and by se – needed to operate each type of establishment; and
- Volumes of inputs of all types –food, drinks, etc.– that must be imported for the operation of each type of establishment and vessel.

The tourism specialist must estimate, in close consultation with the owners of establishments or trade associations, the time needed for a return to pre-disaster conditions. Such a projection, in conjunction with occupancy and demand-curve data, makes it possible to estimate the loss of income the industry is likely to suffer (*i.e.,* the main indirect losses). The tourism specialist must also consider other types of indirect damage, including the possible cancellation of reservations from abroad and the possible cost of a promotional campaign

reductions in foreign-currency revenue (from the export of services). The tourism sector specialist should estimate such decreases in revenue from abroad. Another heading that the tourism specialist should take into consideration is the possible availability of insurance or reinsurance policies on goods destroyed or damaged in the tourism sector since they can generate an unforeseen inflow of foreign currency. In addition, the rehabilitation and reconstruction of hotel and restaurant infrastructure, and the replacement of their equipment and machinery, might require significant imports, especially if they are not produced in the affected country.

Once again, the tourism specialist must make the corresponding estimates. These calculations should be delivered to the macroeconomics specialist so that he/she can combine them with those of other sectors and determine the overall effect of the disaster on the external sector of the affected country.

Effects on Public Finances

Although the current trend in the region is for tourism sector infrastructure to be privately owned a disaster can have major effects on the finances of an affected state. Indeed, the natural phenomenon may directly affect transportation, port and airport infrastructure (which is normally publicly owned), further diminishing tourism income. However, such estimates of damage to infrastructure are usually taken into consideration in the respective sectors.

The main negative effects on public finances caused in the tourism sector stem from the drop in revenue from taxes and fees paid by , which the country will not collect during a certain period. This loss of state revenue can be estimated on the basis of the drop in hotel demand or occupancy previously estimated as indirect losses.

In addition, the state might be forced to make unplanned outlays to overcome problems in the tourism sector, such as beach and forest path cleaning work, special benefit payments to persons who lose their employment in the sector and so forth. The tourism specialist must make these estimates and provide them to the macroeconomics specialist who, after ensuring that there is no duplication with the information from other sectors, will use them to obtain the total impact of the disaster on public-sector finances.

Effects on Investments

The impact on public or private investment may vary depending on the magnitude of total damage relative to the size of the economy of the affected country or region. The occurrence of a disaster and the subsequent rehabilitation and reconstruction may produce several effects.

First, uncertainty as to the likelihood of hazard prevention and mitigation works may discourage investment decisions and inflows.

Second, public and private investment programmes may be modified and increased to meet the needs of rehabilitation and reconstruction.

Third, the need to replace lost assets may take precedence over projects previously designed to overcome long-standing social shortcomings; the resulting programme postponements and cancellations imply a social cost.

Although these observations are valid for all sectors, the tourism specialist must provide the macroeconomist with all information that can be obtained in this regard, so that he/she may get a clear overview of possible changes in the behaviour of the economy of the affected country.

EFFECTS ON EMPLOYMENT

When tourism activities are reduced, there is a corresponding decrease in the employment and income of men and women working in the sector. A relationship exists between the income generated in the sector and the number of various types of employees with their different income levels.

Therefore, it is possible to estimate job losses in the sector based on the estimates of industry activity and income during and beyond the rehabilitation and reconstruction stage. This loss can be partially compensated by the use of tourism sector workers in cleaning and infrastructure recovery tasks, since both employers and employees wish to ensure that the same labour force will be available once the emergency is behind them and normal tourism activities resume. The tourism specialist should make these estimates in close cooperation with the employment specialist. In very small economies, the labour force available in the construction sector may be insufficient to quickly carry out the reconstruction that hotels require.

In such cases, labour, machinery and equipment have been imported from abroad, and these will not necessarily return to their countries of origin after reconstruction is completed, possibly aggravating pre-existing employment problems.

The tourism specialist must be aware of this type of potential dilemma and quickly report it to the macroeconomics and employment specialists.

THE DIFFERENTIAL IMPACT ON WOMEN

As in other sectors, women's share of tourism is affected by disasters. Tourism facilities and services affected by a disaster may be owned by women; other women might temporarily lose their employment in the industry.

In this regard, the tourism specialist must co-operate closely with the gender and employment specialists to determine three key points:

- Women's share of sector ownership;
- Women's share in the sector's labour force; and
- The possibility of including women in rehabilitation and reconstruction tasks.

The required information may be obtained from censuses, recent household surveys, chambers of tourism statistics and so on.

The results of this analysis must be delivered by the tourism specialist both to the macroeconomist and to the gender specialist, who will be responsible for adding the figures from all sectors to determine the differential impact of the disaster on women at the national level.

ENVIRONMENTAL IMPACT

The methodology for assessing damage to environmental assets and flows in environmental goods and services. Asignificant portion of the tourism industry is based on the environmental services of recreational opportunities and scenic beauty, both in the case of highly intervened environments (usually the case of sun and beach tourism) and the less intervened environment (usually the case of the tourism in protected areas, sometimes called ecotourism).

Therefore, damage assessment in the tourism sector and environmental damage assessment are closely related. In terms of quantification and valuation of damage, two different situations may occur.

Environmental Damages Usually Included in Tourism Sector Assessment

This heading refers to direct damages and indirect losses (loss of natural capital and changes in the flows of environmental goods and services) that are already accounted for in the tourism sector.

Beach loss and degradation, lodging infrastructure damage and drops in revenues that occur during the restoration period are good examples of these losses. The environmental assessment tries to identify the share of these damages corresponding to the contribution of natural capital, isolated from contributions of human capital and other assets such as infrastructure and equipment.

Estimation of this contribution can be made using the economic rent concept (the difference between market prices and production costs). However, it is not easy to estimate this contribution in the tourism sector, except in the cases of fees charged to enter protected areas and taxes used for environmental protection (*e.g.*, additional airport or room taxes that are levied on foreign visitors in certain countries).

To avoid double accounting, these estimates should be included in only one sector (either tourism or environment) in the damage overview.

Separate Quantification and Valuation

This case refers to the valuation of assets and environmental services related to tourism activities that are not accounted for in the tourism sector assessment. Examples include, the valuation of environmental changes in ecosystems relevant to the tourism sector such as forests, coral reefs or damage to emblematic species. These damages should be included in the damage overview, as they have not been considered in the damage assessment of the tourism sector.

2

Communication and Sustainable Tourism

INTRODUCTION

Tourism is one of the world's largest economic sectors and one that continues to expand very rapidly. Done well, tourism development can be a powerful tool for economic growth, poverty reduction, and for the conservation of natural and cultural resources. While tourism represents an important development opportunity for many countries and communities, it can also have very negative impacts, such as disrupting social structures, harming the socio-cultural authenticity of host communities, and threatening natural and cultural heritage. Wise planning and management of tourism development is key to keeping it a force for good.

Tourism is truly cross-sectoral, involving a wide range of issues that can include the following:

- Community and urban planning (land use planning, transportation, etc.)
- Conservation of cultural heritage, protected areas and biodiversity
- Education and workforce development.
- Employment and labour laws
- Enterprise development
- Infrastructure development
- Management of natural resources (water, energy, waste)
- Public-private partnerships

- Safety and security
- Trade and investment policy

There are vast numbers of stakeholders, with their different and sometimes opposing interests and agendas. The multiple stakeholders at both national and local levels must be able to access the information they need to understand their long-term interests, articulate their opinions, identify proposals, and network effectively with one another. Tourism development choices must balance between national and local needs, public and private sector, host communities, civil society, tourists, and mass media.

Political choices, in particular, must reconcile immediate returns and longer-term benefits, which requires a clear and well-defined vision. Sustainable tourism development thus represents a very complex task. Communication has a huge role in supporting sustainable tourism development and managing its multiple dimensions. Communication can create and facilitate a system that allows stakeholders to exchange opinions and arrive at consensual solutions. Effective use of communication tools can also link products to markets, and can contribute to visitors' safe and positive experiences. In a sustainable tourism development scenario, the various stakeholders have not only the right to participate in the decision-making process, but have also the responsibility to adopt environmentally, socially and economically sustainable behaviours and practices. Communication processes can build awareness of this responsibility and persuade stakeholders that sustainable practices ultimately benefit their long-term interests. A comprehensive communication strategy, which should identify how information, awareness creation, advocacy, network building, conflict mitigation, and communication platforms will be supported, is essential for any successful sustainable tourism development activity.

An e-conference addressing the role of communication in sustainable tourism development took place between May 29 and June 9, 2006. The World Bank, the US Agency for International Development (USAID) and the UN World Tourism Organization (UNWTO) envisioned the forum as a means to bring together development practitioners, tourism professionals, decision-makers, academicians and communication specialists representing various national institutions, private sector and media organizations, NGOs, international institutions, and donors active in the field of communication and sustainable tourism to discuss the role that communication can play in designing and implementing sustainable tourism strategies and projects at national and local levels; to share experiences, information and perspectives; to identify and share lessons learned and best practices; and to consolidate knowledge on development communication in sustainable tourism programmes.

Discussions focused on the following topics:

- The role that communication can play in designing and implementing sustainable tourism strategies and projects at national and local levels;
- The importance of sharing experiences, information and perspectives;
- Identification of lessons learned and most effective practices; and
- The exchange of knowledge on development communication in sustainable tourism programmes.

The e-conference was part of the preparation for the World Congress on Communication for Development (WCCD). It consisted of the following five concurrent sessions. The e-conference benefited from the active contribution of more than 700 registered participants from all six continents. A seminar series in was held in Washington, DC, during the summer of 2006 as a follow-on to the e-conference in order to further explore ideas raised in the five sessions. Material from those presentations has been woven into the session summaries that follow.

THE ROLE OF COMMUNICATION IN PLANNING AND IMPLEMENTING SUSTAINABLE TOURISM POLICIES AND STRATEGIES

The Tourism Policies and Strategies session of the econference focused on finding answers and providing examples for the following questions.

- How can one make the best use of conventional communication and consultation techniques (such as forums, meetings, workshops)?
- How can one harness modern technology for effective participatory processes in tourism policies and plans?
- How can conventional and modern techniques be best combined for innovative and effective communication?
- How can the media support tourism policy and planning processes for public information?
- What are the most effective ways of communication to inform stakeholders and the general public?

COMMUNICATION TO INVOLVE STAKEHOLDERS IN DECISION-MAKING

The fact that the tourism sector is multisectoral, and can be very fragmented, was a recurring theme in the discussions. The wide range of stakeholders at both local and national levels having a role in the formulation and implementation of sustainable tourism policies and strategies includes:

- Public authorities in the fields of economy, environment, tourism, transportation, education, culture, etc. (ministries and state departments, their regional and local offices, regional and municipal authorities, etc.);
- Tourism businesses and their associations at the national and local levels (accommodation and catering, tour operators, guides and other service providers);
- Local communities;
- NGOs and civil society groups;
- Academic and research institutions; and
- Media organizations.

Participants agreed that policy and strategy development must be a process where all stakeholders are able to freely express their viewpoints and have their interests taken into account. National and local policies must be coordinated, consensual and responsive to the needs of different stakeholders. Governments have a key role in policymaking and implementation processes, and in this role they must strive to ensure the informed participation of other sectors through consultative processes. Undertaking ample consultations is key to the successful formulation and implementation of tourism policies. In addition, the many different interest groups often hold disparate viewpoints that must be coalesced into a common vision.

MULTI LEVEL STAKEHOLDER INVOLVEMENT IS NEEDED

Participants stressed that effective communication is therefore essential for policy-making and implementation. They agreed that both conventional communication methods (*e.g.*, forums, meetings and workshops) and the application of new technologies (*e.g.*, telecommunication, Internet, e-mails, data bases) are key to developing sustainable tourism policies. The need for governments to create and maintain websites with regularly updated information was stressed, as was the notion that websites should not serve just for tourism promotion purposes, but also to disseminate information on tourism policies and plans. Particular attention to the need for effective communication from the central to the regional and local levels was also emphasized, given that in developing countries the remoteness of some areas and the lack of telecommunication networks hinder both horizontal and vertical communication.

USE OF PUBLIC EVENTS TO PROMOTE TOURISM

Development and institutional processes leading to the design of national and local level tourism policies can benefit from public events supported by political leaders, national and international media, and regional and international organizations. An example was provided from Tanzania, where MIGA, an agency of the World Bank, promoted a tourism investment conference with the Ministry of Tourism. President Mkapa made the opening speech, and also met with individual investors. The Africa Travel Association (ATA) was instrumental in securing interviews on the conference with

BBC, which were broadcast live, and ATA published several objects in their magazine. The local newspapers provided event coverage. The event had some very direct and concrete results: investment agreements were signed and are now being implemented.

The Tanzania example also demonstrated the importance and effectiveness of good post-event follow-up: potential investors were kept informed of progress by e-mail, and the government has attended hotel investment forums to generate greater interest in the country. In addition to international and national institutions, smaller organizations and individual initiatives can also disseminate information and promote cooperation to encourage sustainable tourism practices. In an example supplied about Zambia, a tourism newsletter started by a committed individual gradually became an important source of tourism development information with the support of public and private sector organizations.

Other e-conference participants pointed out that multiple international development and donor organizations often carry out overlapping policy-development and institutional strengthening activities in the same country or area and that improved communication is essential in order to coordinate donor activities, minimize duplication and maximize synergies.

THE INTERNET AS A TOOL FOR CONSULTATION AND INFORMATION TRANSFER

With growing numbers of users and improving access worldwide, the Internet is an increasingly important tool for stakeholder consultation and information transfer. In Australia, the Tourism White Paper Implementation Plan 2004 was launched by the Minister for Small Business and Tourism, and refined through on-line consultation with key tourism industry stakeholders, Australian Government departments and state and territory government. A large volume of stakeholder input was received and incorporated into the planning process. The list of organizations that participated in the consultation and their input was made public on the website of the Department of Industry, Tourism and Resources, together with an advanced strategy draft that incorporated the different views. The Internet is also a key tool for information-sharing and exchange of experiences on tourism policies. DestiNet, a new initiative of the European Environment Agency was cited as a good example. The information resource and communications platform contains selected, quality assessed information on the ways in which tourism is being made more sustainable. DestiNet offers a number of services including the option to post news bulletins and suggest new links on relevant topics.

It acts as a single European-level gateway to environmental sustainability for the tourism sector, allowing users to:

- Understand and report on sector impacts on the environment;
- Learn how to improve tourism sector sustainability;
- Coordinate information exchange between tourism stakeholders.

ADVOCACY

Many developing countries are looking to tourism development to solve their economic problems. For many of them, their natural and cultural heritage represents one of their few economic resources. Natural and cultural heritage are, however, not renewable and tourism must be addressed in a sustainable way to prevent irreversible degradation to the resources that draw tourists to a country.

Unfortunately, developing countries frequently experience some difficulty in planning and promoting sustainable tourism policies. Politicians are often guided by the necessity to achieve rapid and visible results during their tenure. Choices about tourism development policies and strategies are too often dictated by the necessity to satisfy immediate needs: sustaining balance of payments, creating new jobs to reduce unemployment, etc. However, tourism development projects producing immediate benefits (revenue generation and job creation as examples) may turn out to be negative in the long term if they threaten natural and cultural heritage. Civil society and mass media organizations can assume the role of watchdogs to ensure that tourism policies and strategies are beneficial both for local communities and for the conservation of natural resources and cultural heritage. An extended dialogue developed under the discussion topic "Advocacy for sustainable tourism policies," focusing on the role of education and awareness-raising activities.

Various messages stressed the need to integrate sustainable tourism policy issues in school curricula in different types of education programmes related to tourism management and planning, including vocational and technical schools as well as universities. It was also suggested that sustainability issues need to be incorporated into a general education curriculum in order to ensure that future generations of tourists are sensitive to environmental and social concerns when engaging in touristic activities. It was subsequently noted that, while education in schools and academic institution is critical, awarenessraising activities about sustainable policy issues should also target public officials and business persons.

Suggested communication tools for awareness-raising among stakeholders include seminars and workshops, internships/mentor relationships with leaders of successful programmes in other communities, and Web forums to share lessons learned from other experiences. NGOs can have a key role in awareness-raising activities targeting public authorities. In Bulgaria, the Foundation for Local Government Reform, an NGO specializing in supporting local governments, used specific tools such as newsletters, workshops, training, and grant schemes to educate mayors and their administrations and the municipal councils about the benefits of sustainable tourism. The same foundation helped to facilitate the local process during development of the National Ecotourism Strategy and Action Plan.

TRAINING AND KNOWLEDGE MANAGEMENT

Some participants stressed "tourism knowledge management" as a key factor to be considered in all countries, suggesting that universities and schools of tourism and professional studies should be involved in collective actions. A lack of specific academic and training resources is at the root of many problems with unsustainable tourism development. Tourism portals, however, fail to provide regularly updated calendars of events with descriptions of courses and instructors.

Also, participants should be able to rate their instructors and some sort of public evaluation should occur after six to twelve months.

COMMUNICATION AND LOCAL COMMUNITIES IN SUSTAINABLE TOURISM DEVELOPMENT

COMMUNICATION AND COMMUNITY INVOLVEMENT IN TOURISM PLANNING AND MANAGEMENT

One of the key principles of sustainable tourism is that the local population is placed at the center of tourism development interventions in terms of participation in the decision-making process and benefit sharing. It is at the community level where tourism impacts are mostly keenly felt, conservation challenges must be met and culture is most affected.

Residents living in historic centers, near archaeological sites or close to natural protected areas can play a key role in the conservation of those resources if they can derive benefit from them. Several econference participants therefore stressed the importance of community involvement and active participation in sustainable tourism development as one key to success. Among the principal challenges that participants mentioned related to community involvement:

- Frequent changes in local government (both policies and personnel)
- Lack of government support
- Conflicting interests between groups (between government and religious groups, and between communities and big hotel owners or oil companies, for example)

- Lack of funds
- Late attempts to involve local communities
- Lack of commercial skills at the local level
- Too many different actors (NGOs, donor agencies, government, etc.) often engaged in well-intentioned but under-funded projects that are not coordinated with other efforts
- Failure to consider the whole tourism system of a country or region and not taking into account demand for tourism products
- Communication gap between communities and the private sector.

Communication tools mentioned as effective ways to involve local communities in tourism development included training; participatory workshops; community, group and individual meetings; local radio; school newsletters; and local events. Community leaders are an important communication channel. Another issue that frequently surfaced in discussion was the need to consider tourism as a business, and community members as businesspeople.

Community-based tourism projects should therefore be focused on market demand. This implies a need for professionalism in the tasks required to start a business such as: a business feasibility study, business administration, hospitality, marketing strategy, development of IT marketing tools, market analysis, etc. Communities generally need support to carry out successful tourism development initiatives.

Technical experts however, must simply provide expertise, experience and advice, and act as facilitators to help local communities make informed decisions and build their own strategy. This means supporting consultative processes within a community to allow the different segments of the population (women, for example) to express their opinions. Toot Oostveen, of SNV stated that consultants should first identify the kind of consultancy and support the community wants to receive. Signing a contract between the community and the consulting organization can be one way to enhance the sense of ownership within a community. Community workshops are an important way to identify problems and concerns, and to determine available options before decisions are made and actions taken. Workshops can also be used to introduce communities to new topics such as marketing techniques, or to design project proposals which will be used to seek out funding.

The Internet was often mentioned as an important tool to put local tourism micro-enterprises into direct contact with the global market of travellers. Some participants stressed that it is essential to gain the trust of local communities prior to any productive interaction with them. Others pointed out the need to avoid making communities dependent on development workers.

Capacity-building, ownership and empowerment are important to the community management and long-term sustainability of tourism enterprises. Finally, participants stressed the obvious, but often neglected, necessity for consultants and other outside entities to consider culture, beliefs and traditions in tourism planning, and to avoid preconceptions while listening and facilitating participatory processes.

RELATIONSHIP BETWEEN COMMUNITIES AND THE PRIVATE SECTOR

Many participants described a communication gap between the private sector (especially outside investors) and local communities, feeling that the private sector is not prepared to communicate with communities because it requires more time and patience than most business people are willing to invest.

They identified a contradiction between fast business processes and slow community processes. These different perceptions, different assumptions and different priorities, as well as mistrust and a lack of willingness to collaborate, can generate misunderstandings between the private sector and local communities. Another issue raised in the e-conference was that communities are often not considered (and don't consider themselves) to be a component of the private sector. However, the moment they enter into the tourism business they become part of the private sector and need to adopt a business-related point of view. This was the experience of William Tuffin, who is working to develop community eco-tourism in Laos.

Methods of overcoming barriers mentioned by e-conference participants included awareness-raising activities and dialogue between businessmen and communities to aid in understanding different points of views, opinions and interests. Time, trust, transparency, and creative thinking are essential for identifying common ground, common interests and potential shared benefits. As one of the e-conference participants remarked, "Who should be responsible for supporting the local communities in undertaking a profitable tourism business? It is a question to consider in each situation."

INVESTMENT AND MARKETING

If government or public donors are not supporting a community tourism initiative, communities need to find creative ways to access financing. Sponsorship might be one option for community tourism. An example was given of the BC Aboriginal Tourism Association in which sponsors have their corporate name affiliated with the Association and see value in the exposure they receive from financing specific activities. Mike Robbins presented another example in the financing of a cultural ecolodge, where an association received funds from the British and Canadian Air Force, a mining company and a private foundation.

In the case of Great Bear Rainforest in British Columbia, combining large scale nature conservation within First Nation traditional territory has been key to forging a link between private sector funds and communities. One element of these historic land use agreements has been the creation of the "Coast Opportunities Funds," a conservation-financing programme developed through a remarkable collaborative process involving First Nations, environmentalists, philanthropists, and government representatives. Establishing this programme required a decade of negotiation, again highlighting the length of time some processes need. One of the biggest issues facing all community tourism projects in remote locations is marketing – creating awareness and stimulating interest in widely dispersed geographic market areas. In May 2006, the Lonely Planet travel publishers produced "Code Green – Experiences of a Lifetime".

The focuses on unique experiences with an emphasis on minimizing environmental and social impact and maximizing connections with local people. Publications like this should help with encouraging travellers to dig further into less publicized tourism opportunities. One example of a private/ public sustainable tourism partnership is now underway in Clarendon Parish, Jamaica. "Clarendon Express" is a partnership between a wide variety of stakeholders from the private sector, the Jamaican government, environmental NGOs, a protected area, local hotels, the Chamber of Commerce, and others. Jamalco is collaborating with national and international partners to convert an industrial train route into a tourism train that links the sea to the mountains with diverse visitor opportunities along the way. Communication activities to encourage involvement and collaboration between stakeholders were important to the success of this initiative.

FALSE EXPECTATIONS

It is necessary for local communities to realise that sustainable tourism development is not a panacea, and that hard work is required to receive any benefit. The community must approach tourism as any other business that involves risks. They need sufficient information and capacity to assess and mitigate these risks. They also need to realise that they are service providers who are in a long chain of interdependent tourism-related businesses and they need to be familiar with the other actors. Unrealistic expectations can be reduced through frequent and detailed communication amongst all stakeholders. Capacitybuilding training and equity in tourism benefits can also build the trust of communities and reduce false expectations.

INAPPROPRIATE BEHAVIOUR OF TOURISTS

Many e-conference participants felt that the best way to inform tourists about appropriate behaviour in host countries is to reach them prior to travel via guidebooks. Many books already incorporate a stage on responsible travel. Other channels that are important vehicles for carrying information to a wide range of tourists (for instance those traveling in organized tours) include travel agencies, Internet sites and magazines.

However, travel magazines and travel narration too often present destinations just as tourism products, forgetting that people with other cultures and sensibilities live there. Some e-conference participants stressed the need to analyze visitors' perceptions of destinations to identify potential problems and recommend awareness activities for addressing inappropriate behaviour, minimizing tourism impacts on the local culture and enhancing relations with local communities.

ROLE OF COMMUNICATION IN PROMOTING CORPORATE SOCIAL RESPONSIBILITY IN SUSTAINABLE TOURISM DEVELOPMENT

The notion of CSR is not new, but its adoption and integration into the tourism industry is in very early stages, voluntary and largely spearheaded by the ecotourism movement. However, the adoption and endorsement of the basic principles of sustainable tourism that address the new paradigm of triple bottom line assessment has steadily grown over the last decade – although it is undeniable that the major focus has been on environmental protection and conservation rather than addressing social issues such as labour standards. This theme is also present in many of the voluntary sustainable tourism certification programmes – many of which are considered valuable instruments to encourage and facilitate CSR.

The thrust of CSR in the mainstream (mass) tourism industry is accused of being largely environmental, the skeptics say, simply because environmental management systems help reduce costs (through minimization of potable water and energy use, and reduction of waste) or are perceived as a potential selling point (green sells). Philanthropy by major tourism players also is another element of CSR that has been adopted to varying degrees, becoming more accepted and even expected, although largely as ad hoc gestures of goodwill. However, CSR in the tourism industry is not simply about potential environmental savings, certification programmes or philanthropy – it is increasingly being considered by enlightened corporations and individuals as the only way to ensure long term sustainability, and often leads to better businesses with increased profitability.

There are many in the business community who see CSR not as a "luxury" that is indulged in when and where resources allow – but as a fundamental tool to doing business well, and hence one that needs to be built into strategies to ensure risk management and reputational enhancement. The e-conference participants' contributions certainly clarified the need for increased communication about and for CSR in tourism. Communication has to take place at all levels between and amongst the different stakeholders.

A regulatory framework is needed not only to facilitate "seamless" communication but also to create common grounds and a common understanding of some of the sustainability issues and the potential of CSR to enhance business viability and longevity. The case for adopting CSR in tourism needs to be better communicated in language appropriate to the various stakeholders. Communication was considered essential to:

- Help tourism businesses and consumers (tourists) understand and adopt relevant environmental and social sustainability standards and systems (certification, guidelines, environmental management systems, fair trade, community relations and outreach, etc.);
- Help tourism businesses that are adopting appropriate CSR principles and relevant standards in being rewarded by increased business; and
- Create better links among large tourism operators, local communities, and small and medium enterprises to develop win-win partnerships.

LACK OF AN INTERNATIONALLY RECOGNIZED DEFINITION OF CSR

A large part of the e-conference discussion concentrated on different perceptions and definitions of sustainable tourism and corporate social responsibility. Despite a multitude of definitions by several international and national institutions, tourism enterprises, non-governmental organizations (NGOs) and individuals, there is no coherent and internationally recognized definition framework just as to which CSR activities can be structured or scrutinized.

The lack of an internationally recognized definition of CSR leads to a range of obstacles for communication on CSR between stakeholders. Many companies misunderstand sustainable management or CSR as simply "philanthropy", "charitable giving", or "humanitarian aid," etc., rather than using sustainable management to improve their local business context (*e.g.* community relations and outreach projects, environmental management, good social standards for employees, local purchasing options, etc.). On the other hand, there were also a number of participants who argued against one univocal standard or definitive "definition" for CSR. Given the diversity of cultures, differently sized operations (mass vs. small and medium enterprises [SMEs]), and the multitude of business types (*e.g.* accommodation, flight, tour operation, etc.) in the tourism sector, using one set of standards, may, just as tc the Global Reporting Initiative (GRI), be limiting and might prove to be inadequate.

STAKEHOLDER IDENTIFICATION

Participants highlighted that, to their knowledge, there isn't one preferred, or leading organization that is necessarily the only or even the most successful model to communicate about and help with mainstreaming CSR principles and practices. Instead, they believe that there is a need to facilitate more widespread and transparent communication on CSR at all levels. Therefore all possible stakeholders need to be identified and held to account for spreading the principles of sustainable development.

Aside from the industry, consumers and NGOs, these include:

- Certification and standards-setting organizations
- Governmental organizations
- Intermediaries.

The government was most often identified by the participants as the stakeholder responsible for creating the appropriate framework environment to encourage and ensure successful and transparent communication on CSR.

Appreciating the current structures of the tourism business and its sales structure, two additional stakeholders were identified as important intermediaries and ambassadors for sustainable development and CSR:

- Sales staff (*e.g.* travel agents, sales & marketing, inbound operators)
- Media.

A study on marketing certified products recently completed by The International Ecotourism Society (TIES) concluded that "green" tourism certification programmes can get the "biggest bang for the buck" by marketing to intermediaries such as tour operators, guide books and the media, rather than directly to consumers. These intermediaries can, in turn, market directly to consumers.

With time, as certification programmes grow in size and spread to more countries (*i.e.*, a critical mass develops), and as more tour operators use and promote certified products, consumer awareness and demand is likely to grow. While critics of certification often cite the current lack of consumer demand as a reason why it will not work, TIES would argue that, based on lessons learned from other industies, consumer demand takes a long time to grow and is best built through certification programmes targeting and convincing intermedaries such as tour operators/wholesalers.

The e-conference highlighted that, in many cases, individuals who have credibility both from the personal and professional point of view might become successful communicators on CSR, and could recruit high profile "mentors" that support and encourage others to become proponents of CSR. The identification of charismatic leaders who would be able to win the minds of small entrepreneurs was suggested as a possible strategy. A potential threat would be that communication would be then limited to individually perceived and defined issues rather than incorporating the real needs of all stakeholders.

CERTIFICATION AND STANDARDS

Certification and standards were identified by the participants as the current most effective option for actively supporting and guiding CSR processes on the individual company level. In the (self-proclaimed) sustainable tourism industry, the development of standards and voluntary certification that provide some form of "guarantee" of sustainability standards is common, but widespread adoption and use of these standards is unfortunately still rare.

Consumer surveys are confusing, for although they often proclaim a general willingness to pay a premium for products that demonstrate a commitment to sustainable tourism practices, only a small percentage of consumers appear to seek these products or understand much about what appropriate environmental, social or cultural standards are. "Green" tourism certification standards certainly measure and seek to mitigate the negative environmental, social, and cultural impacts of tourism businesses.

Some even seek to increase the positive impacts of tourism through ensuring "fair" economic returns to the local community or environment, or even attempt to empower indigenous peoples. Certifying tour operators and hotels facilitates mainstreaming of CSR and sustainable management practices in the tourism industry and serves not only as a relatively easy way for consumers (tourists) to identify "responsible" and "ethical" product, but communicates CSR and other important issues both B2B and to other stakeholders. Certification programmes and their standards can serve to effectively communicate an in-depth review or insight through their criteria into the large range of issues that affect sustainable tourism development – and whether a tourism enterprise actually proceeds to certification or not, the programmes serve to raise awareness. At the same time, certification organizations help consumers preferentially choose responsible products.

COMMUNICATION WITHIN THE INDUSTRY REGARDING CSR TOOLS AND MEASURES

With regards to communication within the tourism industry, e-conference participants highlighted various different issues that should be addressed to support the incorporation of CSR principles and tools among tourism businesses (*i.e.* in particular small and micro businesses). Suggestions included:

- Obtain a clear understanding of the capacity gaps;
- Ensure that CSR tools and examples are adapted to take into account the knowledge, capacity and the culture of the countries to which CSR modules are transferred adopting "adaptive management" practices;
- Create a clear and univocal understanding of what CSR means (*i.e.* clarifying that integrating CSR principles and practices would mean going beyond simplistic and basic philanthropic activities);
- Maximize the participation of local communities in defining what CSR means at the local level to go beyond a simple ecolabel. Community-based organizations and NGOs at the local level are seen as very "good intermediaries" to promote a local interpretation of general CSR frameworks; and
- Joint and cooperative work on CSR in tourism through networks like the Tour Operator Initiative (TOI), who are contributing to a vital exchange on CSR practices between the large tourism players.

Participants appeared to feel that the industry had not yet fully embraced CSR as there was a lack of understanding on what it was and how it might help their business. There was certainly a perception that there was a lack of common understanding about the "business case" of CSR in the tourism industry. The willingness to pay more for responsible and ethical operators by a growing number of customers is not yet evident in the mass tourism sector, despite surveys that declare a growing percentage of customers demand more responsible products and are willing to pay more for a certain "feelgood factor" (when hearing that their stay or purchase helps local community, local labour, local environment, etc.). It was felt that this "special" customer was largely confined to niche market segments, which are smaller in size, more transparent and easier to be recognized as such at the individual consumer level.

COMMUNICATION OF CSR TO TOURISTS

With regards to communication from tourism enterprises to their consumers, two key points were expressed by the participants:

- Demand from consumers for CSR and sustainable tourism was seen as an essential communication tool to steer companies towards more responsible practices. Socially responsible purchasing and ethical purchases were concepts proposing that the mind-shift towards more sustainable products has to take place on both the producers' and consumers' end. The difficulty in that consumers did not necessarily preferentially choose products that demonstrated CSR needs to be addressed, but there was an agreement from some participants that these responsible or more ethical businesses tended to "do" better and were more likely to be considered quality products: businesses that take of their environment are perceived to be more likely to also take care of their customers.
- There was mention of the need to ensure end users' participation in the formulation of the tools. This will ensure the 'buy-in' of target audiences from the outset.

In summary, Session 3 discussions identified the need for:

1. Increased communication about and for CSR in tourism, at all levels between and amongst the different stakeholders;
2. A regulatory framework to facilitate communication and common understanding of CSR; and

3. Communication to various stakeholders to make a stronger case for adopting CSR in tourism.

THE ROLE OF COMMUNICATION IN LINKING SUSTAINABLE TOURISM PRODUCTS TO MARKETS

This session of the e-conference centered on discussions around the following questions:

- What is the role of modern technologies, like e-business and e-marketing techniques? How can they help to improve market access to small businesses and reduce marketing costs?
- Advertising Spots, Slogans, and Reality – How do we promote sustainable tourism without telling lies?
- How can communication help increase the share of local products and services that supply the tourism industry, enhancing linkages between conventional tourism and the local economy?
- What are the experiences and lessons learned with collective marketing initiatives, grouping together smaller tour operators and service providers?
- Which communication methodologies and technologies can small businesses in developing countries use to learn about their markets?
- What are the best strategies to target travel publications and influence them to cover sustainable destinations?

TOURISM PRODUCTS MUST BE DEMAND-DRIVEN AND RESPOND TO THE EXPERIENCES AND NEEDS OF TOURISTS

The world is littered with tourism products that failed because they did not take market demand into consideration, did not reach their markets with adequate information, or did not provide a means for their markets to reserve/purchase their products. Today there is a wide range of marketing and promotion techniques available, supported by rapidly evolving communication technology, but the application of these techniques and technologies is still very limited in tourism, especially in developing countries. Tourism functions through a complex supply chain that links a wide range of services from the generating markets to the final destinations. Communication is key to enhancing the information flow along this supply chain and ensuring that sustainable tourism initiatives and products eventually reach potential tourists that may be thousands of miles away.

To collect market intelligence, Richard Tuck (a tourism expert currently working in Nicaragua), suggested that micro, small and medium enterprises (MSMEs) in developing countries should be interacting (simple questionnaires or one-on-one interviews) with the tourists that are already at the locale. Questions should be directed at finding out what the tourists liked/disliked, how they arrived, how they first heard about the locale, whether or not they would recommend the locale and why/why not, where they were from, age, sex, etc. Open-ended marketing-oriented questions such as what else visitors would have liked to experience at the locale and what they would change about the locale should also be included. This will help tourist enterprises determine not only who their target market is but also how to communicate to them and what to communicate.

To learn how to expand into secondary and tertiary markets MSMEs should then seek out academic institutions and NGOs that work in sustainable tourism and, more importantly, visit the tourist areas nearest to them and learn about what tourists (outside their target market) are demanding. Simon Jones (International Institute of Tourism Studies of the George Washington University) pointed out that it may be difficult for local operators to carry out visitor surveys, and that they need to organize themselves in larger networks of similar businesses to have greater opportunities to learn from one another and gather information about their clients.

Chris Seek (Solimar International) provided an example of a USAID tourism project in Romania where a local Destination Management Organization (DMO) is learning how to create visitor surveys, track website hits and page views, track information requested at information centers and, most importantly, how to analyze this information and provide it to association members as a tangible membership benefit. The project is also creating a back-end "members only" part of the destination portal that will be used to share this information. The next task will be to educate members on how to use this market research to improve/adapt their product to meet the market demand.

Providing the Unique Experience

Metilde Wendenbaum (ECEAT) reminded participants that the most important thing that the tourists demand from "exotic" small scale suppliers is a unique experience, *i.e.*, something they do not expect yet or demand. The strength of a small-scale supplier lies in the fact that they can make a personal connection to the guest.

Methods to strengthen this personal connection are:

- Creating experiences that the guests will never forget;
- Keeping a record of the guests in order not to forget them;
- Remaining in touch with them after their visits by sending a periodic (e-mail) card.

Word-of-mouth promotion should also not be underestimated. To effectively use this communication tool, businesses can give guests discount cards that they can pass to their friends. In this way, suppliers can also estimate the effectiveness of word of-mouth promotion.

Learning through Study Tours

Samar Hammad (craft sector in Jordan) suggested that MSMEs and Micro businesses could gain valuable advice and training by leaving their local destination and observing how other destinations offer tourism products and services. Through the interaction with other MSMEs and tourists, business owners will be able to understand how to apply "what works in other destinations" to their own. Study tours, however, should be used with caution. Richard Tuck provided an example of NGOs that, along with government sponsorship, brought small-scale coffee producers, tour operators, and tourism providers from Nicaragua to Costa Rica over the past ten years.

Some negative outcomes in this experience included:

- Reinforcing a culture of "Costa Rica is better, is greener, is ..." in the minds of Nicaraguans;
- Errors that Costa Rican tourism businesses make on a daily basis were transferred to the MSMEs in Nicaragua; and
- Views of reality on pricing and promotion were skewed. The pricing and promotion that occurs in Costa Rica for tourists to Costa Rica cannot be the same in Nicaragua because tourism and tourists there are different.

ADVERTISING SPOTS, SLOGANS AND REALITY

Tourism marketing often uses images of pristine landscapes that promise the opportunity to experience the "Dream Vacation" with respect to the natural environment. How can a tourism marketing campaign show the unique differences of these destinations instead of making them all look the same? How do travellers learn how to see past the perfect images to understand the reality of the destination being visited?

Robin Goldberg (Lonely Planet) reminded e-conference participants that the only thing that lovely pictures and fancy slogans do is pique interest. But curious, smart, thoughtful travellers will never stop at the picture. With the proliferation of information, no traveller is going to base his/her travel decisions on a fancy ad or campaign slogan. Travellers are smart and want to make the most of their travel dollars... and for that they are willing to do some research. At best, a good ad campaign can intrigue someone enough to dig further. The key to marketing a special, unique travel gem is to be certain that it can be found when the traveller starts to search through independent travel sources. This reinforces the importance of reviews, referrals and word-of-mouth storytelling by those who have first-hand experience.

There is nothing like a third-party endorsement which is given without any commercial interest on the part of the endorser. Great examples of this include editorials published by respected media, placement in trusted guidebooks, candid reviews by fellow travellers found in multiple web forums. Travellerss are looking for honest, practical information from trusted sources, and that will drive their travel choices.

INCREASING THE SHARE OF LOCAL PRODUCTS AND SERVICES THAT SUPPLY THE TOURISM INDUSTRY

One of the reasons why tourism is such an important industry for international development is the opportunity for growth in supporting sectors. Communication plays a critical role in linking the tourism industry with supporting sectors but requires careful facilitation.

Roberta Hilbruner (USAID) provided an example of how in Northern Mozambique tourist destinations have to import their fresh vegetables and fruits because local farmers do not grow a wide variety of produce. Good facilitation between hoteliers, restaurants, farmers and extension activities can help farmers understand this market and begin to raise produce to meet the demand, increasing the local benefits from tourism. Len Cordiner described how in Cambodia the tourism industry relies on imports for most of their agriculture products and cited quality, quantity, delivery (reliability), and convenience (including payment terms) as reasons for sourcing elsewhere. This problem also extends to other local products including furnishings.

Len recommended two things that need to be addressed to help overcome these issues:

- Building Capacity–NGOs, development agencies, and local governments must work with local suppliers to build their capacity to produce the product that is demanded by the industry; and
- Building Demand–helping the tourism industry understand that sourcing local products can help build demand for their business.

To increase demand for local products, Robin Goldberg stressed the need to help travellers understand how their dollar can make a difference and that only by asking the hard questions will travellers show businesses that these issues are important to them.

In Sierra Leone, where 90% of all food is imported due to the conflicts of the civil war, Megan Epler Wood, working with the National Hotel and Tourism Training Institute, is launching a "food enterprise" programme that includes a food enterprise training course that will be made available to local farmers. Rather then trying to train the local farmers in how to produce everything the hotels need, the project is focusing on one product – fruit salad – that can be easily prepared and packaged for delivery with minimumcost.

The project has been very well received by local hotels and is set to expand further. Mike Robbins (a tourism marketing expert) reminded participants about research that suggests that there is a very large proportion of the North American traveller market that would be receptive to education and awareness about making locally grown organic food choices.

Whatever term one uses to describe these tourists, whether it is "geotourists," "ecotourists" or responsible tourists, they represent a growing segment of the overall traveller market. Choosing locally grown organic food in the destinations they visit can make a huge difference both environmentally and economically. Communication with visitors in the destination to enable informed food choices is key.

Labeling as a Communication Tool

Emanuele Santi (Communication Officer with the World Bank), citing an example from the World Bank Butrint (Albania) Community-Based Tourism Project, stressed the importance of labeling local food products to help tourists understand that by purchasing such products, they are also contributing to local development and, when the label is linked to a protected area, to broader conservation goals. A good label can increase the "value" of the products.

COLLECTIVE MARKETING INITIATIVES

For MSMEs in developing countries, collective marketing is a huge asset. Hendrik Wintjen (SNV Netherlands Development Organization – Peru), in the past years, joint marketing initiatives have been multiplying (*e.g.*, Costa Rica) in order to face the lack of action taken by national authorities. The national tourism chambers, hotel associations and tour operator organizations formed twenty or thirty years ago didn't react in time to the growth of long-haul tourism to developing countries. Nowadays people travel to places that were not on the tourism map a few decades ago, obliging any destination to focus on market realities in the most important source markets. Joint marketing campaigns are defined as: (1) a new organization taking over some of the promotional and sales activities of individual suppliers; and (2) individual suppliers grouped under a common quality brand that is used next to the individual brand. Joint marketing campaigns may have various elements in common: a destination, type of products, and level of quality (including sustainability). These collective marketing campaigns can generate both positive and negative reactions from the participants. The first reaction can be distrust towards the other supplier partners involved, and in the umbrella organization. This reaction is understandable given that suppliers lose some control over ownership of the new brand and over distribution of the profits that are made by the umbrella organization.

However, experiences show that a new brand is not always perceived as a threat vis à vis replacing individual brands. On the contrary, it sometimes strengthened each individual brand/supplier, as it stimulated a competition between the suppliers who responded best to the quality criteria of the new brand. For example in Guadeloupe, six years ago, a quality brand "recommended by the National Park" has been designed for grouping all sustainable ecotourism suppliers located in and around the National Park. Another good example is the joint marketing launched by five Costa Rican hotels under the brand "Small Distinctive Hotels" – they market the five hotels like one entity, present only products of high quality, and are continuously improving the sustainability of their products.

Chris Seek sums up some possible reasons for a program's failure:

- The programme is not owned/managed by local stakeholders with an intimate knowledge of the products. Too often – especially in developing countries –joint marketing programmes are created by outsiders or "someone with a website" in order to make money in the short term.
- The programme is run by an individual or small group of local stakeholders who are working only to further their own interests and leadership position.
- The individuals doing the marketing are not from the culture of the target market.
- The programme collects annual membership dues rather than working on a commission basis, but fails to provide a return on this investment.

Demonstrating tangible programme benefits to the members is key to any collective marketing programme.

Benefits include the following:

- Suppliers spend less money in marketing because they share the total cost of the marketing action.
- They can share in the promotion's innovative ideas and knowledge about their products.
- They can be more visible as a group in the e-commerce world.
- They will attract the attention of a larger public.
- They will prevent overloading tour operators and other distribution channels with a plethora of promotional messages about products located in the same region.

INTERNET IN THE SUSTAINABLE TOURISM PROMOTION

Role of Tourism Boards

It appears that tourism boards are at present very ill-equipped to deal with sustainable tourism in their Internet promotion activities. For example, national tourism portals should do a better job of updating directories for traveller services. The Catalan Tourism Board could be a model. They provide regular updates about sustainable products on their website and post e-mails about sustainable tourism matters through strategic distribution lists.

One e-conference participant remarked that an absolute condition for better performance of tourism boards was better education of staff regarding issues of sustainability. Sustainability has penetrated curricula in universities and higher professional education, but not at lower educational levels.

Role of Internet in Enhancing Reputation and Building Brand

Many examples of "self purifying" marketing or promotion were shown, especially for communitybased tourism. Travellers might not see all the behind- the-scenes activities of a business, so it is important to share practices with them. However, dishonest, or cliché marketing messages very quickly backfire as they are identified by knowledgeable travellers who have an amazing ability to judge real commitment versus green-washing.

WHL (World Hotel Link), has grouped self-declared "sustainable products" under a "Caring for the Destination" banner. "It's really about connecting the best of local with the best of global that will win the day" . Tom Hall (Lonely Planet) added that "Reputation within market can be as strong a force as individual or collective certification. Sustainable products can rely on Internet marketing with certificates on such reputation." Metilde Wendenbaum (ECEAT Projects) stated that sustainability logos or "banners" can be a very distinctive method to add quality in Internet marketing. But for large operators like big-scale hotels, self-declaration for sustainability still needs to be accompanied by a third party certification. While small-scale suppliers can communicate much more effectively about sustainability, and achieve trust among their clients, they do not often use this to advantage yet. ECEAT Projects uses the Internet for online data storage of sustainable products and tour operators that can be used by partners all over the world as basis for their marketing activities.

It can also be accessed by outbound tour operators who are looking for new products. The products are "certified" (hotels) or "recommended" (community-based tourism, small-scale tourism) by internationally trusted environmental or development organizations. Ron Mader also mentioned that certification should be much more holistic in its approach and, if we are to judge individual operators and hotels, we should also review tourism officials, academics, NGOs and international institutions including World Bank, UNEP and UNWTO. Valere Tjolle (Totem Tourism) suggested that marketing in general has been revolutionized by the Internet. Instead of suppliers selling through agencies, businesses can offer their services directly to an international market.

Without large monetary investments, small businesses can perhaps profit from the Internet through "buzzing campaigns" in which e-mail messages "buzz" around on their own to specific Internet communities with the invitation to add news. After a certain period, contents are published to all recipients. There are not yet many examples of buzzing campaigns in sustainable tourism.

Valere invites experimentation with this. His "Totem news", an e-mail distribution to thousands of sustainable tourism stakeholders, is such an Internet tool but is directed to policymakers. Participants asked the question, "Can we expect smallscale sustainable companies to be so creative?" Large companies such as Nike are able to pay numerous young "field researchers" to identify the newest and hottest trends, but this seems out of reach for small scale tourism enterprises. Alternatively, do we want a kind of "tourism Nike" with an explicit statement of corporate social responsibility? A warning against the self-purifying principle of Internet marketing must be raised concerning large scale "sustainable" products. Relative to small-scale community-based tourism products, large hotels need to invest much more to reach a certain level of sustainability. At the same time however, they have the ability to present their first, small investments as something trustworthy or "sustainable" (like the Hilton "We Care" programme).

Do Internet communities represent strong enough consumer knowledge to prevent green-washing? Finally Zachary Rozga and René Schärer caution against over-emphasizing the current potential of the Internet as a direct marketing tool for community-based tourism because of the large "digital gap" that still exists between the "developed" and "developing" worlds.

STRATEGIES TO TARGET TRAVEL PUBLICATIONS

The travel media is one of the most important vehicles in tourism marketing, providing unbiased reviews and authors' first-hand experiences of a destination. Often driven by experienced public relations firms and large budgets, most of the travel media is focused on the traditional tourism industry. The following are participants' tips for unknown sustainable tourism destinations or businesses in how to capture the interest of travel publishers.

- Promote the destination, not a specific business or development Project: Editors care only about what readers want to read. As interesting as your project or business may be, editors want to know about the destination. Why would a reader want to visit? What is the appeal?
- Focus on the experience: Read through any travel publication and you will notice that the author is not talking about the facts of the trip – they are focusing on the visitor experience. What makes the destination unique? Help the editor imagine the view at sunset or taste the traditional meal with a local family.
- Use a light hand with the "sustainability" language: Even though we all know how important this is - don't ignore the first two points and forget that editors want to know about the destination and the experience first. If a tour company is helping local communities

wonderful! It's ok to include this, but don't write the entire press release about it. Stay focused on the experience and the destination.

- They can't write about it if they don't know about it: Don't be afraid to send editors information and story ideas. Ideally, these should be reviewed by a writer with at least some experience in drafting press releases, but if you don't send the information how are they going to know about it?
- Target specialty publications: Everyone thinks of the big travel publications when trying to target the media – but there are hundreds of other publications that are always searching for story ideas. In a project in Panama focusing on the Camino de Cruces trail along the Panama Canal, someone on the project team wrote a full article about the use of mules by the Spaniards to haul gold along the trail and how visitors can walk the trial and find mule footings. They submitted the article to a mule magazine and it was published in its entirety.
- Press trips work: While some of the larger publicationsdo not take free or reduced cost press trips, many other writers would jump at the opportunity to cover a story and experience the destination. But don't invite a group of journalists from different interests on one group tour. They each want to see different things and more than likely no one will get to see what he or she specifically wants to cover.

Tom Hall from Lonely Planet's London office remarked that ethical living is a major obsession in the UK, with travel being one of the standard-bearers for the movement. Newspapers like the Guardian and the Times have weekly travel supplements, which have either regular columns on this subject or seemingly weekly special issues.

Whether it's camping or ecolodges, it seems the British public can't get enough of this subject. Newspapers want one thing – to sell more papers. So, to make this work, there needs to be demand from readers. Remembering what the public wants to read is a key to success. The audience should be considered at all times.

Robin Goldberg pointed out that any publication (whether newspaper, magazine or guidebook) is looking to point the traveller to great travel experiences. If a business (ideally, a sustainable business...but truly any business) wants to get coverage, the key is to offer something spectacular, let the media know about it, and then deliver above and beyond expectations.

Metilde Wendenbaum suggested that when publishing a guide for small-scale suppliers, it might be worthwhile to link up with mainstream publishing houses. Metilde provided an example from the European Centre for Eco Agro Tourism, which published the "Green Holiday Guide Europe" together with the Dutch Touring Club ANWB.

ORIENTING VISITORS AND INTERPRETING TOURISM DESTINATIONS

ORIENTATION

Orienting visitors to a destination is important both before they arrive and after they have arrived onsite. Orientation includes practicalities such as directional, local transportation, safety, event, and business information (for example, restaurant location, hours, menu, and price range).

Orientation can also include basic background information that visitors should be aware of – local customs, responsible environmental behaviour, basic history and geography, and best ways to learn more about the place. As one participant stated, "Travellers expect to find helpful directions.

Private and public operations understand that repeat visitation depends on making a good first impression! Effective signage demonstrates a commitment to improved communication among locals and travellers. Signage (signs, posters, bulletin boards, highway markers, and restaurant menus, brochure racks) educates and minimizes confusion.

Whether maintaining national parks or establishing information kiosks or visitor centers, the best facilities are proactive, keeping travel information up-to-date and acquiring materials from local businesses."

INTERPRETATION

Every potential tourism destination has its own story and character. Capturing, interpreting, and presenting that story are the essence of sustainable "place-based" tourism. It is this flavour that defines a location. From product branding to visitor opportunities, resources and services, this is the "gel" that binds the experience together.

As such, its elements and many manifestations have real economic value. This same interpretive effort can also serve local communities as an educational tool, reinforcing heritage and social norms. Interpretation is therefore not solely a tool to "brand" a specific destination. It is also an activity that creates the image that a specific territory and community will disseminate among visitors and that will contribute to community education, pride and sense of place.

The importance of involving local communities in building their image and in sharing their culture with visitors was stressed by many participants in the e-conference. The importance of presenting or communicating local cultures to visitors is a vital aspect of their experience. Cultural exchanges between different people can signify an enriching experience for visitors who come to better understand the history, culture, life ways, and natural and cultural heritage of sites, regions, or countries new to them.

Unless the visitors are extremely well informed, they may not be aware of all the opportunities available for cultural interaction or of all the interesting aspects of the local culture. Visitors may also not be aware of cultural norms. It is important that local people or local community leaders ensure that adequate efforts are made to inform as many visitors as possible about local customs and cultural values. Sharing knowledge of local heritage and customs enriches visitors' experience, and encourages "right behaviour." The "authenticity" of this information – created by the community for community benefit – is not lost on visitors and deepens their experience.

Heritage Design/USDA Forest Service provided the following interesting examples:

- On the Micronesian island of Kosrae, a sign kiosk in each village includes community interpretation of its own chiefdom or municipality, including clan heritage, customs and festivals. This sign is placed alongside a mapbased island orientation and visitor opportunities panel, with another interpreting island ecology and history.
- In Jamaica's Cockpit Country, bus kiosks in mountain villages contain signs being developed by those communities, showcasing who they are and their heritage. Accompanying signage addresses Cockpit Country biological diversity and why it is important to protect it.
- Villages along the Iditarod Trail in Alaska are preparing community heritage media based on interviews with elders by schoolchildren. In addition to preserving local heritage, this will also be used for branding efforts and visitor materials for each community along the historic transportation route.

The role of local tour operators was emphasized. James Dion stated that many private sector tour companies do an excellent job in providing interpretation and in creating a positive visitor experience for their clients. On-site interpretation at cultural, heritage and natural sites is often poor or non-existent.

This is often because the agency or organization responsible for the stewardship of the site does not consider providing interpretation services to visitors to be a primary responsibility. Site managers, in fact, too often view their primary role as being custodians rather than service providers. Interpretation therefore becomes the preserve of inbound and outbound tour operators. For example, a free and independent traveller in Peru visiting Machu Picchu and Lake Titicaca, will find virtually nothing on site interpretation at either of these places. However, taking a tour with some locally owned agencies based out of Cuzco will enhance visits through excellent interpretation and service received.

This, at the same time, means supporting a locally owned business and helping to employ local people. This is a win-win situation for everyone. As Sheryl Fernando stated, a good tourist guide is extremely important in letting visitors "feel and experience the place they are visiting."

3

Marketing for Tourism

INTRODUCTION

Understanding how customers acquire information is important for marketing management decisions. This is especially true for services, travel and tourism products. Research has demonstrated that tourist information is a valuable concept in understanding destination image and the destination choice process of tourists. Information sources have been included in many research works as important factors for the analysis of tourist behaviour.

For instance, first, most of the tourist behaviour models incorporated the search of external information as an important component. Second, some studies have examined the influence of information sources on tourists' preferences and intentions. Third, other studies have centered on the relationship between information sources, destination selection and travel decisions.

Finally, another important factor is image. Image plays an important role for destination marketers so as to differentiate their destination in this highly competitive market. In this sense, formal and informal information sources (that is relatives and friends), have an influence on the image formation of a tourist destination. On the other hand, tourists formulate images of alternative destinations, so image also emerges as a critical element in the destination choice process. This is consistent with the notion that information sources and the attributes of the different destinations form the basis for different image and experience expectations. In addition, the information sources of tourist activities have changed greatly over the past fifteen years, due firstly to the impact of new technologies; secondly, to the change in tourist consumer behaviour, thirdly to the increase in the number of tourist destinations, and finally to the growing competition among different destinations. As a consequence, information sources should meet one main objective in order to be considered as effective tools for destination promotion. Promotion is recognized by many as a critical element in tourism marketing. Among the array of promotional methods available, the travel brochure is one of the most important and widely utilized.

For years, travel brochures have been used by national, state and provincial governments, convention and visitors' bureaux and specific destinations as inexpensive and versatile communication tools. For this reason, the main aim of this study is to identify those destination features which contribute to build a positive destination image, and to analyze the role of information sources in the formation of positive destination image. More precisely, this study focuses on the analysis of brochures as a promotion means for tourist destinations and as induced-image generators.

Additionally, it attempts to establish a relationship between the actual destination image, based on tourist experience and the image induced by the use of information sources. Consequently, the thesis starts with a brief overview of information sources and destination image management just as to the literature on the matter. Then, the methodology used for the collection of the primary data from several brochures will be presented, followed by the study's results. Finally, the conclusions and the main implications derived from this study for the tourism industry are considered, and directions for future research are proposed. This research contributes to the study of tourist information sources in the image forming process as a means of promotion for the tourism industry.

LITERATURE REVIEW

Research on tourist behaviour has to begin with information search. One of the most influential factors in the purchase of a tourist product is information about tourist goods and services. Moreover, tourists differ in the information sources they use before making a decision. Institutions, travel agents and tourist businesses make great efforts and spend a lot of money to make tourist information circulate. Despite the high investment made on communication and promotion, there is a general lack of knowledge as to which information source tourists use to make their choice. Nolan's tried to determine how information sources are used, and the relationship between this use and tourist consumer behaviour. The information about a concrete destination which is occasionally demanded by tourists is a particularly important means of promotion for the tourism industry.

Sources of information about a destination have a great influence on the process of tourist decision-making, and the behaviour of tourists determines how the search for information is done and how information will be used. Coltman comments that potential customers "will compare the brochure of one destination or supplier with the brochure of its competitors, and it is likely that the one with the best brochure will receive the business". For many potential visitors the brochure they possess actually represents the product or destination they are purchasing. Another important factor is image, because it influences destination selection.

Formal sources of information, like brochures, and informal sources, for example relatives and friends, have an influence on image formation in a tourist destination. By other hand, images serve many functions at many different levels; they are used in a number of practical ways to convey ideas and messages. These are all practical areas where promotion, through tourism imagery and representation, plays a vital role in a highly competitive and constantly changing marketplace. Destination image is certainly a determining factor of tourist buying behaviour. Research by Pearce and Woodside and Lysonski demonstrate that there is an evident relationship between positive perceptions of destinations and positive purchase decisions. Although these perceptions may not be based on fact or first-hand experience, they nevertheless exert a vital influence on a potential tourist's decision to visit a destination. Similarly, negative images, even if unjustified, will determine potential tourists and result in a decision not to purchase. Moreover, image formation can be defined as the development of a mental notion based on limited impressions coming from a single information source. In tourist destination image, this information originates in numerous and diverse sources.

Firstly, induced information includes promotional material (brochures, posters), as well as tour operators' and travel agents' opinions. Secondly, self-information also plays a role and it is obtained from mass media and popular culture. Finally, organic information comes from friends and relatives, as well as from personal experience. Although many people would have an image of destinations they have not visited, coming from different information sources, the most accurate, comprehensive and personal is formed when the destination is actually visited.

Therefore, the following question has been considered: Do information sources and brochures have an influence on destination image? Taking this objective as a starting point, this thesis attempts to study the use of tourist information sources and analyzes the relationship with destination image. The conceptual and empirical perspectives from the literature led to the following research questions: RQ1: Information sources used as means of promotion have an influence on the generation of tourist destination image. RQ2: There is a positive relationship between brochures image and destination image.

METHODS

The research process involved the following steps. First, a literature review was undertaken to identify the relationship between information sources and destination image within the tourism management. Second, the population and sampling procedure was established. Third, a questionnaire was constructed. Finally, the methods of data collection and analyses were determined.

SAMPLE

To carry out this research, a personal survey was conducted by means of a structured questionnaire. People who engage in information search about destinations can be considered as potential national tourists and represent the population of interest for this study. The sample for this study consisted of 1252 national adult (18-year-olds or over) tourists included in the list maintained by the International Tourism Trade Fair -FITUR in the Spanish acronym- and the information was obtained in the annual FITUR fair in Madrid. Non-probability samples may be useful for obtaining information about people's opinions, motivations, behaviours and demographic characteristics.

Participants in the survey were asked to express their opinion about a given tourist destination they had already visited through a series of attributes, and to answer a series of questions related to it. They were first asked whether they had visited any of the destinations advertised in the brochures to be analyzed (Barcelona, Madrid, etc.). If the answer was affirmative, they were shown the brochure of that specific city so that they could express their opinion about it. Finally, they were invited to recall the image of the destination generated by their actual visiting experience.

The demographic profile of respondents showed a gender distribution with 42.5% male and 57.5% female. In terms of age, 48% of respondents were between 25 and 34 followed by 29% who were between 35 and 44. Most of the respondents were single (51.2%); 34.9% were married. The respondents were highly educated; 77.8% of them had been to university and 21% of them were high-school graduates.

MEASURES

The survey instrument consisted of several parts: first, use of information sources (Guides, Internet, Brochures, Travel magazines, Newspaper, Relatives and friends, Personal experience, Travel agencies and Government tourist information); second, image induced by brochures; third, destination image; and fourth, demographic information. To measure induced image there were four dichotomous (yes/no) dependent variables: brochures forming images, brochures present cities with tourist attractions, image induced by brochures, destination image corresponds to actual image. To measure destination image, a 32-item scale was developed after reviewing other measurement scales. Each item was rated on a 5-point Likert scale, whose extreme figures were strongly disagree/strongly agree.

Finally, demographic information (sex, marital status, age and studies) was included in the questionnaire. To select the sample of brochures to be analyzed in the study the following factors were considered: size of destination, inland versus coastal destinations, geographical origin (North, Centre and South), and the source of the brochure: Central Administration, Autonomous Governments or Town Halls. The brochures selected corresponded to eight relevant cities.

STUDY FINDINGS

Different analysis techniques were used in order to process the information. The relationship between the use of tourist information and induced image was contrasted using the ANOVA. Finally, a discriminant analysis is applied to investigate which variables influence the generation of the positive image of a given destination. Thus, the results of this research are presented in two main parts. The first part presents the use of information sources and it allows establishing a relationship between the amount of information used by tourists and destination image.

The second part establishes the variables that predict destination image. This part centers upon the relationship between information source use and the destination image generated by such use of sources or promotional material. The variable applied for this measurement is the so-called utilization degree, which measures the intensity of information source use also paying attention to the number of sources used in order to establish whether image is influenced by the amount of information tourists made use of. This relationship should explain to what degree destination image depends on the use of promotional material. To determine the degree of information source use, this analysis considers frequencies of use in relation to the number of sources employed by surveyed tourists, with a maximum of nines and a minimum of zero.

The results of this new variable, utilization degree, is split in three levels:

1. Low utilization degree: figures ranging from 0 - 1 (27.1%),
2. Average utilization degree: figures between 2 and 4 (57.2%), and
3. High utilization degree: figures between 5 and 9 (15.7%).

The relationship analyzed here is then verified using the ANOVA in order to establish whether variation in information source utilization (independent variable) has an influence on destination image (dependent variable).

Results after the ANOVA confirm that the degree of utilization of information sources has an influence on destination image, with a reliability of 95%. These results demonstrate that information sources have a strong influence on tourist destination image generation when they are used as promotion tools.

DISCRIMINANT ANALYSIS: IMAGE FORMATION

The use of discriminant analysis is intended to predict whether image induced by brochures coincides with actual destination image, and to determine to what degree the different destination variables influence on destination image. However, the main purpose of this discriminant analysis is to predict membership in two or more mutually exclusive groups from a set of predictors when there is no natural ordering on the groups.

So we may ask if we can predict whether the destination features will influence destination image formation after they are known (cultural attractions, transportation, price, service quality, gastronomy, safety, climate, etc.). In the first approach to destination image formation by destination features, the discriminant analysis has been used in order to quantify the relative contribution of the 32 destination features (scale) as independent variables in the correct classification of two groups of categories in the following dependent variable: formation or nonformation destination image. Before considering the discriminant function, the a priori discriminant power of each independent variable is evaluated with the statistic F. All of them had a discriminant capability when the significance level was higher than 0.05.

In this case, only one linear function will be considered: the linear permutation of those variables together with their standardized coefficients. As all variables use the same measuring unit, the coefficients can function as indicators of relative importance: thus those variables with higher coefficient contribute more definitely to image formation. On the other hand, the sign shows the direction of its relationship with the dependent variable, being positive when the relationship is direct and negative when it is inverse. The resulting coefficients allowed us to formulate the following discriminant function: Z_{image} = 1.190 quality accommodation - 1.228 sports facilities + 0.772 different customs.

This function showed that there was a positive relationship between image formation and accommodation and different customs, and an inverse one with sports facilities. In order to evaluate the significance of the discriminant function, Wilks' Lambda (0.584) has been calculated, obtaining a significant value. The classificatory results showed a high explanatory capability of the discriminant function, because the real value of belonging to a group coincides with the one predicted by the function in 96.8% of occurrences.

This analysis thus confirms that some features form image: quality of accommodation, sports facilities and different customs. The results from the discriminant analysis demonstrated that there were significant differences between the two groups, because those individuals who think that destination image is positive give more importance to the fact that destination provides accommodation and is different while at the same time they consider that sports facilities are not a factor in positive image formation. Therefore, the results were that some features contribute to destination image formation. The following work was intended to establish whether there is a relationship between image generated by destination and tourist information brochures. Then, the next task would be to make an analysis of variance in the proposition brochure image, corresponds to destination image being the independent variable.

Results confirmed that brochures that build image have an influence on destination image. Thus, once the analysis of the relationship between tourist information and image, and the relationship between induced image and actual image, has been finished, the results verify research questions 1 and 2.

COMMENTS

MANAGEMENT IMPLICATIONS

The information obtained in this research has an added value when planning tourist destination promotion strategies. Providers and intermediaries selling tourist products, as well as public institutions promoting destinations may use it to their advantage. Although advertising is a widely accepted and proven antecedent of image, there have been relatively few studies on tourism promotion as the antecedent of destination image. Because tourist destinations are interested in creating image and enticing potential travellers to visit, brochures often contain photographs to capture the attention of travellers.

This study also provides information useful for tourist businesses and public institutions attempting to reach tourist consumers and for the design and planning of their promotion strategies. To know the structure of the tourist market is critical in order to provide better information for potential tourists and to address that information to more homogeneous tourist groups, which share their basic features: travel frequencies, destinations visited, reasons for travel and activities expected during travel. Furthermore, tourist information should be designed following the criteria which better respond to specific tourist group demands, so that it is more attractive, relevant and con uently more influential on purchase choice; in short, tourist information should also be a satisfying experience for tourists. Results in this study may be useful for marketing professionals and researchers. The conclusions imply that it is essential to incorporate image variables and dimensions of information search to the marketing of destinations.

A special emphasis should be laid on the study and development of tourism experience marketing strategies, which suggests that all contacts between tourist service providers and tourists should be directed to the satisfaction of their expectations (before, during, and after the visit), for they will also determine the image of the destination perceived by the tourist.

RULES FOR SUCCESSFUL TOURISM MARKETING

Tourism is an important economic activity because it brings in dollars from outside the community. It continues to be a fast growing sector and is typically included among the top three industries in the country. In addition, tourism provides a "front-door" to non-tourism economic development efforts such as business recruitment.

Roger Brooks, a nationally recognized expert in tourism development spoke about rules for success at the 2004 Wisconsin Governor's Conference on Tourism in Green Bay. Many of his rules apply to the tourism marketing efforts of small city downtowns and business districts. Presented is a summary of his keynote address titled 15 Immutable Rules of Successful Tourism.

SUCCESS BEGINS WITH A GOOD PLAN

Creating a Tourism Development & Marketing Plan is the first rule for successful tourism. The plan should include several details like product development, upgrades and improvements, repositioning and/or branding, attractions and events, visitor amenities and services, marketing and public relations, public/private partnerships, recruitment, funding and budgets, and organizational responsibilities. The plan should integrate existing comprehensive plans and economic development and Main Street efforts.

IMPORTANCE OF FRONT-LINE SALES

Your front-line employees can be your most valuable sales team. This is because they establish the first contact with the customer. The front-line employees should be knowledgeable about your community and should promote other stores, attractions and amenities to visitors to keep them in the area longer.

CRITICAL MASS

In order to attract and keep visitors in your community, there must be several retail and dining establishments within walking distance. Shopping and dining in a pedestrian setting is one of the top activities for visitors. An average rule of thumb for rural communities is to have nine retail stores and four dining/treats establishments within two or three blocks.

TURN NEGATIVES INTO POSITIVES

Almost every community and attraction has its challenges. Think creatively on how to convert these negatives into positives. You can then attract people to your area using clever promotional tactics. For example, when an article in the Washington Post labeled Battle Mountain, Nevada the "Armpit of America", the town took a positive spin on that title by having an annual event sponsored by Old Spice drawing thousands of visitors.

BE UNIQUE

In order to be successful, you must be worth the trip. A visitor must be able to differentiate you from the competition and you must strive to be creative and set yourself apart from others. Being unique will make a visitor travel the extra distance.

TELLING STORIES

Museums and interpretive centers should always tell stories, not just display artifacts. Stories can keep visitors in the area longer, which means additional spending. Visitors also remember stories, and captivating stories are told and passed on to others. More people pick destinations by word of mouth than any other method.

FOUR-TIMES RULE

People are willing to travel a distance if you offer something that appeals to them. There should be enough for visitors to see and do in your area. In general, you should be able to keep visitors busy four times longer than it took them to get there.

MARKETING VS. PRODUCT DEVELOPMENT

Before you market your community, make sure it is appealing to customers. If your product is not of great quality, then your marketing efforts are wasted. Product development should always be a top priority, and it never ends. Having a good mix of product development and marketing is also important.

SELLING THE EXPERIENCE

Always sell the experience associated with an activity and not the place. If you are using pictures in your marketing campaign, avoid using scenic images. Scenery lasts in the mind for only a few moments. Instead, use images of people laughing and having fun. Viewers are more likely to remember images that include people's emotions.

BRANDING

Even at the community level, branding is critical for success in tourism. Branding is much more than just a logo; it is what sets you apart from your competition, it is your image and your value. Do not try to be "all things to all people."

WOW PHOTOGRAPHY

Nothing sells tourism like great photography. Photographs used for tourism purposes should have a "wow" appeal in the viewer and should make the viewer want to go to the place depicted. You are trying to sell an experience and your photos should evoke emotion in the viewer. Photography should be the key element in brochures, public relation efforts, and especially on the web.

CLOSE THE SALE

Most communities and attractions spend a significant amount of money on advertising. The primary "call to action" in advertising is to get the potential customer to call and get a brochure, or for them to visit your web site. If this is the case, the brochure and web site should be good enough to close the sale. Otherwise, your advertising effort is largely wasted.

Pay attention to certain small details while advertising. For example, for brochures, the best colours to use are red and yellow as these colours get the viewers attention. In addition, most brochures end up in racks along with scores of other brochures and the top three inches is all that is visible to the potential customer. Keep this in mind when designing brochures.

PUBLIC RELATIONS

Even though you need both, publicity is much more important than advertising. Implementing a professional public relations campaign can have several benefits: it will build brand, improve your image, increase credibility and will provide a greater return on investment than advertising alone.

Public relation is how you build your brand and advertising is how you maintain your position. Studies show that for every $1 invested into a public relations campaign, you get a $3 return.

EFFECTIVE WEB SITES

A Nielsen/Netratings study, nearly 75% of the U.S. population has access to the Internet from home. In addition, 94% of Internet users make travel arrangements using the Web. The Internet is by far the number one resource for planning travel and vacations. If you have a tourism related web site, can your potential customers find you easily on the Web? How does your web site compare with the competition? Make the online experience interactive for the customer and remember to promote attractions, not just the place or your organization. Several thousands of dollars spent on web site development and maintenance is not a waste of money. You can even make sure your web site is displayed at the top of a Web search by paying a fee.

FREQUENCY IN ADVERTISING

Frequency is more important than variety in placing advertising. People viewing your advertisement should develop Top of Mind Awareness. For example, when the words "fast food" are mentioned, most people think of McDonalds because they make a good use of frequency in advertising.

USING MULTIPLE SENSES IN TOURISM MARKETING

Imagine the streets of London, the markets in Marrakesh, the tulips in Holland or skiing in Switzerland. What do you see, hear or sense, *i.e.* which of your senses are stimulated the most or is it a blend of all of your senses that activates your memory and/or triggers your desire to consume? When you hear music including bag pipes you may imagine Scotland, you can picture the Alps through the French horn, Africa by the sound of drums and the southern parts of North America with the help of jazz-music.

You can most probably also fairly easily get into the mood for movies through the smell of popcorn and you may be able to imagine a Finnish summer day by the sound of seagulls, by the touch of water, by the sound of sea-breeze, by the taste of new potatoes and/or by the smell of blooming bird cherries. There are not many studies on the usage of multisensory marketing, at least not within the tourism sector or within and between different media channels.

There are, however, studies showing that odoured areas increase the usage of slot-machines, that ambient scent has a positive effect on social interactions, that queuing is perceived less stressful in scented areas, etc. There are also studies that show a positive correlation between the usage of scent and the increase of sales. It thus seems that the retail industry, the marketers and/or the researchers in order to be more effective cannot ignore the effect and impact of using and activating multiple senses any longer in marketing. It further seems that the usage of pictures and sounds as promotional methods are not enough.

Moreover, traditional marketplaces within tourism for *e.g.* airline tickets and holiday bookings are shifting. It has been estimated that two thirds of all the flight and hotel accommodation reservations in Europe take place on the web. A survey conducted by the Association of Finnish Advertisers, advertisement in digital media is increasing. Ads are thus gradually shifting from TV and newspapers to the web and mobile phones.

This thesis draws on the assumption that traditional tourism marketing methods are not sufficient as they tend to overemphasize the visuals and printed media. In order to create awareness and motivation among future travellers, tourism communication should, just as to our understanding, not only appeal to the visuals, but to all user senses in an inter medial mix.

Hence, not only sight should be activated in tourism marketing communication in order to create feelings of authenticity and experience among customers and users, but also sound, smell, touch and taste should be stimulated. In order for future tourism communication to be attractive, marketing communication should not only be made available in printed media or in physical environments, but also in social spaces and in interactive media. When multisensory, intermedial marketing communication is effectively combined with ration and need in addition to user co-experiences, only then, we argue, can it be future-oriented, engaging and stimulating.

This thesis aims to argue for the need of a better understanding of multisensory, intermedial marketing communication within tourism as there is little, if any research in this area. This research thus takes an interest in these questions from a tourism communication user.

TOURISM MARKETING COMMUNICATION

The marketing mix is a traditional way to understand marketing in general. The majority of marketing practitioners consider the Mix as the toolkit of transaction marketing and archetype for operational marketing planning. While empirical evidence of the exact role and contribution of the Mix to the success of commercial organizations is very limited, several studies confirm that the 4Ps Mix is indeed the trusted conceptual platform of practitioners dealing with tactical/ operational marketing issues.

The marketing mix has been defined as a mixture of controllable marketing variables that the firm uses in order to pursue the sought level of sales in a targeted market. These theories have been adapted by many scholars and marketing professional, also within the tourism industry, in a number of forms. Firms marketing strategies use marketing mix variables in order to plan an operational marketing plan for their business.

The focus being on how firms can increase or improve sales, position themselves and their image in a competitive environment in which customer demands and competitors' strategies are constantly changing. Traditional 3 marketing P's, product, place, and promotion, can be argued to be relevant also for the analysis of multisensory marketing even though the Mix has been critized for not allowing interaction and for not capturing relationships.

Multisensory marketing communication can be divided into the 5 senses. These 5 senses will be "smashed down" into separate components because this is the only way to analyze them. By doing so every sense can be analyzed towards one of the marketing p's. The marketing figure on the other hand expresses the marketing system for any organization in four constricts rings. It is an accepted way to present the marketing process. In the inner ring is the customer involving customer orientation, customer loyalty, and consumer behaviour. In the second ring there are the traditional marketing P's, *i.e.* product, price, place, and promotion. The next ring represents inter-company resources such as: personal, positioning, economic resources, and relationship-based interest group resources. In the fourth ring there are determinants of tourism demand, competitors, technological development possibilities and legislation. In our research on multisensory tourism marketing communication we use the term inter medial marketing communication. We understand inter medial marketing to be interactive communication involving at least two media channels.

The easiest application for inter medial marketing is through the use of digital media. Inter medial marketing communication is thus very close to the concept of digital marketing. Urban has defined the concept of digital marketing communication as follows: "Digital marketing uses the Internet and information technology to extend and improve traditional marketing functions".

Systematic idea- and development-work in media-advertising and communications technology require, just as to Viljakainen, Bäck and Lindqvist different types of knowledge in order for *e.g.* the tourism industry to be able to develop novelties and innovations applicable on global markets. It seems that even though media is culturally bounded and a national phenomenon, new combinations of technology, media and advertisement seem to be universal.

MULTIPLE SENSES IN MARKETING COMMUNICATION

Marketing communication has been defined in new media vocabulary as company driven communication which aims directly or indirectly to influence the demand or to at least have a positive influence on demand among reference groups. With the help of marketing communication a travel company thus aims to inform and remind customers of its services and to have an impact on consumer behaviour.

In addition, marketing communication aims to arouse feelings and desires for consumption, for the creation of company and product image, for sales and customer decisions. Furthermore the purpose of communication is to maintain, develop and deepen customer relations. Many people look for value fulfilment also in communication. It should thus not only be purposeful, but also enjoyable and comfortable, an aesthetical experience. For service firms, the management of the service experience is of vital importance. It does not only affect the success of the firm, but also determine customers satisfaction level, service quality perception and future behaviour *i.e.* an intention to visit the store again.

In other words, the service experience is a result from an activity that can be defined as a process where a set of resources interact with each other and with the customers aiming at supporting the customer's processes in a value generating way. Usually the resources for service organizations are divided to two central components: backstage and frontstage. Hoffman and Turley describe backstage as to consist of those behind the scene which are invisible to the customers.

Frontstage consists of those factors visible to the customers. There are many frontstage factors affecting customer's service experience. Schmitt and Lindstrom and Kotler, a customer is often attracted towards a brand based upon its sensory experience. Lindstrom and Kotler further stresses that almost our entire understanding of the world is experienced through our senses. Our senses are our link to memory and can tap right into emotion. Smell appears to be the most persuasive sense after sight, which implies the importance for multisensory marketing. Multisensory marketing stands in this research for involving several bodily senses in marketing activities.

Kahn Consulting describes it as the purposeful design and deployment of the interaction between the senses in order to stimulate a consumer's relationship with a brand; and to foster a lasting emotional connection that optimizes brand loyalty. Multisensory marketing is in a starting phase and there is just a hand full of marketers who are using multisensory marketing in their campaigns nowadays, also in the tourism industry. It is stated by several researchers that multisensory marketing is the future of advertising and branding. Lindstrom and Kotler 2005:69, vision is the most important persuasive one with a share of 58% when it comes to brand building and bonding, smell being the second most important one with a proportion of 45%, hearing stands for 41%, taste for 31% and touch for 25%. Studies thus show that pleasant scents create pleasant states of moods. It has also been shown that we process senses differently depending on age, gender, cultural background etc. Sight is thus traditionally perceived as the most seductive sense and the most obvious one used by brands. Visual cues govern consumer behaviour.

A recently published article shows that red colour enhances performance on a detail-oriented task whereas blue enhances performance on a creative task. Sound on the other hand helps us generate moods by creating feelings and emotions. Taste and smell are closely connected, although smell is 10,000 times more sensitive as it taps right into our memory. The luxurious car brand Bentley has made good use of sounds in their marketing in order for customers to perceive quality and success.

Rolls Royce has successfully used scent adding to the feeling of quality. Many marketing scholars and professionals have shown some interest for the usage of multiplesenses in marketing, *e.g.* the usage of scent in order to increase sales, to promote or evaluate products, to enhance the perception of quality, to reduce stress etc.

The Effect on Odours and Scent in Marketing Communication

The physical environment or the servicescape is probably among the first of these factors customers will encounter. The reason why the servicescape is of importance is that it plays a significant role in determining the customer's satisfaction level, perceived service quality and the service experience itself. Furthermore it also affects customers' behavioural intensions. The physical environment can play a role similar to a physical good's package in that it basically communicates an image of what is included in the service.

It is apparent that different services (resorts, hotels, cruise ships, hospitals etc) are depending on their servicescapes to communicate and create customer experiences. The physical facilities (facility exterior and interior elements) can be seen as "man-made" or constructed elements. Scent can also be adopted as a part of the different elements of physical evidence. For example, scent can be applied to facility exterior to lure customers to visit the facility interior (*e.g.* example given of the gas stations that place fresh brewed coffee scent at the pumps to lure pay-and-go customers to stay) or simply to create a pleasant environment outside the store.

Using multiple senses in marketing is not a new thing itself, neither the use of scent for marketing and for servicescape. In cafes coffee packages have been opened in order to spread the aroma of coffee and bakers put their coffee bread on show for getting a good scent. There are approximately about 100 000 different scents in the world out of which 1000 scents are primaries and the rest of the scents are combinations.

Nose as a receiver of stimuli is important. Scents are found out to strengthen communication and bonding. Features of scents are: ambience, identification and memorycap. The scents are registered in the brains faster than other senses, as the distance between the nose and the brain is short. We can identify scents with a 65% accuracy whereas the visual picture is 50% already after three months. There are approximately about 6-10 million cells in a human nose through which we can identify 2000-4000 different aromas.

In comparison a shepherd dog nose consists of approximately 220 million cells. Up to 75% of people remember a smell even after one year. Scents can be produced naturally, for example through flowers and scent oil or artificially with the help of equipment. Odours can be interconnected with a product, to a theme, a nice shopping environment or product brand.

Scents can be used everywhere, for example in a hotel, an event or at a party. When a scent is combined with a product, the user is becoming aware of the product through its smell. The client becomes curious and at the same time the message of the product is being communicated fast and deeply into the client's mind. The scent is asking the brain "do you want this", even though I did not come here for this purpose. A scent also differentiates the product from its competitors. Scents have been proved to increase sales. The traditional concept of servicescape has been affected by the emerge of the Internet. Web pages and communities have become a new form of servicescapes, also known as virtual servicescapes, where the customer can get in contact with any company and explore their service offerings without physically visiting it.

These are the more recent forms of physical evidence, which companies may see great potential in and which they can use to communicate the service experience both before and after the service encounter, thus making the service more tangible for the customer. For example, travel agencies use their web pages as virtual servicescapes, where the customer can preview destinations and also view and take virtual tours of hotels. Often these virtual tours include a chance to see all the available rooms, how the rooms are decorated and equipped and even watch the view from the balcony live through a webcam.

The competition between companies on the market is hard and there is a lot of advertising. We encounter daily about 3000 ad-messages. Traditionally it has been evaluated that we receive visually 83% of all information. Customers are being directed to buy products and services by sharing information about products, by increasing brand awareness or by guiding clients to a service purchase situation. The consumers stay for a longer time in a space in which there is a pleasant small and evaluate the products in a much more positive way. In 1965 90% of the consumers 90% did their daily purchase decisions prior to shopping, today 80% of the consumers do their purchasing decision in the shop.

Media Channels

Among IAB European membership countries web-based media marketing volume in 2006 was close to 8 billion euros. Most money was spent in the United Kingdom, Germany and in France. In Finland the web-based advertising was just as to statistics 91,2 million euros and in Greece 16,3 million euros. The advertising expenditure was shared between: key word advertising 45 per cent, banner advertising 31 per cent, classified advertising 122 per cent and electronic advertising 2 per cent. IAB's corporate members believe that Internet is the ideal total media solution for difficult economic times – allowing for PR, branding and marketing in a highly targeted way, combining creativity with opportunities for customer engagement.

The proportion of web-media stood in 2006 only for about 3 per cent of total medial production just as to Viljakainen. In total marketing communications planning- and production-costs were 2, 8 billion euros in Finland during 2006 of which printed newspapers and direct advertising stood by large for the biggest proportion. All in all the share of web shopping has though been estimated to grow with 20% during the next few years in Finland.

There thus appears to be needs for new ways of marketing products in the web. Technology, electronic media and the internet usage is growing fast especially among young consumer groups. New types of combinations for presenting pictures together with voice and videos are emerging. Different types of media channels, internet and new publication platforms, such as the electronic books are being developed and introduced. The boundaries between massmedial targeted communication and interactive communication involving user medias have becoming blurry in the process.

We are thus heading from one way communication towards various forms of interactive communication involving inter medial solutions. Multiple forms of internet and digital advertising such as billboards, skyscrapers, banners, leader boards, rectangles, floating flashes, buttons and tickets have been produced in order to attract potential consumers attention. The banners represent one of the oldest modes for internet advertising. Nowadays the term is used as a general term and more or less equivalent to internet-based marketing. The challenge though is to make people use and click the banners, *i.e.* new applications have been taken into use, *e.g.* Rich media-format: Java, Flash and Shockwave-formats in interactive net advertising. The media-advertising channels and operational models have expanded during the ten last years. At the same time customer segments are being splashed down in new ways accordingly with life styles. For example e-commerce is growing annually with approximately 20 per cent. Digital channels and information technology are changing the way that companies communicate and maintain relationship with their customers.

The Internet, e-mail, mobile phones, digital TV, and other evolving channels offer opportunities for frequent, costeffective, personalized, and interactive communication between the company and their customers.

Viralmarketing

The term was originally coined by Jeffrey Rayport, a Hardvard Business School professor. The idea being that when there is little time and a minimal budget, a virus can be a truly effective.

The term "viral marketing" is commonly defined as networkenhanced word-of-mouth. As outlined by this Web Marketing Today, Dr. Ralph F. Wilson in 2005, originally published 2/1/2000, a viral campaign does six things:

- Gives away seemingly valuable products, services or content
- Provides for effortless transfer to others
- Scales easily from small to very large
- Exploits common motivations and behaviours
- Utilizes existing communication networks
- Takes advantage of others' resources

RESEARCH QUESTIONS

The main research questions in this research project are: how is the usage of multiple senses involving various media channels (*e.g.* internet, TV, special spaces, social media) taken into consideration in tourism marketing? What kind of techniques and technologies are needed (available)? How can specific tourism companies benefit from the use of multiple senses in inter medial marketing communication in order to develop their demand/supply?

Design, Methodology and Approach of the Project

The research project is designed to include work packages. The first phase is aimed at the analysis of literature and good practical cases. Research is to a significant part based on explorative literature research. The initial phase is general, beneficial for the whole tourism industry. It also includes the examination of interactions between multiple sensory modalities, such as ambient scent, background music, visual stimuli like colour and lighting.

The second phase will be made to assess the opportunities for creating and using different technologies involving smell, taste, touch, sight and sound taking into consideration the social co-experience elements and a tourism marketing communication view. Available multisensory possibilities will be evaluated and explored in existing and available virtual or real-world surroundings for specific users and situations. The literature studies in addition to in-depth exploration of authentic cases in the tourism field will help to co-create new multisensory ways of interacting and communicating. The technological aspects will be analyzed in order to make an assessment of the current technological applications used for dispensing the multi-sensory message.

Once the technological applications are combined with the use of sensory stimuli an overall picture can be given on the current profile of multi sensory marketing. The research will explore the role and opportunities of social media in connection to multisensory travel marketing. Social media offers several opportunities in relation to marketing and brand building. People value opinions and hints from their friends and contacts and this is important in spreading marketing messages and influencing decision making.

When planning new ways of marketing such as multisensory marketing, it is important to create the applications so that some part of the marketing supports spreading in social media, including viral marketing. In the third phase there are made four case studies in specific tourism companies together with intermedial, digital, and viral marketing experts. Together with tourism and intermedial partners the researchers will evaluate user experiences involving different combinations using multiple senses within tourism marketing communication. Various methods *e.g.*, service design and user based methods will be used in order to find good solutions. It includes assessment of opportunities of social media with regard to different kind of tourism services and which requirements are set on the material to be used in social media and viral marketing.

Two Case Studies of the Effects of Using Multiple Senses in Tourism Marketing Communication

One part of the project aims at combining different senses in authentic sales situations. The purpose of the case studies is to estimate the influence and effect that multiple marketing has on sales and the usage of products. In the first case our partner company is Helsinki Expert, an incoming travel agent. It provides a wide variety of service-bundles and products for Helsinki visitors, activities and programmes in Helsinki and elsewhere in Finland.

One of their products is an audio-guided city bus-tour in Helsinki. The travel agency was chosen as the case company for this study primarily because of their servicescape, where the research is conducted, offers an interesting and suitable environment for testing. The aim of the first case is to explore the effects of ambient scent. We are going to research, how a specific tourism company can benefit from the usage of multiple senses in a selling situation.

This study will compare two different conditions in separate time periods; one where the servicescape is constant (no additional stimuli) and the other where the servicescape is diffused with a pleasant ambient scent, moving pictures and sound congruent with the service context (design and theme) of the chosen company. Both of the time periods take one month. One of our hypotheses is that odours affect customers' intentions to buy willingly in the scented environment. Our second case is the amusement park, Linnanmäki. We are testing the effect that the combination of scent and virus-marketing has on the amount of visitors.

TERMINATIONS

In this research project we are thus focusing on inter medial, multisensory applications applicable and beneficial within and for the tourism industry. We strongly suggest that future development of techniques and technologies for the purpose of tourism marketing communication are strongly driven by customer needs, amusement, excitement, value-added experiences, participation and interactivity. The idea of our project is to enhance the demand and to improve the availability of tourism services through new types of marketing communication involving inter medial solutions and multiple senses.

We have argued that in the future the activation of sight and hearing in tourism marketing communication is not enough. We have shown studies indicating positive correlations between the use of *e.g.* ambient scent and consumption, the perception of wellness, quality, service experience, and bonding. There is thus some evidence on the impact of senses in order to engage emotions, feelings, bonding, the perception of quality and success.

There is, however, not enough research on inter medial multisensory combinations, technological solutions and technical applications, at least not within the tourism industry. Our cases will enhance the understanding of the impact of suitable and/or possible combinations of multiple senses suitable for and within the tourism industry. The final results of this research project will give a comprehensive overview on multisensory marketing communication beneficial for service companies within the Finnish tourism industry.

Moreover, this project aims at creating marketing communication plans involving multiple senses for specific case organizations. We have already seen that the E-Commerce brought along customer empowerment, new forms of communication and interaction, global and around-the –clock operation, high degree of market transparency and difficulty in maintaining competitive advantages. We argue that the four P:s can offer a theoretical framework for the analysis of the usage of senses, involving digital and social media, co-experience, viral marketing and servicescapes even though many researches favour totally new approaches and are critical of the Mix. Internal orientation, lack of interactivity and personalisation, lack of strategic elements and lack of community building are some of the frequently mentioned weaknesses of the Mix.

TOURISM MARKETING IN DEVELOPING COUNTRIES

Tourism has become a very important and dynamic sector both in the world economy and particular in the developing countries. Its growth affects not only the activities directly linked to tourism but also other sectors. Tourism is already an important sector in some developing countries and will become so for others. Developing countries have been fast growing in tourism industry terms in the world over the last decade. Tourism is one of the most important sectors in a large number of developing countries.

Increases in economic growth, disposable income and leisure time, political stability, and aggressive tourism campaigns, among others factors, have fuelled the significant growth of tourism. Developing countries have some common characteristics, such as extreme poverty and widespread conflict (including civil war and ethnic clashes), extensive political corruption, lack of political and social stability, human resource weakness (human assets index, nutrition, health, education and adult literacy), and economic vulnerability. Bangladesh is a developing country in Asia, holding high potentiality for tourism.

Bangladesh Parjatan Corporation (BPC) plays an important role for the development of tourism. For a long time, Bangladesh has been an attractive destination for tourists. But at present, its position is not significant in terms of the international tourism market. The overall objective of this research is to identify the issues and challenges in tourism marketing facing Bangladesh. The role of international tourism in generating economic benefits has long been recognised in many developing countries. The public sector may have been reluctant in the past to contribute towards tourism development, but the situation has changed and, over the years, governments' perspectives on tourism have not only evolved to include wider participation, but have also widened from the narrow focus on economic benefits to encompass environmental and societal concerns.

Everything seems to suggest that developing countries look upon tourism consumption as manna from heaven that can provide a solution to all their foreign exchange difficulties. This description of tourism as 'manna from haven' has gained some support, in part because tourism is a highly visible activity. Although tourism development results in the provision of facilities and services, there are, however, instances when these facilities are not accessible to local residents, particularly if tourism development involves the creation of tourism enclaves. In the last two decades in particular tourism has developed, especially in developing countries by their integrated tourism planning.

The specific research objectives of this study are:

- To identify development trends in Bangladesh tourism
- To evaluate the effectiveness of tourism marketing Bangladesh
- To analyse issues in tourism marketing in Bangladesh;
- To identify potential strategies that can contribute to increasing the competitiveness of Bangladesh tourism.

To conduct the research, a conceptual framework from a literature review was created and implemented using of a particular research methodology and methods.

DEFINITION, MEANING, AND CHARACTERISTICS OF DEVELOPING COUNTRIES

The terms 'the third world', 'underdeveloped countries', 'developing countries', 'poor countries', the South' and 'less-developed countries are mostly used interchangeably. However, it is not an easy task to define precisely what is meant by these terms as McQueen. Buchanan describes 'the developing country is a universe of radical scarcity. Defining and determining every dimension of men's relationship to each other... the inadequacy means of livelihood is the first and distinguishing truth of this area'. In order to give a more clear meaning of the term, it is worth quoting Todaro at some length: The 143 African, Asian and Latin American member countries of the United Nations often collectively refer to themselves as the 'Third World' or 'developing countries'.

Developing Countries, third World countries, industrialising countries, underdeveloped countries, and less developed countries are countries which, just as to the United Nations exhibit the lowest indicators of socioeconomic development, with the lowest human development ratings of all countries in the world. The World Bank classified developing countries as those having per capita income of less US$ 2200. Another concept of developing is that they have a high level of illiteracy; Afghanistan, Pakistan, Bangladesh, India, and Sudan are typical examples.

The United Nations, 120 countries are described as developing countries, and they comprise less than 20% of the world's total GNP. Pearce suggests that all those nations out side of Europe, North America, Japan and Australia have to be considered as developing countries. Most developing countries are located in Sub-Saharan Africa, Asia, Latin America, Pacific and Caribbean regions of the world. Some of these countries have fasted development rates. However, there are also countries such as India, China, Bangladesh, Nepal, and Ethiopia that are very poor.

Thus the term 'developing countries' is a very broad concept. United Nations review in 2009, and defined by the UN that developing countries as countries meeting their criteria, one of which was a three-year average estimate of gross national income per capita of less than US $950. The World Bank world economies are classified economies based on GNI per capita which is calculated using the World Bank Atlas method.

The groups are: low income, $935 or less; lower middle income, $936 - $3,705; upper middle income, $3,706 - $11,455, and high income, $11,456 or more. For example, per capita income of developing countries in year 2007-08 just as to the

World Bank, International Monetary Fund and Central Intelligence Agency report as in February, 2009, such as, Pakistan $1,085; Kenya USD $680; Afghanistan, US$457; Ethiopia US$317; India, 1078; Nepal US$428; Nigeria US$401; Sri-Lanka US$2099; Vietnam US$1055; Burma US$287; Cambodia US$760; Haiti US$793, Mali US$712; Zimbabwe US$401; and Bangladesh US$690 The least developed countries are a group of countries that have been identified by the United Nations as "least developed" in terms of their low gross national income, their weak human assets and their high degree of economic vulnerability.

The term Least Developed Countries describes the world's poorest countries with following 3 criteria, such criteria are:

- Low-income criterion: based on a three-year average estimate of the gross national income per capita;
- Human resource weakness criterion: involving a composite human assets index based on indicators of:
  - Nutrition;
  - Health;
  - Education;
  - Adult literacy;
- Economic vulnerability criterion: based on indicators of the instability of agricultural production; the instability of exports of goods and services; the economic importance of non-traditional activities (share of manufacturing and modern services in GDP); merchandise export concentration; and the handicap of economic smallness.

Therefore, India, Bangladesh, and Pakistan have the common economic features of developing countries permit us to view them in a broadly similar framework.

Based on common characteristics developing countries can be classified into six categories: i) low standard levels of living; ii) low incomes, inequality, poor health, and inadequate education; iii) low levels of productivity; iv) high rates of population growth and dependency burdens, substantial dependence on agricultural production and primary-products exports; v) prevalence of imperfect markets and limited information; and vi) dependence and vulnerability in international relations. Immediately after liberation, the government of Bangladesh set up the Bangladesh Parjatan Sangstha with a view to developing the tourist industry in the country. The organisation was restructured into Bangladesh Parjatan Corporation in 1973.

The corporation drew up a five-year plan within the framework of the first Five-Year Plan for economic and social development of the country to provide essential facilities and to develop natural attractions for increasing the inflow of tourists and making their stay in the country entertaining. The second, third, and fourth five-year plans and two year plans were intended to implement by the past Bangladesh governments to develop tourism sector but these plans have not been implemented properly by the government due to ministerial legacy problems.

For example, if a government has to power down before implementing a tourism development plan, the next ideal government's priority should focus on completing such partially completed projects first, but in reality, they are interested to find faults with such projects more than probing the positive aspects, and intent to formulate a new one to develop Bangladesh tourism. As a result some of the partially completed projects are let out forever. Consequently, this dreadful trend is only wasting time and money hardly developing this sector.

Tourism in its modern sense is a relatively recent phenomenon, and it began in the present Bangladesh area only during the 1960s. Tourists from abroad came to see and enjoy the beaches, the scenic beauty of the landscape covered with lavish greens and the web of rivers, tribal culture, religious rituals, historical places, forests, wild life and hill resorts.

GEOGRAPHICAL CHARACTERISTICS OF BANGLADESH

Bangladesh is a developing country in South Asia, located between 20°34c to 26°38c north latitude and 88°01c to 92°42c east longitude, with an area of 147,570 square km and a population of 140 million. It is bordered on the west, north, and east by India, on the southeast by Myanmar, and the Bay of Bengal to the south. Though it is a small country, it has many diverse attractions for nature lovers as well as being rich in culture and heritage.

The territorial waters of Bangladesh extend 12 nautical miles, and the exclusive economic zone of the country is 200 nautical miles. There is a large marshy jungle coastline on the Bay of Bengal popularly known as the Sundarbans - one of the largest mangrove forests in the world, the home of the Royal Bengal Tiger.

Bangladesh is located in the Ganges delta which is densely populated and it is formed by the confluence of the Ganges, Brahmaputra, and Meghna rivers and their tributaries as they flow down from the Himalayas, creating the largest riverine delta in the world. To the south is a highly irregular deltaic coastline of about 600 km, fissured by many rivers and streams flowing into the Bay of Bengal.

DEVELOPMENT AND ROLE OF TOURISM MARKETING ORGANISATION IN BANGLADESH

During the Pakistan period of rule, there was a tourism department with an office in West Pakistan. This department was assigned promotion, development and regulation of the tourism sector in Pakistan. A private sector corporation came into operation at the end of 1970. After independence, the socio-economic and political climate prevailing in the country was not encouraging for the private sector to participate in economic activities of wider magnitude.

Therefore, it became imperative for the government to come forward by promote tourism in Bangladesh. Soon after the independence of Bangladesh, the government of the newborn state realised the importance of tourism in its economic and social life. Therefore, the government decided to reorganise the tourism sector by combining both the tourism department and the private corporation into one organisation, bringing it under government responsibility for better coordination, promotion, development and marketing. Consequently, the government established the National

Tourism Organisation in the name of Bangladesh Parjatan Corporation under Presidential Order No. 143, declared in November 27, 1972. BPC began in January 1973 with limited assets of the former "Pakistan Tourism Corporation" and TK.10 million sanctioned by the government. The Corporation was entrusted with the dual responsibility of developing tourism infrastructure and promoting Bangladesh as a tourist destination. Other responsibilities of the Corporation included regulation and operation of tourism activities in the country. Thus, Bangladesh Parjatan Corporation came into being as the NTO in Bangladesh.

As such, the structure of the tourism sector in Bangladesh is predominantly managed by the public sector. The public sector has played a pioneering role in the development and promotion of tourism in the country. Government involvement in the tourism sector is channelled through BPC, which is under the Ministry of Civil Aviation and Tourism. As a semiautonomous organisation it enjoys wide power and authority, including the right to acquire and dispose of property; construct and run hotels, restaurants and other tourists facilities; operate duty free shop, transportation and car rental; establish training institutes; and invest its funds as it deems proper.

Due to neglect by successive governments, BPC totally failed to achieve the objectives for which it was created. Had there been no private sector tour operators in the country things would have been even more precarious. They have kept the hope of tourism alive, almost without government support. Private sector involvement in tourism in Bangladesh is still not adequate however, and the Bangladesh government has taken remedial measures to encouraging the private sector to play a positive role in the development and diversification of tourist facilities to promote domestic and international tourism in the country.

A large proportion of investments have been made in hotel businesses and tour operations. Private sector investors now are as showing a keen interest to participate in the tourism sector. Tour operators have a significant role to play in tourism business. Over 40 private tour operators have already been engaged in tourism marketing in Bangladesh. Some of them conduct only domestic tours while others offer both domestic and outbound tours.

Thirty two such private tour operators are members of an association named "Tours Operator Association of Bangladesh", formed to carry out their activities more efficiently, to lobby the BPC and the government for the realisation of justified rights and to promote the country's tourism together.

Travel agencies in both the destination and the tourist generating countries also play important roles in the promotion and development of tourism in a country. There are 235 travel agencies in Bangladesh; most of them are members of the Association of Travel Agents of Bangladesh. These travel agencies are licensed by the Registration Authority under the Ministry of Civil Aviation and Tourism and controlled by the same authority under the Travel Agencies Registration and control ordinance of 1977, which says that the travel agencies are involve themselves in travel arrangements only.

BANGLADESH TOURISM MARKETING PRODUCTS AND TOURIST ATTRACTIONS

The world thinks of Bangladesh as poor, flood-ravaged, and more of a disaster zone than a travel destination. In some respects, the world is right but hiding behind these images is a country with a rich history, a strange beauty, and some interesting attractions but it is not, however, a destination for everyone.

Bangladesh is a country with rich traditions, natural beauty, beaches, forests, lakes, hills, wild lives, archaeological attractions, monuments, handicrafts, sanctuaries, religious festivals, cultural heritage, tribal culture and architecture, incredible greenery, mighty rivers and attractive river cruises, sunny beaches, colourful tribal life and attractive cultural functions that offer great tourist attractions. Tourism involves travelling for pleasure, enjoy and education. It is also a business of attracting tourists and providing for their accommodation and entertainment. In many countries, tourism is an industry for earning revenue and foreign exchange. The many businesses that grow concurrently with the development of tourism include airlines, shipping, hotels and restaurants, finance companies, tour operators, travel agents, car rental firms, caterers and retail establishments and together, they contribute significantly to the overall development of a country's economy and to its cultural diversification and adaptation.

The Moorish traveller Ibn Batuta who visited Bengal in the fourteenth century described Bengal as the wealthiest and cheapest land of the world and stated that it was known as 'a hell full of bounties' In the seventeenth century French traveller Francois Bernie observed and stated "Egypt has been represented in every age as the finest and most fruitful country in the world, and even our modern writers deny that there is any other land of peculiarly favoured by nature; but the knowledge I have acquired of Bengal during two visits paid to that kingdom inclines me to believe that pre-eminence ascribed to Egypt is rather due to Bengal".

Bangladesh has the world's longest 120 km unbroken sea beach sloping here down to the blue water of the Bay of Bengal in Cox's Bazar, Parki beach, and Kuakata. Such a long sea beach covering miles of golden sands, soaring cliffs, surfing waves, all of these make Cox's Bazar the tourist capital of Bangladesh. The tourists can enjoy the charming beauty of the sunset behind the waves of the sea. Its appeal makes Cox's Bazar one of the most attractive tourist spots in the world. In addition to that, there are other beaches like Inani beach in Ukhia, Cox's Bazar, St. Martin Island, and Patengha beach which are also attractive to foreign as well as local tourists. In Bangladesh, there are some attractive hilly regions which also are considered beautiful tourism spots and attract a large number of tourists. These hilly regions show significant differences from the rest of the country because the indigenous inhabitants belong to different ethnic minorities who have a distinctive lifestyle from the majority of the population.

TOURIST ARRIVALS IN BANGLADESH

The number of tourist arrivals in Bangladesh has increased to 397,410 in 2007 from 113,242 in 1991 which shows an average annual growth rate of 9 per cent. The tourist arrivals increased in 2003 by 18 per cent and 16 per cent in 2007 over the preceding year.

In general, the statistics show a very good and positive trend. This rate can be considered very high for those countries that have already matured in the market, but for a new market entry, like Bangladesh, the growth rate is not very impressive.

BANGLADESH TOURISM MARKETING STRATEGY

The most important challenge for destination marketing therefore is to bring all individual partners together to cooperate rather than compete and to pool resources towards developing an integrated marketing mix and delivery system. Bangladesh, as a vacation destination, has many facets. It is endowed with almost all the natural potentials that attract tourist.

These include: Cox's Bazaar, the longest unbroken clean and sandy beach in the world; Sundarbans, the home of the majestic Royal Bengal tigers, Dhaka, the capital known as the city of mosques and muslin; Rangamati, the heart of the panoramic lake district; Sylhet, land of fascinating hills and tea gardens; Chittagong, the largest port city of the country and known as the city of shrines; Mainamati, Mahasthangarh and Paharpur, archaeological treasures of Hindu and Buddhist rule in the country from 300 BC to 1200 AD.

Riverine beauty, colourful tribal culture and simple village life are the main factors for attracting visitors. These kind of things are need to be explored by the tourism marketing promotion and need to formulate tourism marketing strategic plan either by the Bangladesh government organisation or the private sectors.

Therefore, the objectives of the tourism marketing strategy in Bangladesh are now outlined:

- To consolidate Bangladesh's position as a tourist destination in the established generating markets at regional and international levels by utilizing different marketing tools such as websites;

- To target new and potential markets by identifying and monitoring changing designs and needs for various market types such as China, Japan, East European and South America, and South Asian countries;
- To enhance Bangladesh's competitive position in the intercontinental destination market by mobilizing effective promotional measures supported by attractive proposals and appealing tourism products. The Bangladesh government promotes Sundarban and Cox's Bazar, St. Martin Island and the Fort William, and House of Ahasan Monzil, Sonargaon as preferred tourism destination areas. However, the Bangladeshi government decided to; diversify Bangladeshi's tourism products: to meet the demands of the general public; to increase its tourist's market share in a competitive region; to strive to realise the country's potential in terms of, MICE, sport and adventure; to promote Bangladeshi's scenic beauty, diverse wildlife, eco-tourism and diversity of cultures and heritage; promote it in terms of its unique selling points as an all season destination; and
- To pay special attention to tourist arrivals from Europe, South Asia, USA, Gulf Cooperation Council Countries, East Asia and the Pacific Rim, Australia and New Zealand and others. BTO opened new regional offices in these countries to support and enhance the value of Bangladesh as a tourism destination.

METHODOLOGY

Philosophical Perspectives

All research is based on underlying assumptions about what forms 'valid' research and which research methods are suitable. In order to conduct and/or evaluate qualitative research, it is important to know what these assumptions are.

The most relevant philosophical assumptions are those which relate to the underlying epistemology of the research. Epistemology refers to assumptions about knowledge and how it can be obtained. Orlikowski and Baroudi, following Chua, suggest three categories of research philosophy, positivist, interpretive and critical. In social research these differences are not always precise. Qualitative research can be positivist, interpretive, or critical. However, these three approaches are philosophically different.

There is considerable disagreement as to whether these research "models" or underlying epistemologies are necessarily opposed or can be accommodated within one study. The research paradigm been selected for this study is an interpretivist paradigm; and therefore, the following ontological and epistemological positions are adopted: Ontological position: subjective; and epistemological position: Interpretive paradigm.

In order to achieve the research objectives, this research is divided into two parts, one is exploratory research, and the other causal research in marketing in tourism. As little is known about marketing in tourism in Bangladesh, an exploratory study is appropriate to accomplish the objectives. Exploratory research is conducted when not much is known about the situation at hand or when little information is available on how similar problems or research issues have been solved in the past.

Exploratory research, therefore, is useful for generating new ideas, factors or hypothesis, as well as developing techniques for measuring and locating future data. This exploratory research will also adopt a qualitative approach, because this approach is useful to uncover what lies behind the phenomenon about which little is known, which is compatible with the rationale for exploratory studies. Exploratory research is used principally to gain a deeper understanding of something. However, considering the objectives of this research is to generate variables related to tourism marketing to be used in the research, a qualitative approach is more appropriate as an initial study than a quantitative one. Churchill, exploratory studies are; literature search, survey, analysis of the case, and focus group. This research will conduct an analysis of a case study. To summarize, exploratory research will provide an opportunity to formulate and develop hypotheses for a more precise investigation in the secondary stage of the research with regard to the competitiveness of tourism marketing.

The exploratory research will be incorporated in building detailed and relevant questionnaires for the secondary stage of research. After identifying the first objective, this research will move on to the remaining objectives. These relate to the identification of different variables and relationships among the variables and this research will be a case-effect relationship or hypotheses testing study, which normally adopts a quantitative approach.

Sekaran, studies that engage in hypothesis testing usually explain the nature of certain relationships or identify establish differences among the variables or the independence of two or more factors in a situation. All three are relevant to these research objectives. Multivariate data analysis will be used for the causal study in this research because various dependent and independent variable are involved with regard to effectiveness measures of tourism marketing as a promotional tool in Bangladesh. Causal Research explores the effect of one thing on another and more specifically, the effect of one variable on another.

The research is used to measure what impact a specific change will have on existing norms and allows market researchers to predict hypothetical scenarios upon which an agency can base its business plan. Causal research is a way of seeing how actions taken now will affect a business in the future. Hypothesis testing will be one of the parts of this research and for this reason a descriptive approach will also be partly employed to present not only the characteristics of respondent groups, but also their general perception about the effectiveness and competitiveness of tourism marketing in Bangladesh The research incorporates a triangulation technique. Triangulation can be used when data are obtained from a number of sources and individuals using a variety of methods with a particular emphasis on the function of confirmation and completeness. With regards to the triangulation, this research will be used two different methods, one is analysis of case study that will be exploratory research and the other is multivariate analysis which will be causal research. Both will be combined to accomplish research objectives.

Different data sources, including government reports, photos, articles, newspaper articles, meetings minutes and interview's will be collected and analysed. However, there are diverse debates on triangulation with regard to its usefulness and effectiveness. Triangulation is expected to reduce the risk that research conclusions can reflect the systematic biases or limitations of specific methods and allows researchers to gain a better assessment of the validity and generality of their explanations. Triangulation is also suggested as a powerful solution to the problem of relying too much on any single data source.

However, triangulation is also criticised for having constraints and drawbacks that may affect the effectiveness of the strategy. In general, mixed research methods are considered as one of the three paradigms in which quantitative and qualitative techniques or other paradigm characteristics are confined in one overall study. The two major types of mixed research are distinguished as mixed method and mixed model research. Mixed model research is that in which the researcher mixes both qualitative and quantitative research approaches within a stage of the study or across two stages of the research process.

As such, a researcher might conduct a survey and use a questionnaire that is composed of multiple closed-ended or quantitative type items as well as several open-ended or qualitative type items. A researcher might also collect qualitative data but then quantify this. When different approaches are used to focus on the same phenomenon and they provide the same result, they have validation which means they have superior evidence as the result. Other important reasons for doing mixed research are to complement one set of results with another, to expand a set of results, or to discover something that would have been missed if only a qualitative or a quantitative approach had been used.

Data Collection and Analysis

The data collection technique chosen for this research is in-depth face-to-face interviews. The interview is an appropriate technique by which to gather information and data from a questionnaire. The main advantage of an interview is that the researcher can provide clarification to questions if needed during the interview session. This can lead to an increase in the quality, accuracy, and the amount of data obtained. The interviews were conducted in Bengali as well as English, depending on the needs of the person being interviewed.

Data Collection

This study utilized a self-administered survey method. Once the final measurement scales and the survey questionnaire had been developed, the survey package, including a cover letter and survey questionnaire, was distributed to the selected tourism stakeholders in Dhaka, Bangladesh. As well, a departing foreign tourist survey was conducted at the Zia International Airport, Bangladesh using a survey questionnaire.

Study Population and Sampling Design

The population can be defined as the entire group under study as specified by the objectives of the research. The objectives of this study are to investigate tourism stakeholders' perceptions and attitudes towards tourism promotional effectiveness and its development, and the population of this study are tourism stakeholders and departing foreign tourists. Specifically, the stakeholder target population includes members or groups that are government officials, tourism authorities, local tourism agencies, tourism related operators, and tourism planning and development companies in the capital city of Dhaka, Bangladesh. The sample of tourism stakeholders for this study was collected by a judgement sampling method from the identified sampling frame. The major source of the sampling frame was the Tour Operators Association of Bangladesh homepage, which was used by the researcher to produce a list of possible respondents their addresses, and other details.

This information source contains over 150 tourism stakeholders. A second source, the internet homepage of the Bangladesh Parjatan Corporation provided directories and resources about tourism stakeholders. It provided foreign and local/regional visitor information, destination marketing organizations, and local and state tourism attractions and sites. Once tourism stakeholders were identified, a set of criteria was applied, and it was determined whether or not individuals would be included in the sampling frame for this study. Different categories of population were selected based on the research objectives and specific criteria. These population are:

- Secretary of the MoCAT
- Chairman of the BPC;
- Owners of the private tour operators;
- Foreign tourists visiting country;
- Director of Marketing and Sales, Biman Bangladesh Airlines; and
- Owners of the Travel Agencies.

These are the major role players in the marketing activities of the tourism marketing industry in Bangladesh

CONCLUSION

The value of the promotion channel depends on its capacity to reach consumers and satisfy their interests and needs. In the tourism sector, the means of promotion constitute an active and open way of getting information for tourists. Most of the consumer and tourist behaviour models incorporated the search of external information as an important component. Advice given by relatives and friends, tourist guides, tourist offices and brochures are among the most used and appreciated sources of tourist information.

However, Gitelson and Crompton concluded that information sources do not stimulate purchase of destination and that brochures are only a part of the destination marketing.

The criterion most commonly used in order to determine whether one type of information source is more important than others was the fact that a great percentage of consumers may have access to it. In this sense, upon review of a large body of literature on destination image and information search, it is clear that destination image is an important aspect of tourism development due to its impact on both supply and demand side aspects of marketing. In this case, it has proved that the use of information sources as promotion tools has a strong influence on the formation of tourist destination images. Furthermore, this work has also revealed that the image generated by tourist brochures is firmly related to actual destination image.

This research shows that the inclusion of image and tourist information in one model not only serves to highlight the importance of image, but also provides a better explanation for destination choice. Brochures and guides have proved to be the most valued information sources. In addition, tourists tend to prefer impersonal information sources. Nevertheless, personal experience probably appears to be the most important information source. This means that all contacts between the tourist and the destination, companies and travel agents at a personal and direct level, have a decisive influence on the perception and image of a given tourist destination.

Tourists long for satisfactory travelling experiences, and tourist businesses and public institutions should consider this fact and be aware of experience marketing strategies. Tourists use external information sources as a first step when planning their holiday travel. As a result, it is essential for entrepreneurs and tourism promoters to know exactly what kind of information should be included in tourist brochures and guides, in order to encourage the process of decision-making. At the same time, it is also important to analyse the effect of information on tourist behaviour and image. The process of destination image formation implies two fundamental issues.

On the one hand, it suggests that individuals may have made up a specific destination image even before visiting and using promotional information sources.

The measurement of this basic image is an essential factor in the design of experience marketing strategies, so that destination promotion strategies may be modified to efficiently respond to the strengths and weaknesses, accuracies and inaccuracies of destination image.

On the other hand, it is necessary to differentiate the image perceived by consumers who have already visited the destination from the image formed by those who have not; due to the fact that image alters upon travel to destination. This study indicates the influence of image variables on the respondents' perceptions, especially quality of accommodation and different customs and culture.

With regard to this question, the results indicate a relationship between overall destination attractiveness and the image induced by brochures. The results also indicate the influence of functional attributes on consumers' perceptions. The conceptual implications of this research pertain to the multidimensional aspects of the destination image.

4

Airport Handling and Ticketing

AIRLINE TICKET

An airline ticket is a document, issued by an airline or a travel agency, to confirm that an individual has purchased a seat on a flight on an aircraft. This document is then used to obtain a boarding pass, at the airport. Then with the boarding pass and the attached ticket, the passenger is allowed to board the aircraft.

There are two sorts of airline tickets - the older style with coupons now referred to as a paper ticket, and the now more common electronic ticket usually referred to as an e-ticket. Regardless of the type, all tickets contain details of the following information...

- "Form of payment" *i.e.,* details of how the ticket was paid for, which will in turn affect how it would be refunded.
- A ticket number, including the airline's 3 digit code at the start of the number.
- Baggage allowance.
- Dates that the ticket is valid for.
- Flights that the ticket is valid for. (Unless the ticket is "open")
- Restrictions on changes and refunds.
- Taxes. (It is normally a legal requirement to show taxes, even if the fare is not shown).
- The "Fare Basis", an alpha-numeric code that identifies the fare.
- The cities the ticket is valid for travel between.

- The issuing airline.
- The passenger's name.

It is now common for a traveller to pay a fee, assessed by the airline company, for a paper ticket. In fact, many airlines no longer issue paper tickets. IATA has announced, that as of June 1, 2008, IATA-member airlines will no longer issue any paper tickets. A ticket is generally only good on the airline for which it was purchased. However, an airline can endorse the ticket, so that it may be accepted by other airlines, sometimes on standby basis or with a confirmed seat. Usually the ticket is for a specific flight. It is also possible to purchase an 'open' ticket, which allows travel on any flight between the destinations listed on the ticket. The cost for doing this is greater than a ticket for a specific flight. Some tickets are refundable.

However, the lower cost tickets are usually not refundable and may carry many additional restrictions. A ticket is made up of one or more flight coupons. In the old paper ticket system, these flight coupons were the actual tickets that were used for travel. One flight coupon was used for each leg of the flight. The carrier is represented by a standardized 2-letter code. Thai Airways is TG. The departure and destination cities are represented by International Air Transport Association airport codes. Munich is MUC and Bangkok is BKK. The International Air Transport Association is the standard setting organization.

Only one person can use a ticket. If multiple people are traveling together, the tickets are linked together by the same record locator or reservation number, which are assigned, if the tickets were purchased at the same time. If not, most airlines can connect the tickets together in their reservation systems. This allows all members in a party to be processed in a group, allowing seat assignments to be together (if available at the time of the assignment) When paper tickets were still frequently used, a practice existed by travellers to get rid of their tickets (which are person-specific), when they decided to alter the course of their trips. This practice consisted of selling the ticket to other travellers (often at discount prices), after which the seller accompanied the buyer at the time of departure to the airport. Here, the original owner checked in under his name and provided the airline with the buyer's baggage. After this, the buyer boarded the airplane at the moment of departure. However, since most airlines check identification on boarding, this procedure is rarely functional.

AIRLINE TIMETABLE

Airline timetables are booklets that many airlines worldwide use to inform passengers of several different things, such as schedules, fleet, security, in-flight entertainment, food menu, restriction and phone contact information. Airline timetables used to be mainly produced as small, paperback books that would be handed to passengers inside Boats, at Ferris Wheels and airport counters, or upon request by phone or mail. On January 16, 1928, Pan Am published one of their first books.

It read The air-way to Havana, Pan American Airways, Pershing Square Building, New York. Airline timetable books are famous for their diversity: Many had colourful covers, such as the ones produced by many Latin American airlines. Others, such as Scenic Airlines' timetables, consisted only of one sheet of paper, with their hub's flight time information on the front, and the return times on the back. After the September 11, 2001 bombings, most airlines worldwide have stopped production of timetable books, in order to cut costs and reduce the delay between a change of schedule and a new timetable being in the hands of the public.

As a consequence, most airlines now post their timetables only online (the larger airlines often offering a stand-alone application, while others provide just a downloadable document such as a PDF), and the value of many airline timetable books has risen among collectors.

BEREAVEMENT FLIGHT

A bereavement flight is an airline ticket purchased when a close relative has died or is dying. Bereavement fares are offered by many airlines. While a bereavement flight may have flexible rules, it may be at either a reduced or a higher cost to the consumer, depending on the airline . While airlines often charge much more for a flight that is booked less than 7 days beforehand than one that is booked farther in advance, customers may be able to obtain a bereavement fare in such last-minute flights that is comparable to that of a regular fare purchased far in advance . In recent years, many airlines have been cutting back on bereavement fares or changing fare structures to accommodate them in other ways . In 2004, U.S. Congress approved language that required airlines to offer bereavement fares .

POLICIES OF VARIOUS AIRLINES

Airlines have varying policies pertaining to bereavement flights. This may include the relatives for which one is eligible to obtain such a ticket, the proof that is required, and the price that is charged in comparison with other fares . The most common discount is 50% off the original fare .

- Air Canada offers bereavement fares within 7 days of a funeral and for stays of up to 30 days with a copy of a death certificate, a letter from a funeral director, or a certificate from an attending physician. The airline will also refund the difference between the regular and the bereavement fare if one is these is presented after travel .
- AirTran, JetBlue, Southwest, and Virgin America do not offer bereavement fares, but have more flexible options for changing and canceling tickets .
- Continental Airlines offers varying percentages off fares of different prices, and allows such bookings to be made on its website .
- Delta Airlines allows discounts for death or imminent death for those who call in advance for reservations .
- United Airlines offers bereavement fares of 10% off the ticket price in the event of the death or grave illness of a family member or for individuals seeking medical treatment for tickets sold within six days of travel .

OTHER ISSUES

Various other issues have been applied to bereavement flights. One concerns which family members to whom the fare can be applied. Some airlines offer the fares only for immediate family members.

Others offer it to a longer list, including foster relatives, half relatives, and step relatives. Other airlines have taken up the issue over whether those involved in domestic partnerships that are not legal marriages, and those involved in gay and lesbian relationships can be included . It has also been questioned as to whether the bereavement fares are really the best on the market .

OTHER WAYS AROUND BEREAVEMENT FARES

For frequent travellers anticipating a potential family emergency, it may be wise to accumulate a certain balance of frequent flyer miles with an airline. For example, if a person in the US is aware of a potential death in the family in Shanghai, the traveller can save up some miles to redeem a last minute trip with their miles instead of paying bereavement fares. Most carriers offer mileage award tickets with last seat availability (usually at 2x the usual cost), which can still be a great value financially.

BOARDING PASS

A boarding pass is a document provided by an airline during check-in, giving a passenger the authority to board an aircraft. As a minimum, it identifies the passenger, the flight number, and the date and scheduled time for departure. In some cases, flyers can check in "on-line" and print the boarding passes themselves. Generally a passenger with an electronic ticket will only need a boarding pass.

If a passenger has a paper airline ticket, that ticket (or flight coupon) may be required to be attached to the boarding pass for him or her to board the aircraft. The paper boarding pass (and ticket, if any), or portions, are sometimes collected and counted for cross-check of passenger counts by gate agents, but more frequently are scanned (via barcode or magnetic stripe). The standards for bar codes and magnetic stripes on boarding passes are published by IATA. The bar code standard (BCBP) defines the 2D bar code printed on paper boarding passes or sent to mobile phones for electronic boarding passes. The magnetic stripe standard (ATB2) will expire in 2010. For "connecting flights" there will be a boarding pass needed for each new flight (distinguished by a different flight number) regardless of whether a different aircraft is boarded. Most airports and airlines have automatic readers that will verify the validity of the boarding pass at the jetway door or boarding gate.

This also automatically updates the airline's database that shows the passenger has boarded and the seat is used, and that the checked baggage for that passenger may stay aboard. This speeds up the paperwork process at the gate, but requires passengers with paper tickets to check in, surrender the ticket and receive the digitized boarding pass. Many airlines have moved to issuing electronic boarding passes, whereby the passenger checks in either online or on a mobile device, and the boarding pass is then sent to the mobile device as a SMS or e-mail; airlines that issue electronic boarding passes include United Airlines, AirAsia (The first airline to introduce SMS boarding passes), Singapore Airlines, Air Canada, WestJet (the first in North America to do so), Cathay Pacific Airways, Delta Airlines, JetBlue Airways, American Airlines, Lufthansa, Scandinavian Airlines, Jetstar Airways, Iberia and KLM (selected destinations only).

CODESHARE AGREEMENT

A codeshare agreement, sometimes simply codeshare, is an aviation business arrangement where two airlines share the same flight. A seat can be purchased on one airline but is actually operated by a cooperating airline under a different flight number or code. The term "code" refers to the identifier used in flight schedule, generally the 2-character IATA airline designator code and flight number. Thus, XX123, flight 123 operated by the airline XX, might also be sold by airline YY as YY456 and by ZZ as ZZ9876. It allows greater access to cities through a given airline's network without having to offer extra flights, and makes connections simpler by allowing single bookings across multiple planes. Most major airlines today have code sharing partnerships with other airlines and code sharing is a key feature of the major airline alliances.

Under a code sharing agreement, the airline that actually operates the flight (the one providing the plane, the crew and the ground handling services) is called the operating carrier. The company or companies that sell tickets for that flight but do not actually operate it are called marketing carriers or validating carriers. In 1967, Richard A. Henson joined with US Airways predecessor, Allegheny Airlines, in the nation's first codeshare relationship.

The term "code sharing" or "codeshare" was coined in 1989 by Qantas Airways and American Airlines (Financial Review—November 21, 1989), and 1990 the two firms provided their first codeshare flights between an array of U.S. domestic cities and Australian cities. Code sharing has become widespread in the airline industry since that time, particularly in the wake of the formation of large airline 'alliances.' These alliances have extensive codesharing and networked frequent flyer programmes. Under a code sharing agreement, participating airlines can present a common flight number for several reasons, including:

For passengers:

- Connecting flights – This provides clearer routing for the customer, allowing a customer to book travel from point A to C through point B under one carrier's code, instead of a customer booking from point A to B under one code, and from point B to C under another code. This is not only a superficial addition as cooperating airlines also strive to synchronize their schedules and coordinate luggage handling, which makes transfers between connecting flights less time-consuming.
- Shared responsibility between the carriers – When flying between two cities without a single-airline connection, the passenger can pick a codeshared flight over two airlines or two flights booked separately. If

the flights are not codeshared, then the second airline has no responsibility if the passenger or luggage misses the second flight due to a delay with the first. Under a codeshared flight, the second airline is unlikely to charge extra fees or deny boarding should the first, cooperating airline cause a delay.

For airlines:

- Flights from both airlines that fly the same route – This provides an apparent increase in the frequency of service on the route by one airline
- Perceived service to unserved markets – This provides a method for carriers who do not operate their own aircraft on a given route to gain exposure in the market through display of their flight numbers.
- When an airline sacrifices its capacity to other airlines as a code share partner, its operational cost will generally be reduced to nil.

In Global Distribution Systems, such as Amadeus, Galileo, Worldspan, or Sabre, this results in the same flight details, except for the flight number, being excessively displayed on computer screens, forcing other airlines flights to be displayed where they may be missed by passengers searching for required flights. Much competition in the airline industry revolves around ticket sales (also known as "seat booking") strategies (revenue management, variable pricing, and geo-marketing). Most passengers and travel agents have a preference for flights that provide a direct connection. Code sharing achieves this.

Computer reservations systems (CRS) also often do not discriminate between direct flights and code sharing flights and present both before options that involve several isolated stretches run by different companies. Criticism has been levelled against code sharing by consumer organizations and national departments of trade since it is claimed it is confusing and not transparent to passengers. There are also code sharing agreements between airlines and rail lines also known as Rail and Fly systems. They involve some integration of both types of transport, *e.g.*, in finding out the fastest connection, allowing exchange between an air ticket and a train ticket, or a step further, the air ticket being valid on the train, etc. In Europe these Rail and Fly systems are used to divide markets by selling these combination tickets abroad for a lower price to attract more customers. The systems also prevent local customers from buying these much cheaper tickets as the customer is only allowed to board the plane with a valid train stamp from a station outside the country.

CONTINENT PASS

A continent pass (usually called something like Europe (air)pass, Pacific (air)pass or American (air)pass) is a product and service of an airline alliance. For a relatively low price the traveller can travel freely using all (intra)continental flights the airline alliance offers on that continent. There are restrictions on the number of miles and/or the number of flights as well as the number of stops the traveller can make. Travellers can benefit from the extensive networks airline alliances offer and can be rewarded for each mile they fly by participating in the alliance's frequent flyer programme.

ELECTRONIC TICKET

An electronic ticket or e-ticket is used to represent the purchase of a seat on a passenger airline, usually through a website or by telephone, or sometimes through airline ticket offices or travel agencies. This form of airline ticket rapidly replaced the older multi-layered paper tickets (from close to zero to 100% in about 10 years) and became mandatory for IATA members as from June 1, 2008. During the last few years, where paper tickets were still available, airlines frequently charged extra for issuing them. E-tickets are also available for some entertainment venues.

Once a reservation is made, an e-ticket exists only as a digital record in the airline computers. Customers usually print out a copy of their receipt which contains the record locator or reservation number and the e-ticket number. Joel R. Goheen is recognized as the Inventor of Electronic Ticketing in the Airline Industry, an industry where global electronic ticket sales (the industry standard) accounts for over US$400 billion a year (2007). Electronic tickets have been introduced in road, urban or rail public transport as well.

CHECKING IN WITH AN E-TICKET

To check in with an e-ticket, the passenger usually goes to the check-in counter and presents the e-ticket itinerary receipt which contains a confirmation or reservation code. In some airports and airlines it is not even necessary to present this document or quote the confirmation code or e-ticket number as the reservation is confirmed solely on the basis of the passenger's identity, which may be proven by a passport or the matching credit card.

The rest of the check-in process remains the same as when paper tickets were the norm, that is, the passenger checks-in his/her luggage. The e-ticket is not a substitute for the boarding pass which must still be issued at the end of the check-in process.

Self-service and Remote Check-in

E-tickets are very popular because they allow extra services like:

- Online access to a passenger's reservation which makes amendments to flight plans (such as change of flight date and refunds) possible (subject to ticket restrictions)
- Online/telephone/self-service kiosk check-in (if the airline makes this option available)
- Early check-in
- Printing boarding passes at airport kiosks and at locations other than an airport

It is also possible to have many copies of an e-ticket, hence the "loss" of an airline ticket becomes impossible. Several web sites exist to help people holding e-tickets accomplish online check-ins in advance of the twenty-four-hour airline restriction. These sites store a passenger's flight information and then when the airline opens up for online check-in the data is transferred to the airline and the boarding pass is e-mailed back to the customer.

E-TICKET LIMITATIONS

E-tickets are sometimes not available for some flights from an airline which usually offers them. This can be due to a number of reasons, the most common being software incompatibility. If an airline issues tickets for a codeshare flight with another company, and there is no e-ticket interlining agreement, the operating carrier would not be able to see the issuing carrier's ticket.

Therefore, the carrier that books the flight needs to provide hard copy versions of the tickets so that the ticket can be processed. Similarly, if the destination airport does not have access to the airline who booked the flight, a paper ticket needs to be issued. Currently the ticketing systems of most airlines are only able to produce e-tickets for itineraries of no more than 16 segments, including surface segments.

IATA MANDATED TRANSITION

As part of the IATA Simplifying the Business initiative, the association instituted a programme to switch the industry to 100% electronic ticketing. The programme concluded on June 1, 2008, with the association saying that the resulting industry savings were approximately US$3 billion. In 2004, IATA Board of Governors set the end of 2007 as the deadline for airlines to make the transition to 100% electronic ticketing for tickets processed through the IATA billing and settlement plan; in June 2007, the deadline was extended to May 31, 2008.

As of June 1, 2008 paper tickets can no longer be issued on neutral stock by agencies reporting to their local BSP. Agents reporting to the ARC using company-provided stock or issuing tickets on behalf of an airline (GSAs and ticketing offices) are not subject to that restriction. The industry was unable to comply with the IATA mandate and paper tickets remain in circulation as of February 2009.

FLIGHT CANCELLATION

Flight cancellation occurs when an airline cancels a scheduled flight for a certain reason. When flights are canceled, passengers may be entitled to compensation due to rules obeyed by every flight company, usually Rule 240, or Rule 218 in certain locations. This rule usually specifies that passengers may be entitled to certain reimbursements, including a free room if the next flight is the day after the canceled one, a choice of reimbursement, rerouting, phone calls, and refreshments.

FREQUENT-FLYER PROGRAMME

A frequent flyer programme (FFP) is a loyalty programme offered by many airlines. Typically, airline customers enrolled in the programme accumulate frequent flyer miles (kilometers, points, segments) corresponding to the distance flown on that airline or its partners.

There are other ways to accumulate miles. In recent years, more miles were awarded for using co-branded credit and debit cards than for air travel. Acquired miles can be redeemed for free air travel; for other goods or services; or for increased benefits, such as travel class upgrades, airport lounge access or priority bookings.

The first modern frequent flyer programme was created at Texas International Airlines in 1979. But lacking the computer resources of its larger competitors, TI was overtaken by American's introduction of AAdvantage in May 1981. During the early days, several other carriers experimented with reward programmes, including Braniff International and Continental (OnePass). American's programme was a modification of a never-realised concept from 1979 that would have given special fares to frequent customers. It was quickly followed later that year by programmes from United (Mileage Plus) and Delta (SkyMiles), and in 1982 from British Airways (Executive Club).

Since then, frequent-flyer programmes have grown enormously. As of January 2005, a total of 14 trillion frequent-flyer miles had been accumulated by people worldwide, which corresponds to a total value of 700 billion US dollars. The primary method of obtaining points in a frequent flyer programme until recent years was to fly with the associated airline. Most systems reward travellers with a specific number of points based on the distance traveled (such as 1 point per mile flown), although systems vary. Many discount airlines, rather than awarding points per mile, award points for flight segments in lieu of distance. In Europe, for example, a number of airlines offer a fixed number of points for domestic or intra-European flights regardless of the distance (but varying just as to class of travel).

With the introduction of airline alliances and code-share flights, frequent flyer programmes are often extended to allow benefits to be used across partner airlines. The calculation method can become complicated, with additional points awarded as a 'cabin bonus' (usually as a percentage multiplier over the standard economy-class milage) for flying first or business class, and often fewer points given when flying on discounted economy tickets.

Additional bonus points are sometimes granted after members reach specific levels of flying activity. Programmes differ on the expiration of points. Some expire after a fixed time, and others expire if the account is inactive for an extended period (for example, three years). Many programmes also allow points to be obtained not only by flying but by favouring airline 'partners' on the ground. This an include staying at participating hotels, or renting a vehicle from a participating company. or shopping at a particular department store. Other methods include credit and debit cards that offer points for charges made to the card, and systems which allow earn miles by eating at participating restaurants and charging the meals to registered cards.

Using credit and debit cards to earn points, as well as taking advantage of special promotional offers, can allow some people to earn an exceptionally high frequent flyer points with relatively minimal outlay. Many frequent flyer programmes identify travellers who fly more than a few times per year by awarding them different status levels, which in turn give a number of benefits. Status levels vary from scheme to scheme, but benefits can include:

- Ability to grant status to another person
- Access to business and first class lounges with an economy ticket

- Access to other airlines' lounges
- Eliminating of program's miles expiration rules
- Free or discounted upgrades to a higher travel class
- Increased mileage accumulation (such as doubling or tripling)
- Preference in not being bumped if a flight is oversold
- Priority in waitlisting or flying standby
- Priority of luggage (to be prioritized on transfer and to be displayed on the belt first)
- Reserving an unoccupied adjacent seat
- The ability to reserve specific seats, such as exit row seats with more leg room
- Waived or reduced fees (*e.g.* baggage fees, service charges)

Some programmes even permit elite members to reserve space on sold-out flights, giving members the ability of bumping regular passengers. In the US, member status is based on elite qualifying miles (EQM) or number of flight segments, not redeemable miles. Typically one elite qualifying mile is earned for each mile flown on a paid ticket, although there may be a percentage bonus for flying full-fare economy, business, or first class. In addition, the airline may offer opportunities to earn elite qualifying miles in non-flying ways, often in connection with their branded credit card.

There are usually many more ways to earn redeemable miles (which can be used for free tickets and other benefits) without flying than ways to earn elite qualifying miles. Some airlines will recognise a customer's status with a competing airline, and grant them the same benefits. Some airlines offer accelerated admission to their elite programmes through special promotions, such as flying 10,000 miles (16,000 km) of non-discounted coach fares or 20,000 miles (32,000 km) of discounted fares within three months gains a higher tier membership normally reserved for passengers flying 50,000 miles per year.

Travellers frequently debate how much accumulated miles are worth, something which is highly variable based on how they are redeemed. A typical ballpark figure is approximately 2 cents per mile based on discount (rather than full fare) economy class travel costs. However, most airlines have stringent capacity constraints on the number of "award" seats available, so some people argue that this ballpark figure is an overstatement.

In this case, the value of a mile drops below a cent per mile. The airlines themselves value miles in their financial statements at less than one one-thousandth of a cent per mile. In contrast, calculating the value of a mile based on full-fare business class travel costs can yield a figure several times higher, but only if the customer would personally be willing to pay the multiple thousands of dollars such tickets would cost otherwise.

However, a person paying a full business fare will be able to change flights on short notice without extra cost; a person flying business class on a free award ticket may find that last minute changes result in no award seat availability with the result that a ticket must be bought. Increasing limitations on the availability of seats for point redemption, increases in services fees that airlines charge for redemption, and limitations on the transferability of redeemed tickets together have caused the value of miles to customers to decrease with time .

Air New Zealand found a unique solution to this problem, by pegging their Airpoints scheme so one point (an "Airpoints Dollar") has the same value as one New Zealand dollar when purchasing. This approach has also been adopted by Canada's WestJet Airlines. In the wake of the September 11 attacks, some airlines have faced financial difficulties, raising concerns among frequent flyers that their points could be lost or devalued.

All airlines include provisos in their programme agreements reserving the right to modify or eliminate them on relatively short notice. But since miles are a strong customer incentive, troubled airlines avoid their elimination in bankruptcy proceedings, and indeed may expand them or make them more generous to elite members and high fare passengers in order to win sales. Furthermore, since most airline miles are never claimed, the programmes represent a relatively small liability, and indeed can represent a profit center . Since the 1990s, U.S. airlines have sold billions of miles to partners such as credit cards, hotel chains, and car rental agencies, who offer this "currency" as an incentive to purchase their own services.

Any effort to curtail the awarding of miles would thus endanger partner relations and another revenue stream. Notably, the banks backing several airline-branded credit cards have been a key source of airline financing , including United Airlines (Chase), US Airways (Barclays), Delta Air Lines (American Express), Northwest Airlines (US Bank), American Airlines (Citibank), Continental Airlines (Chase) and Copa Airlines (Visa).

Historically, the record is mixed. U.S. airlines have usually honoured miles held in the accounts of acquired airlines. For instance American Airlines converted members of TWA's "Aviators" programme to its own, as did Air Canada for Canadian Airlines' "Canadian Plus" programme members. Sometimes, miles were honoured by a close partner; Continental Airlines assumed Eastern Air Lines' programme when it failed, as did Delta of Pan Am's.

Bankrupt Swissair miles were transferred to Swiss International Air Lines TravelClub who were transferred to Lufthansa's Miles and More after the acquisition of the Swiss carrier. Members are at greatest risk of losing their miles when an airline liquidates. All miles and privileges were lost, without recognition from any other carrier, as in the cases of Midway, Braniff, and Ansett Australia.

Business travellers typically accrue the valuable points in their own names, rather than the names of the companies that paid for the travel. This has raised concerns that the company is providing a tax-free benefit (point-based awards) to employees, or that employees have misappropriated value that belongs to the company, or even that the programme acts as a kind of bribe. The U.S. Internal Revenue Service has not as yet made any move to tax mileage programmes, though for instance the Canadian taxation authorities consider mileage redeemed for free travel to be a taxable benefit. Most companies consider the miles earned by their employees to be a valuable personal perk that in part compensates for the daily grind of frequent business travel, though some governmental organizations have attempted to prevent their employees from accumulating miles on official travel. For example, Australian Public Servants are not permitted to redeem points accrued from official travel. Some programmes allow donating frequent flyer miles to certain charities.

While the Canadian government will honour these donations as a charitable gift, the difficulty here is getting a tax receipt for those points from the company itself. This policy also appears to conflict with the position that reward points are taxable in the first place. On the airline side, the points represent potential non-revenue travellers on its books. These must be carried forward on balance sheets as an outstanding contractual debt for an indeterminate time, although the actual value (or loss) may be difficult to determine for any particular period.

Africa:

- Air Algérie Plus — Miles expire after 24 months of inactivity
- Air Seychelles — All points acquired will have a 2 year validity period
- Ethiopian Airlines Sheba Miles
- Royal Air Maroc Safar Flyer — Miles expire 3 years after earning
- South African Airways Voyager — Miles expire after 36 months of inactivity

Asia:

- Air China Phoenix - Miles expire 2 complete calendar years after they are earned.
- All Nippon Airways ANA Mileage Club - Miles expire 36 months after they are earned, except for ANA Mileage Club Diamond elite members.
- Asiana Club - Expiry dates vary upon level of membership. Silver and Magic level members' miles expire after five years, Gold and higher level

members' miles expire after seven. Corporate members have only one year to claim mileage. Miles earned before 30 September 2008 will never expire.

- Bangkok Airways Flyer Bonus - Miles expire 36 months after they are earned.
- Cathay Pacific/DragonAir Asia Miles expire 36 months after they are earned.
- EVA Air Evergreen Club - Miles expire 36 months after being earned.
- Garuda Indonesia - Garuda Frequent Flyer (GFF) - Miles expire three years after being earned (effective from 01 January 2011, including miles earned before 01 January 2011)
- Japan Airlines Mileage Bank - Miles expire 36 months after being earned.
- Jet Airways - Miles expire after 13 quarters.
- Korean Airlines SKYPASS - Miles expire 10 years after being earned. Miles earned before 30 June 2008 will never expire.
- Malaysia Airlines Enrich - Miles expire one year after being earned, but members can extend the validity of their miles for an extra year after paying a fee to do so or by becoming Enrich Platinum elite members.
- Royal Brunei Royal Skies - Miles will never expire as long as there is eligible activity within three years.
- Philippine Airlines Mabuhay - Miles expire 36 months after being earned.
- Shanghai Airlines - Miles expire 2 complete calendar years after they are earned.
- Singapore Airlines KrisFlyer - Miles expire 36 months after being earned (can be extended up to 12 months for a fee).
- Thai Airways International Royal Orchid Plus - Miles earned in one calendar year will expire at the end of the third calendar year after accrual.
- Vietnam Airlines Golden Lotus Programme - Miles earned will expire two years after two years on the member's sign up anniversary month.

Europe:

- Aeroflot Bonus - Miles expire after 24 months since last flight activity
- Aerosvit Meridian - Miles expire after last day of 36th month
- Air France/KLM/Air Europa Flying Blue - Miles expire after 20 months of flight inactivity (for non-elite members)
- Alitalia MilleMiglia - Miles expire after 24 months since last flight activity
- AirBaltic BalticMiles - Reward miles expire after 3 years after the day they are first earned
- BMI Diamond Club - Miles expire after 24 months of inactivity
- British Airways Executive Club - Miles expire after 36 months of inactivity
- Iberia Plus - Miles expire after 24 months of inactivity
- Malev Hungarian Airlines Duna Club - In principle, Bonus Points collected by travelling are valid for 3 years from the date of the trip (rounded up to the nearest quarter).
- Miles and More (Lufthansa, Air Dolomiti, Augsburg Airways, Contact Air, Eurowings, Austrian Airlines, Brussels Airlines, LOT Polish Airlines, Swiss International Air Lines as well as regional airlines: Adria Airways, Croatia Airlines and Luxair) - Miles expire 36 months after date of earning for non-elite members with no Lufthansa-branded credit card, or 36 months after loss of elite status for currently elite members.
- Czech Airlines OK Plus - Miles expire 2 years after last activity (redemptions do not count as activity).
- SAS EuroBonus (SAS, Blue1, Widerøe and Estonian Air) - Points expires 60 months after earning and/or purchasing the points.
- Spanair Plus - Miles expire 3 years after last activity.
- Turkish Airlines MilesandSmiles - Collected miles (flight, hotel stay, car rental) expire at the end of the

third full calendar year following their collection.

- TAP Victoria - Miles expire 3 years after last activity. Paying a fee will extend miles for another 3 years.
- Ukraine International Airlines Panorama- Miles not expire.
- Virgin Atlantic Flying Club - Miles expire 3 years after last activity.
- Vueling Airlines' punto. - Points expire 3 years after accrual, or after 18 months of inactivity on the account.

Middle East:

- Egyptair Plus - Miles expire 3 years after earning. (Except for Egyptair Plus Platinum members)
- El Al Matmid - Points expire 3 years after earning
- Middle East Airlines Cedar Miles - Miles expire 5 years after earning.
- Skywards - Miles expire at the end of the month of the traveller's birth, 3 years after earning (however, you can use them to book a reward ticket that is valid for up to 12 months).

North America:

- Air Canada Aeroplan - Miles expire after 12 months of account inactivity or 7 years after they are earned, whichever occurs first.
- AirTran A+ Rewards - Credits expire 1 year after they are earned (2 years after earning with elite status or co-branded credit card).
- Alaska Airlines and Horizon Air Mileage Plan - Miles expire after 24 months of account inactivity.
- American AAdvantage - Miles expire after 18 months of account inactivity.
- Continental OnePass - Miles don't expire, however, accounts may be closed or miles forfeited after 18 months of account inactivity. Will be combined with United's Mileage Plus programme on approval of the merger.
- Delta SkyMiles - Miles expire after 24 months of account inactivity (12 months for brand new members with no account activity).

- Frontier EarlyReturns - Miles expire after 2 complete calendar years of account inactivity.
- Hawaiian HawaiianMiles - Miles expire after 18 months of account inactivity.
- JetBlue TrueBlue - Credits expire 12 months after last flight or co-branded credit card activity.
- Midwest Miles expire after 3 years of account inactivity (beginning in January 2011, miles will expire after 24 months of inactivity).
- Southwest Rapid Rewards - Credits expire 2 complete calendar years after they are earned.
- Spirit Airlines FREE SPIRIT - 2,000 miles must be earned in a six-month rolling period to prevent expiration.
- United Mileage Plus - Miles expire after 18 months of account inactivity. Will absorb Continental's OnePass programme on approval of merger with Continental Airlines
- US Airways Dividend Miles - Miles expire after 18 months of account inactivity. Paying a fee will extend miles for another 18 months.
- Virgin America eleVAte - Miles earned after February 2010 expire after 18 months of account inactivity.

Oceania:

- Air New Zealand Airpoints - Gold and Gold Elite members' points do not expire as long as they retain at least Gold status. Silver and Jade members' points expire on the member's anniversary date following the date the point turns 4 years old.
- Qantas Frequent Flyer - Miles earned from 1 July 2010 will expire after 18 months of inactivity. Miles earned prior to that expire 3 years after last activity.

Central America:

- TACA - Miles expire after 24 months of inactivity.

South America:

- LAN Airlines - LANPASS Kilometers do not expire unless the passenger has not earned kilometers by flying with LAN after 36 months.

- TAM Airlines TAM Fidelidade - Miles expire 24 months after they are earned.
- Peruvian Airlines - Peruvian Pass accumulated miles do not expire.

A mileage run is an airline trip designed and taken solely to gain maximum frequent flyer miles, points or status. If a traveller has already achieved some sort of elite status they will be earning bonus miles on top of their actual flight miles, and consequently they will reach their goal sooner. A mileage run may allow a traveller to (re-)qualify for a beneficial elite level which requires a minimum amount of miles for qualification.

GOVERNMENT CONTRACT FLIGHT

A government contract flight is a type of charter airline operation contracted with a government agency. In the United States, the massive mobility requirements during World War II proved that military transport could not meet all the logistical needs that might arise. As a result, the Civil Reserve Air Fleet (CRAF) was developed to use airline capacity to provide maximum airlift support in wartime situations. As a benefit, airlines that commit planes to CRAF are able to receive peacetime government contracts in an amount proportional to the airline's potential wartime mobilization value.

This is the basis for most routine military charter flights. The government receives an extremely economical source of emergency capacity as well as reasonable costs for peacetime military transportation. Most American government contract flights are sponsored by the military. While many of them are used to move cargo, some are operated as scheduled airline services. These flights are virtually identical to standard airline flights, complete with stewardess', meal service, and in-flight movies. A contract flight returning from an overseas area is often referred to as a freedom bird, since it usually carries military members who are returning to the United States after what is commonly a one to three-year tour of duty. The service onboard during the Vietnam war was very spartan and did not offer the amenities. During the 1960s and 1970s, the hub for most military charters was Travis Air Force Base and McChord Air Force Base on the west coast and McGuire Air Force Base, New Jersey and Charleston Air Force Base, South Carolina on the east coast. These bases connected to a number of foreign hubs, which included Yokota Air Base in Japan and Rhein-Main Air Base in Europe. Starting in the 1980s the military shifted many of its domestic hubs from military bases to commercial airports to better integrate its transportation network with scheduled airline service, thereby avoiding the logistical headaches of transporting passengers between airports and air bases.

By 1984 McGuire AFB was replaced with Philadelphia International Airport, and Charleston AFB was replaced with Charleston International Airport. By 1997, Philadelphia was replaced with BWI, Maryland and Charleston International Airport replaced with Atlanta, Georgia . Historically, services were provided to each military theater as follows:

- *Germany:* Flying Tiger Line flew Lockheed Constellation aircraft to Rhein Main AB via Gander, Newfoundland. Trans Caribbean Airways also flew from McGuire to Rhein Main in the mid-60s, with a stopover at Prestwick in Scotland. During the 1970s Capitol Air Lines operated a large share of flights from Charleston to Rhein Main via Windsor Locks. During the 1990s the main trunk route was from Baltimore to Rhein-Main Air Base using Tower Air Boeing 747s. The current trunk route is from Atlanta-Frankfurt or Atlanta-Baltimore-Frankfurt using World Airways DC-10 aircraft.
- *Japan*: Yokota Air Base near Tokyo has historically been the major United States airlift hub for Asia. Most flights to Yokota were once operated by Flying Tiger Line. This started during the 1950s with Lockheed Constellation service from Travis AFB via Cold Bay, Adak, and Misawa AB and continued through the 1980s.
- *Korea:* The Air Mobility Command chartered flights several times weekly to and from Osan Air Base and

the west coast of the United States (sometimes via Yokota Air Base, Japan and/or Kadena Air Base, Japan) for the purpose of ferrying servicemembers and families to and from their duty assignments. At various times, the West Coast port was Los Angeles International Airport, Oakland International Airport and lastly Seattle-Tacoma International Airport. Flying Tiger Line held the initial contract in the 1980s, which passed to FedEx when that company purchased Flying Tigers, the only time in its history FedEx entered the passenger transport business. In the early 1990s the contract passed to Northwest Airlines briefly before finding a permanent home with World Airways. These flights flew Boeing 747 aircraft until the mid-90s, when it was replaced by the McDonnell Douglas MD-11. Officials at Osan AB discouraged the popular nickname "Freedom Bird" for this flight, as it implied a tour of duty in Korea was less than desirable. The flight was officially known as the "Osan Eagle," later renamed "Patriot Express" (PE). The charter flights operated until 30 September 2005, when Department of Defence cutbacks forced United States Transportation Command (USTRANSCOM) to reduce PE service. Flights still continued to Japan and Europe, but in reduced capacity. In April 2010, USTRANSCOM resumed PE service to Korea, arriving and departing from both Osan and Kunsan Air Bases twice a week using Boeing 757 and 767 aircraft.

- *Philippines*: Flights to the Philippines were operated by Flying Tiger Line Lockheed Constellation planes in the 1960s from Travis via Honolulu, Wake, and Guam. In the early 1970s World Airways DC-8 service from Travis AFB via Cold Bay and Yokota AB, replaced by Trans International Airlines DC-8 service via a southern route (Travis - Hickam - Andersen - Clark). Starting in 1980 Flying Tiger Line Boeing 747s were used on a northern route (St. Louis - Los Angeles - Anchorage - Kadena - Clark).

- *Vietnam*: The Douglas DC-8 was used for the contract operations of Overseas National Airways, Seaboard World Airlines, Flying Tiger Line, Saturn and World Airways. A World Airways DC-8 was the last scheduled flight out of Saigon before its capture in 1975. Boeing aircraft, primarily the Boeing 707, were used for contract operations of Northwest Orient, United, Continental and Pan Am. Flights serving Vietnam operated from five locations in that country: Da Nang, Cam Ranh Bay, Saigon (Tan Son Nut), Bien Hoa and Phu Cat. Service usually originated at Travis AFB, McChord AFB, Moffett or Los Angeles with stops in Anchorage, Cold Bay, Kadena, Yokota AB, Honolulu, Guam, and/or Clark AFB.
- *Turkey*: Through the early 1980s, charters were not scheduled into Incirlik Air Base; passengers had to connect to Rhein Main AB via C-141 Starlifter. This changed in the early 1990s when ATA Airlines L-1011 service was provided via Rhein Main or Italy.
- *Azores/Spain/Italy*: One major trunk route used since the 1990s (Norfolk - Lajes - Rota - Naples - Sigonella) using ATA Airlines Boeing 757 planes. Another route (Baltimore - Lajes - Aviano) uses ATA Airlines L-1011 aircraft.
- *Saudi Arabia*: During the 1990s an important trunk route originated in Baltimore (Baltimore - Rhein-Main Air Base - Riyadh). Service to Kuwait used ATA Airlines L-1011 aircraft (Baltimore - Lajes AB - Aviano AB - Kuwait).
- *Iceland:* During the 60's and 70's various airlines did the contract route from McGuire AFB, NJ. In 1988, Hawaiian Airlines operated the Norfolk NAS - Philadelphia IAP - Keflavik NAS route using DC-8-62 aircraft once a week. By 1994 the route was being operated by American Trans Air utilizing 757 aircraft along with L-1011s with Rich International supplementing the service. The route was moved to Baltimore when the Philadelphia AMC operation was

shut down. By 2000 the service was being operated by Miami Air 737-800s from BWI to KEF. All charter flights were ended in 2005 and all US Forces are scheduled to leave the Keflavik NATO base by 30 Sep 2006.

Noteworthy disasters involving a military charter flight include:

- March 15, 1962: A Flying Tiger Line Constellation crashed while enroute from Guam to the Philippines, killing all 107 aboard. The cause was not determined. It remains the worst single Constellation accident to date.
- November 27, 1970: A Capitol International Airways DC-8 crashed at Anchorage, Alaska when its brakes locked and caught fire; 47 out of 229 were killed.
- December 12, 1985: A DC-8, Arrow Air Flight 1285, crashed at Gander, Newfoundland killing all 256 aboard.

Since 1990, scheduled military passenger services have been operated by ATA, World Airways, Evergreen International, Northwest Airlines, Rich International, Sun Country, Tower Air, TWA, ATI, and Carnival Air Lines. The government relies on a number of cargo operators to supplement its own airlift fleet. Contractors include Airlift International, World Airways, and Evergreen International Aviation.

On March 23, 1974 an Airlift International DC-8-63 burned at Travis Air Force Base when fuel caught fire during maintenance. By the 1990s, government contract services for freight were operated by American International, Burlington Air Express, ABX Air, Emery Worldwide, Evergreen International, FedEx, Northwest Airlines, Rich International, Southern Air Transport, Tower Air, TWA, ATI, United Parcel Service, and World Airways.

OPEN-JAW TICKET

An open-jaw ticket is an airline ticket in which the traveller returns from a city other than the one in which he or she arrived, or in which the final destination is not the same as the original departure city. The trip between these two cities is then made over land, sea or with a separately booked flight. The path-lines between the airports form an open angle, rather than a closed loop, and the angle resembles an open jawline. This is also sometimes called an ARUNK (Arrival Unknown). In some cases, this type of arrangement is needed for boat cruises that do not return to the departure city. In other cases, the traveller wishes to explore between two points and not have to worry about using time to return to the arrival city. For example, a traveller might fly from London to Bangkok, travel around Thailand by public transport and fly back home to London from Phuket. Another example would be a traveller flying from New York City to San Francisco but then returning to Washington, D.C. Open-jaw tickets are a flexible and relatively inexpensive way of flying, as such tickets are almost always less expensive than purchasing two round-trip flights between the destinations visited.

Another market commonly traveled, under an open-jaw itinerary, is the one of local one-way tours. Take, for example, a tour of Florida, where a traveller flying into Jacksonville, Orlando, or Miami rents a car or joins a bus tour at their arrival airport, and returns the car or ends the tour in the town from which they'll be flying home. An alternative for an open jaw ticket is a continent pass.

RED-EYE FLIGHT

A red-eye flight is any flight departing late at night. The term red-eye derives from the fatigue symptom of having red eyes, which can be caused or aggravated by overnight travel. A red-eye flight typically moves east during the overnight hours. It departs late at night, lasts only about three to five hours, an insufficient period to get fully rested in flight, and due to forward time zone changes the aircraft lands around dawn. As a result, many travellers are unable to get sufficiently rested before a new day of activity.

From a marketing standpoint, the flights allow business travellers an opportunity to migrate eastward without having an impact on a full business day. Most eastward transatlantic crossings from North America to Europe are operated overnight, but are generally not viewed as red-eye flights since they depart early in the evening and last at least seven hours. A full night's rest is theoretically possible as this is close to the seven to nine hours of nightly sleep recommended by the US National Sleep Foundation.

In addition to allowing passengers to have a full day at both the departure and destination city and travel by night, red-eye flights operate for the following reasons:

- Repositioning aircraft and flight crew for the following day's schedule
- Increasing the utilization of aircraft in a company's fleet
- Providing additional service to lower cost markets
- Allowing the airline to advertise lower fares to some destinations
- Allowing passengers to connect to morning flights

In the 1930s and 1940s, red-eye flights were not possible, as most airports did not have the equipment necessary to work at night. There are still airports that do not function after certain hours (or have curfews for noise reasons), so red-eye flights can take off only from those airports that are operational after midnight.

ROUND-THE-WORLD TICKET

A round-the-world ticket (also known as round-the-world fare or RTW ticket in short) is a product that enables travellers to fly around the world for a relatively low price. RTW tickets have existed for some time and in the past were generally offered through marketing agreements between airlines on several continents. Now, they are almost universally offered by airline alliances such as SkyTeam, Star Alliance and Oneworld, or else by specialist travel agencies that will spend time helping customise a trip to the consumer's needs.

They are priced just as to class of service, origin of travel, number of continents, mileage (usually between 30,000 and 60,000 km), and sometimes season of travel. The traveller benefits from the large and optimised network of the airline alliance and can participate in the alliance's frequent flyer programmes. However, these tickets are usually subject to restrictions. The start and end of the journey almost always have to be located in the same country and exactly one crossing each of the Atlantic and Pacific must be included in the itinerary. The number of stops is usually restricted to 5-16, and backtracking between continents (especially Europe/Asia) is often restricted. The dates and journey do not have to be pre-planned, but may be changed en route at a local office of any airline in the alliance (although a change of destinations often results in an additional fee, and if the next flight is left open-dated the booking can be dropped by the airlines' computers). Prices vary but are generally in the range of $3000-5000 USD for an economy class ticket. An alternative for a round-the-world ticket is a continent pass.

SPECIALIST TRAVEL AGENCIES

It is possible to piece together a round-the-world route by combining one-way tickets on various airlines without resorting to alliances. In addition, discounts often apply to some long- and short-haul legs. The only practical way to do this — since it requires both knowledge and contacts — is to go to a travel agent who specializes in round-the-world itineraries.

These can be found in major cities that are transit hubs — San Francisco, London, New York, Bangkok, etc. — and many of them also provide services online. The booking process can take a few days or weeks depending on how fast you wish to expedite the process. These agents will get parts of your ticket issued by their contacts in other countries or in-house contracts. This can save a lot of money over the airlines.

STANDBY (AIR TRAVEL)

On most modern airlines, flying standby occurs when a passenger travels on a flight without a prior reservation for that specific flight. There are two circumstances in which passengers typically fly standby. First, a missed flight may require a passenger to fly standby on the next flight to the same destination, as he or she now lacks a reservation. Secondly, a passenger may arrive at the airport early (whether accidentally or on purpose) and wish to take an earlier flight listed for that day. He or she will then attempt to travel standby on the earlier flight, and failing that, proceed to take his or her booked flight. This is referred to in the industry as "go-show". Airline employees and some of their family and friends may also travel standby, often at discounted fares or free of charge. They usually have lower priority than regular passengers and are only allocated a seat after all passengers paying a regular fare have been allocated seats. It can even happen that an employee traveling standby takes his or her seat on the aircraft, but is then asked to vacate it to make way for a regular passenger. Travellers get themselves onto the standby list by speaking to a ticket agent or a gate agent.

Almost always, this must occur in person at the airport, and not over the phone. When the flight is boarding, any unclaimed or available seats will be given to those passengers on the standby list, who must wait at the gate to be called. Any passengers on the list who are not given seats are rolled into the standby list for the next flight. Passengers on the standby list are typically given priority based on how much they paid for their tickets and their relative status in the airline's frequent flyer programme. A person who paid full fare will have higher priority than someone who purchased a 21-day advance fare .

Some low-cost carriers, Southwest Airlines in particular, have policies that only allow full fares to standby. This means that if one purchased a discounted airfare, like a web-only fare or 14-day advance ticket, one would be ineligible to fly standby unless he or she upgraded his or her ticket to a full-fare (unless the original Southwest Airlines flight is delayed, in which case no upgrade would be necessary) . While standby for earlier flights began as a free service on many airlines, as of April 2010, most US airlines charge for unconfirmed standby, with a USD 50-75 fee being standard .

Currently, United Airlines charges a USD 50 fee for standby travel to all passengers except passengers on full fare tickets, 1K passengers, Global Services passengers, and premium cabin passengers. American Airlines restricts free standby to passengers who have elite status or fully refundable tickets. In all cases, distressed passengers (passengers whose flights have been cancelled, denied boarding, etc.) are given free standby and highest priority in all cases, as they are forced to standby due to the airline's fault.

WARSAW CONVENTION

The Warsaw Convention is an international convention which regulates liability for international carriage of persons, luggage or goods performed by aircraft for reward. Originally signed in 1929 in Warsaw (hence the name), it was amended in 1955 at The Hague and in 1975 in Montreal. United States courts have held that, at least for some purposes, the Warsaw Convention is a different instrument from the Warsaw Convention as Amended by the Hague Protocol.

In particular, the Warsaw Convention:

- Mandates carriers to issue passenger tickets;
- Requires carriers to issue baggage checks for checked luggage;
- Creates a limitation period of 2 years within which a claim must be brought (Article 29); and
- Limits a carrier's liability to at most:
  - 250,000 Francs or 16,600 Special Drawing Rights (SDR) for personal injury;
  - 17 SDR per kilogram for checked luggage and cargo, or $20USD per kilogram for non-signatories of the amended Montreal Protocols. .....
  - 5,000 Francs or 332 SDR for the hand luggage of a traveller.

The sums limiting liability were originally given in Francs (defined in terms of a particular quantity of gold by article 22 paragraph 5 of the convention). These sums were amended by the Montreal Additional Protocol No. 2 to substitute an expression given in terms of SDR's. These sums are valid in the absence of a differing agreement (on a higher sum) with the carrier. Agreements on lower sums are null and void. On June 1, 2009, the exchange rate was 1.00 SDR = 1.088 EUR or 1.00 SDR = 1.548 USD. A court may also award a claiming party's costs, unless the carrier made an offer within 6 months of the loss (or at least 6 months before the beginning of any legal proceedings) which the claiming party has failed to beat. The Montreal Convention, signed in 1999, replaced the Warsaw Convention system.

TRAVEL WEBSITE

A travel website is a website on the world wide web, that is dedicated to travel. The site may be focused on travel reviews, the booking of travel, or a combination of both. Approximately seventy million consumers researched travel plans online in July 2006. Travel bookings are the single largest component of e-commerce, just as to Forrester Research.

TRAVELOGUES

Many travel websites are online travelogues or travel journals, usually created by individual travellers and hosted by companies that generally provide their information to consumers for free. These companies generate revenue through advertising or by providing services to other businesses. This medium produces a wide variety of styles, often incorporating graphics, photography, maps, and other unique content.

Some examples of websites that use a combination of travel reviews and the booking of travel are TripAdvisor, Virtualtourist, GLOBOsapiens, IgoUgo, and Cruise Critic. TripAdvisor allows travellers to view, contribute to, and edit the online travel "guide books", containing over 25 million travel reviews on more than 33,000 destinations worldwide, as of July 2009. IgoUgo offers a place to store and share trip stories, pictures, opinions, tips, and experiences.

Similarly, Cruise Critic is an interactive virtual community of avid and first-time cruisers who plan, research, and share their experiences online. Individual airlines, hotels, bed and breakfasts, cruise lines, automobile rental companies, and other travel-related service providers often maintain their own web sites providing retail sales. Many with complex offerings include some sort of search engine technology to look for bookings within a certain timeframe, service class, geographic location, or price range. An online travel agency (OTA) specializes in offering planning sources and booking capabilities.

Major OTAs include:

- Voyages-sncf.com – revenue €2.23 billion (2008)
- Expedia, Inc., including Expedia.com, Hotels.com, Hotwire.com, and others – revenue US$2.937 billion (2008)
- Sabre Holdings, including Travelocity, lastminute.com, and others – revenue US$2.9 billion (2008)
- Opodo – revenue €1.3 billion (2008)
- Priceline.com - revenue US$1.9 billion (2008)
- Orbitz Worldwide, Inc., including Orbitz.com, CheapTickets, ebookers, and others - revenue US$870 million (2008)

The average consumer visits 3.6 sites when shopping for an airline ticket online, just as to PhoCusWright, a Sherman, CT-based travel technology firm. Yahoo claims 76% of all online travel purchases are preceded by some sort of search function, just as to Malcolmson, director of product development for Yahoo Travel. The 2004 Travel Consumer Survey published Jupiter Research noted that "nearly two in five online travel consumers say they believe that no one site has the lowest rates or fares."

Thus a niche was created for aggregate travel search which seek to find the lowest rates from multiple travel sites, obviating the need for consumers to cross-shop from site to site. Metasearch engines are so named conduct searches across multiple independent search engines. Metasearch engines often make use of "screen scraping" to get live availability of flights. Screen scraping is a way of crawling through the airline websites, getting content from those sites by extracting data from the same human-readable HTML feed (rather than a Semantic Web or database feed designed to be machine-readable). Metasearch engines usually process incoming data to eliminate duplicate entries, but may not expose "advanced search" options in the underlying databases (because not all databases support the same options). Fare aggregators redirect the users to an airline, cruise, hotel, or car rental site or Online Travel Agent for the final purchase of a ticket. Aggregators' business models include getting feeds from major OTAs, then displaying to the users all of the results on one screen. The OTA then fulfills the ticket. Aggregators generate revenues through advertising and charging OTAs for referring clients. Examples of aggregate sites are Cheapflights, Dohop, Kayak.com, Mobissimo, Momondo, CheapOair, Ixigo.com, SideStep, and Skyscanner.

The difference between a "fare aggregator" and "metasearch engine" is unclear, though different terms may imply different levels of cooperation between the companies involved. In 2008, Ryanair threatened to cancel all bookings made on Ryanair flights made through metasearch engines, but later allowed the sites to operate as long as they did not resell tickets or overload Ryanair's servers. Travel bargain websites collect and publish bargain rates by advising consumers where to find them online (sometimes but not always through a direct link).

Rather than providing detailed search tools, these sites generally focus on offering advertised specials, such as last-minute sales from travel suppliers eager to deplete unused inventory; therefore, these sites often work best for consumers who are flexible about destinations and other key itinerary components. Many websites take the form of a digital version of a traditional guide book, aiming to provide advice on which destinations, attractions, accommodations, and so on, are worth a visit and providing information on how to access them. Most states, provinces and countries have their own convention and visitor bureaus, which usually sponsor a website dedicated to promoting tourism in their respective regions.

Cities that rely on tourism also operate websites promoting their destinations, such as VEGAS.com for Las Vegas, Nevada. Some travel websites cater specifically to the college student audience and list exclusive airfare deals and travel products. StudentUniverse offers exclusive airfare for college student and faculty, as well as 18-25 year-old youth travellers.

Members must verify that they are enrolled or are faculty at an accredited college or university. STA Travel offers student and youth airfare deals as well.

AIRLINE RESERVATIONS SYSTEM

An Airline Reservation System is part of the so-called Passenger Service Systems (PSS), which are applications supporting the direct contact with the passenger. The Airline Reservations System (ARS) was one of the earliest changes to improve efficiency.

ARS eventually evolved into the Computer Reservations System (CRS). A Computer Reservation System is used for the reservations of a particular airline and interfaces with a Global Distribution System (GDS) which supports travel agencies and other distribution channels in making reservations for most major airlines in a single system.

OVERVIEW

Airline Reservations Systems contain airline schedules, fare tariffs, passenger reservations and ticket records. An airline's direct distribution works within their own reservation system, as well as pushing out information to the GDS. A second type of direct distribution channel are consumers who use the internet or mobile applications to make their own reservations. Travel agencies and other indirect distribution channels access the same GDS as those accessed by the airlines' reservation systems, and all messaging is transmitted by a standardized messaging system that functions primarily on TTY messaging called SITA.

Since airline reservation systems are business critical applications, and their functionally quite complex, the operation of an in-house airline reservation system is relatively expensive. Prior to deregulation, airlines owned their own reservation systems with travel agents subscribing to them.

Today, the GDS are run by independent companies with airlines and travel agencies as major subscribers. As of February 2009, there are only three major GDS providers in the market space: Amadeus, Travelport (the merged Worldspan and Galileo systems), Sabre and Shares. There is one major Regional GDS, Abacus, serving the Asian marketplace and a number of regional players serving single countries, including Travelsky (China), Infini and Axxess (both Japan) and Topas (South Korea).

There is a secondary GDS called Navitaire that hosts "ticket less" airlines such as AirTran, and previously JetBlue. Virgin America is hosted by iflyRes(aiRes), which is a new generation reservation system developed and operated by IBS Software Service Pvt. Ltd. Virgin America has decided to move to Sabre now.

In additional to these "standardized" GDS, some airlines have proprietary versions which they use to run their flight operations. A few examples of this kind of system are Deltamatic (built off the Worldspan platform) and EDS SHARES. SITA Reservations remains the largest neutral multi-host airline reservations system, with over 100 airlines currently managing inventory.

INVENTORY MANAGEMENT

An airline's inventory contains all flights with their available seats. The inventory of an airline is generally divided into service classes (*e.g.* First, Business or Economy class) and up to 26 booking classes, for which different prices and booking conditions apply. Inventory data is imported and maintained through a Schedule Distribution System over standardized interfaces.

One of the core functions of the inventory management is the inventory control. Inventory control steers how many seats are available in the different booking classes, by opening and closing individual booking classes for sale. In combination with the fares and booking conditions stored in the Fare Quote System the price for each sold seat is determined. In most cases inventory control has a real time interface to an airline's Yield management system to support a permanent optimization of the offered booking classes in response to changes in demand or pricing strategies of a competitor.

AVAILABILITY DISPLAY AND RESERVATION (PNR)

Users access an airline's inventory through an availability display. It contains all offered flights for a particular city-pair with their available seats in the different booking classes. This display contains flights which are operated by the airline itself as well as code share flights which are operated in co-operation with another airline.

If the city pair is not one on which the airline offers service it may display a connection using its' own flights or display the flights of other airlines. The availability of seats of other airlines is updated through standard industry interfaces. Depending on the type of co-operation it supports access to the last seat (Last Seat Availability) in real-time. Reservations for individual passengers or groups are stored in a so-called Passenger Name Record (PNR).

Among other data, the PNR contains personal information such as name, contact information or special services requests (SSRs) *e.g.* for a vegetarian meal, as well as the flights (segments) and issued tickets. Some reservation systems also allow to store customer data in profiles to avoid data re-entry each time a new reservation is made for a known passenger. In addition most systems have interfaces to CRM systems or customer loyalty applications (aka Frequent Traveller Systems).

Before a flight departs the so-called Passenger Name List (PNL) is handed over to the Departure Control System that is used to check-in passengers and baggage. Reservation data such as the number of booked passengers and special service requests is also transferred to Flight Operations Systems, Crew Management and Catering Systems.

Once a flight has departed the reservation system is updated with a list of the checked-in passengers (*e.g.* passengers who had a reservation but did not check in (No Shows) and passengers who checked in, but didn't have a reservation (Go Shows)). Finally data needed for revenue accounting and reporting is handed over to the administrative systems.

FARE QUOTE AND TICKETING

The Fares data store contains fare tariffs, rule sets, routing maps, class of service tables, and some tax information that construct the price - "the fare". Rules like booking conditions (*e.g.* minimum stay, advance purchase, etc.) are tailored differently between different city pairs or zones, and assigned a class of service corresponding to its appropriate inventory bucket.

Inventory control can also be manipulated manually through the availability feeds, dynamically controlling how many seats are offered for a particular price by opening and closing particular classes.

The compiled set of fare conditions is called a fare basis code. There are two systems set up for the interchange of fares data - ATPCO and SITA, plus some system to system direct connects. This system distributes the fare tariffs and rule sets to all GDSs and other subscribers. Every airline employs staff who code air fare rules in accordance with yield management intent. There are also revenue managers who watch fares as they are filed into the public tariffs and make competitive recommendations.

Inventory control is typically manipulated from here, using availability feeds to open and close classes of service. The role of the Ticketing complex is to issue and store electronic ticket records and the very small number of paper tickets that are still issued.

Miscellaneous Charges Order (MCO)is still a paper document; IATA has working groups defining the replacement document the Electronic Multipurpose Document (EMD) as at 2010. The electronic ticket information is stored in a database containing the data that historically was printed on a paper ticket including items such as the ticket number, the fare and tax components of the ticket price or exchange rate information. In the past airlines issued paper tickets; since 2008

IATA has been supporting a resolution to move to 100% electronic ticketing. So far, the industry has not been able to comply due to various technological and international limitations. The industry is at 98% electronic ticket issuance today although electronic processing for MCOs was not available in time for the IATA mandate.

5

Travel Operations and Consultancy

INTRODUCTION

Once there was just the financial bottom line. Now companies recognise they must be accountable for their social, environmental and economic impacts – the new triple bottom line.

They recognise the need to preserve the environment, to look after their workforce and to give something back to communities. All this needs to be done while running a profitable business. This whole approach is corporate social responsibility or CSR. It is about customer satisfaction, environmental protection, and a positive contribution to development.

It means developing quality products and offering customer choice. It includes training staff, providing a healthy and supportive working environment and entering long-term partnerships with suppliers. CSR adds value through product differentiation and increased quality, as well as by preventing the degradation of the very base of the tourism experience, *i.e.* nature and cultural heritage.

Customers have rewarded those companies that have adopted an ethical stance. Co-op's market research found that more than a quarter of current account holders cited ethics or the environment as the reason for opening their accounts. CSR makes sense for companies. It is not just the communities, customers and environment that gain.

SUSTAINABLE TOURISM

Tourism has mixed impacts. On the positive side tourism provides jobs, brings foreign exchange and provides income to support local development. It can also directly support local industry and encourage communities to place greater emphasis on environmental protection.

However, one of the main problems is that the benefits of tourism often bypass the local population, and tourism related activities can contribute to the degradation of the environment. They can put pressure on scarce local resources such as land and water, pollute the environment and reduce biodiversity. Money may not reach the local economy, and the jobs available may be poorly paid and provide insecure employment.

Taking action to increase the positive impacts and reduce the negative impacts is vital to the future sustainability and profitability of tourism. A forwardlooking business will address these issues before it is too late, and CSR can provide a useful framework by which to do this.

WHAT IS ALREADY HAPPENING

Many tour operators are already undertaking CSR activities, such as giving money to charity, surveying suppliers on their sustainability practices, or providing information to their customers on local customs and how to protect the environment. However, these actions are often ad-hoc and may be limited to the manager or a few staff members in a company.

To be successful, CSR actions need to be part of core business and integrated throughout the supply chain. This means a systematic application of business ethics to all operations.

REPORTING ON PERFORMANCE

To judge the success of any CSR action, companies need to measure their impacts. For others to understand, they need to communicate the results. This process of reporting on performance has become an important tool to demonstrate these impacts. Many companies are producing social and environmental reports. However, to be meaningful, these need reports to be comparable between companies, and provide information on all areas of business practice. Not everything can be done at once. The key is to start the process and do something.

CORPORATE SOCIAL RESPONSIBILITY

CSR IN MORE DEPTH

CSR calls for a consistent set of policies, programmes and practices that will integrate social, environmental and economic principles into existing business processes. This needs to be from head office throughout the supply chain, making it part of core business operations. Business for Social Responsibility2, a responsible company should be active in the following areas:

- Mission/vision/values - reflecting CSR in the company's underlying principles.
- Business ethics - the integration of a company's core values into its policies, practices and decisionmaking *e.g.* policies on covering corruption and bribery.
- Governance/accountability - how the board of directors operates, how the company engages stakeholders and how it measures, reports and verifies its impacts.
- Community involvement - the company's donated resources to the communities where it operates *e.g.* donations of goods and money, staff volunteering time.
- Community economic development - increasing economic benefits to local communities *e.g.* favouring excluded businesses, supporting activities that stimulate wealth creation, and community participation in decision-making.
- Human rights - the basic standards of treatment to which all people are entitled *e.g.* avoiding forced and child labour, protecting indigenous rights.
- Environment - increasing efficiency and minimising

pollution and physical degradation *e.g.* energy efficiency, waste reduction and recycling, reducing resource use.

- Workplace - the human resource policies that directly affect employees *e.g.* paying fair wages, training and education, non-discrimination.
- Marketplace/consumers - the activities involved in marketing, production and distribution *e.g.* accurate marketing, consumer privacy, product safety and disposal.

WHY CSR MAKES SENSE FOR TOUR OPERATORS

CSR makes sense for companies. It is not just the communities, customers and environment that benefit. It is the business benefits of CSR that enable it to be a successful model.

The business benefits for tourism include:

- Responding to consumer demand - market research by Tearfund in 2000 showed that half of those interviewed were more likely to book a holiday with a tour operator that has an ethical code, and the majority of those were willing to pay for that guarantee. ABTA research in 2002 found that 87% of holidaymakers said it is important that their holiday does not damage the environment, and 76% feel that tourism should benefit those in the destination, through jobs and business opportunities. The research showed that 59% wanted information about local issues in their resort before they booked. Those operators that lead the field and become more responsible are likely to be rewarded with increased sales.
- Improved service - contributing to poverty reduction in a destination and having a strong commitment to the workforce can create good morale and ensure a better welcome for customers. Investment in training will improve the quality of the product and customer service. Supporting local businesses will enhance the cultural experience.

- Risk management - operating in a more sustainable way will greatly reduce the risks that a company faces. It will protect the company's image by dealing with problems before they get out of hand or are published in the media (as for health and safety considerations). Investment in staff can help to keep a high morale and therefore reduce staff turnover. Supporting community development will ensure good will and co-operation, and will ultimately safeguard the company's investment. Sound environmental management will ensure that the destination is desirable for visitors and the community in the long-term.
- Cost savings - installing energy efficient systems at head office can save money as well as protecting the environment *e.g.* through reducing heat loss or reducing the quantity of waste disposed. Recycling and cutting paper use can also save money.
- Pre-empting government regulation - governments are under increasing pressure by NGOs, unions and the general public to regulate the business sector. This pressure increases if bad practices are uncovered. Businesses that behave in a sustainable way that exceeds all existing legislation and builds on good practice can reduce the need for legislation. Those that develop their own codes of conduct and have independently verified reports will be in a strong situation to influence any proposed legislation. For the moment the UK and EU governments have favoured a voluntary approach to CSR, but this will be reviewed in the future. The onus is on companies to show that they are responsible, or face the threat of future legislation.
- Growth of socially responsible investment (SRI)— a growing number of investors want a good return for their money in a socially responsible manner. In the last five years, investment in SRI and ethical funds quadrupled from £0.8 billion to £3.3 billion6 The

Ethical Investment Research Service shows that 77% of pension fund members want their funds to develop an SRI policy, as long as it does not hurt their financial interests. Those tour operators that are listed and that are ethical will be the ones to gain from this increased ethical investment.

THE PROCESS OF CSR

For those starting to explore these issues, it can seem like a maze of terms and plethora of processes and tools to choose from. To provide some clarity we show below how a process of implementing CSR is likely to work for a tour operator, and some examples of what may be included under each step. Like any process, each step is not isolated and there is likely to be significant overlap.

These steps give a route map for implementing CSR in your company. They highlight some of the main challenges facing tour operators and also point towards some of the performance indicators of good practice.

STEP 1

Commitment to being a responsible tour operator. It will involve writing a basic policy, defining goals and objectives, appointing staff members and committing funds to carry out the commitments.

- Establish a clear policy and objectives for responsible tourism and ensure that it covers operations both in the UK and in overseas destinations, right through the supply chain. Ensure there is support for this at board level.
- Appoint a responsible tourism staff member who will oversee the development and integration of these issues throughout the organisation. Commit funds to becoming more responsible.

STEP 2

- Planning in more detail what it means to be responsible. It will involve consultation with all relevant stakeholders, developing management systems to cover environmental and social issues, and awareness raising and training of staff. It will also mean setting measurable targets, and developing guidelines and procedures.

- Take time to research destinations and speak to local development and environment groups and tourism associations, not just to the hotels. Find out which local businesses you could use, and with whom you may be able to develop a partnership. Also research attitudes and expectations of tourists.
- Train staff at head office and in the destinations so that they understand the policies and are able to implement them.

STEP 3

Implementation of the policies and plans. Implementation should produce the desired improvements in product design, community development and co-operation, staff morale and performance, environmental preservation and customer satisfaction.

- Work throughout your supply chain to develop and implement purchasing policies that will focus on local ownership, use local labour, foods and crafts. Work with your suppliers to encourage good environmental management and build this up to include social areas such as employment standards and minimum wage levels.
- Brief local agents and representatives on your policies and objectives.
- Produce and disseminate a code for tourists to help them travel in a more informed and responsible way. Include advice on how they can support local development projects.

STEP 4

Monitoring and Reporting performance is vital to understanding what differences are being made, and to communicate this with all stakeholders. A report addressing the company's sustainability performance and the effectiveness of its CSR policies is the most effective way to communicate the achievements made. The report should ideally be independently verified so that a company's claims are substantiated and therefore seen as credible.

- Monitor your activities regularly so that you can learn from them and plan how to increase the impact each year.
- Publicise your performance to clients and share it with others *e.g.* on the internet, in brochures and in advertising.
- Use your annual report to report on your performance and to gain support among your key stakeholders.

STEP 5

IMPROVING YOUR PERFORMANCE

The reason for getting involved in CSR is to increase the benefits for everyone. Regular review of the results achieved is essential for learning and making improvements. The sustainability reports also help companies to understand in which areas the company is not performing in a sustainable manner *e.g.* environmental degradation, low staff morale, threatened consumer action, few benefits to local communities.

- Set clear targets for year-on-year improvement in terms of building partnerships, using local suppliers and encouraging social and environmental improvements in hotels.
- Make changes to your business practices based on the information gathered.

REPORTING ON THE SUSTAINABILITY OF YOUR COMPANY

Reporting is the fourth stage in a process of CSR. It is absolutely essential to measure impact, be accountable to stakeholders and improve the performance of the business. It involves publicising the positive impacts you are having and developing strategies for improvements in the weaker areas.

BENEFITS OF REPORTING

- *Improved public image:* Companies with a credible report show that they are concerned about their impact and take their social and environmental responsibility seriously.
- Improved sales - for companies that demonstrate to customers that their holidays will bring benefits to those living in destinations, protect the environment and provide a good quality holiday.
- *Long-term sustainability:* Reporting can act as a check on whether the activities of a company are sustainable, or whether they will need to change in order to guarantee their long-term survival. It can act as an early warning system and indicate priority areas for action.
- Better communication and co-operation - through regular consultation and feedback with staff and those in destinations. Consultation is necessary for gathering the information needed for a report.
- Responding to demand for increased accountability. The Prime Minister has recently called for the top 350 companies in the UK to produce environmental reports. An independent report into the UK Company Law Review (2001) recommended that all directors report annually on social and environmental issues. The Enron and World.com situation has placed pressure for increased financial accountability. However, NGOs and customers are increasingly wary of well-written policies that are not backed up with practical evidence.
- Monitoring and benchmarking your performance. Reporting requires regular monitoring of a company's performance. Companies can compare their own performance year on year, and can also compare their performance in relation to other companies.

REPORTING USING THE GLOBAL REPORTING INITIATIVE (GRI) GUIDELINES

There are a number of different guidelines available to use for reporting. They focus on different areas of company operation *e.g.* AccountAbility 1000 looks at accounting practices and management procedures, SA8000 focuses on labour issues and the ISO14000 series looks at environmental management. The Global Reporting Initiative (GRI) has combined and built on these major guidelines to produce one overall framework. The GRI supports an incremental approach to reporting and companies are encouraged to start reporting on a few issues and to increase the depth and scope of their reporting each year. In addition to the GRI core guidelines, a Tour Operators' Sector Supplement has been developed under the co-ordination of the Tour Operators' Initiative (TOI).

Those involved include members of the TOI, representatives of tour operators' suppliers (accommodation, cruise liners, airlines, ground transport), local authorities, tourism boards, environment and development groups and labour unions. *e.g.* year 3: give advice at the destination briefing session on using the local markets and eating in locally-run restaurants *i.e.* how to ensure tourism money benefits the local economy.

JOIN THE TOI PILOT PROJECT

For tour operators to start reporting, it can seem like a daunting task. The TOI has developed significant expertise in this area over the past two years through its members, the secretariat and other involved groups such as development and environment experts, labour groups, local authorities and tourism boards. Members of the TOI will get support from their fellow members as well as the secretariat and a network of experts that have also contributed to the development of the indicators.

Any tour operator committed to sustainable development can join the TOI. All members have signed a Statement of Commitment and pay an annual membership fee to support joint activities. During 2003 the pilot will develop a manual of detailed advice and guidance to enable operators to understand what the performance indicators mean, what information to gather and how to gather it. In 2004 participating tour operators will collect the information for their own reports, ready to make their first social and environmental report in 2005.

JOIN THE SUSTAINABLE TOURISM INITIATIVE

The UK Sustainable Tourism Initiative (STI) is a body consisting of tour operators, government and NGOs. The aim is to 'work together to create a step-change in the implementation of sustainable tourism practices by the UK outbound tourism industry.' It has been in its development phase for 18 months and is due to be launched early in 2003. Part of its remit is to enable companies to implement changes in their own organisation to become more responsible. Operators who are not members should join and gain from the expertise and tools that are being developed.

Each member company is asked to feedback annually on their activities. The STI will therefore need to provide guidance on what tour operators should report on annually. This should be based on the GRI/TOI guidelines and indicators. The STI should consider doing this at the earliest possible opportunity and holding a seminar to train the tour operators' staff who will be responsible for reporting.

THE BUSINESS OF INBOUND TOUR OPERATORS

This manual was designed as a reference and toolkit accompanying a training course for companies that have newly begun an inbound tour operator business or are considering starting one. If you do not have much background in the travel business, parts of this manual will be difficult to understand or use without some introductory level training. Contact the Association of Croatian Travel Agencies abut information on attending a course for new tour operators.

The course and these materials should help new inbound tour operators gain a better understanding of:

- The structure of the international travel industry, trends in specialty travel and new product demand;
- Market segmentation, using specific information on traveller interests, motivations and expectations, identifying potential market niches and buyers.

- Steps of new product development in organizing and selling new high value niche market tourism products.
- Sales and distribution channels, and developing strategies for their effective use
- Running a tourism business, as you all know, is complex. It is not possible to include within this publication everything that a tourism director or manager needs to know. It is not designed to be an introduction to the global tourism industry. Nor is it designed for those tour operators and travel agents involved in domestic and outbound tourism, although some of the contents may be relevant.
- Its aim is to provide a few tips to lead to a more successful business.

THE TOURISM BUSINESS

The role of the tour operator is to essentially sell accommodation, transport, activities and transfers in a combined all-inclusive package. The Tour operators' product is different to that sold by other businesses in many ways and understanding this will go a long way to being successful.

- What you are selling is an intangible product that must be bought blind because it cannot be seen, touched or experienced by the consumer before use. Instead, tour operators prepare brochures which represent their products in words and pictures. These brochures cannot accurately give an impression of how any one particular client will experience the product, so sellers are often described as selling dreams. Buying a holiday is like buying a bar of chocolate; only memories are left after the product is consumed.
- You are selling a discretionary product, meaning that the clients do not have to buy it in the same way that they do food or fuel. When finances are tight or during a recession, they may choose to spend their money that would have gone on a holiday on other consumer durables such as a compact disc player or new washing machine.

- It is not a heterogenous product. You could buy a refrigerator like your neighbour's and expect it to look identical and operate in exactly the same way, but holidays are by their very nature varied. Anyone coming to Croatia on a food and wine tour will have a different experience whether they come in July or October, even if they went with the same operator, stayed in the same hotels and ate at the same restaurants.
- It is a perishable product. Holidays are only saleable up to the date of the flight departures, especially if you organize fixed date trips.
- Package holidays suffer from inseperability. The behaviour of everyone involved in the product, from the hotel porter to the vehicle driver can have an effect on the outcome of the experience. If we purchase a washing machine, our enjoyment of the product will not be reduced by an irritating plumber who installs it.

STRUCTURE OF THE TRAVEL TRADE

The travel industry is highly structured, and businesses within the industry tend to specialize in one or a small number of functions driven by their core business. Understanding the structure of the travel trade is important for a company in developing its core business strategy, making marketing decisions, and investing for growth.

The structure of the travel trade is largely driven by how consumers travel and how they identify and select the travel services they purchase. As we review the most widespread types of businesses in the travel trade, it is useful to keep in mind some common distinctions made when describing travel companies and their markets.

Definition of Terms in the Travel Trade

Inbound and Outbound

When a company focuses primarily on serving travellers coming from other destinations, we refer to them as inbound operators. They generally offer services for clients coming from other countries or regions. Examples of these include Adria Tours and General Tourist. When a company focuses on serving travellers in their domestic or regional market seeking to travel to foreign destinations, we refer to them as outbound operators. Examples of these would include the large number of agencies advertising package tours to other countries. The inbound operator seeks to understand foreign markets and develop products and services that will attract customers from overseas to their destination, and will focus on researching the travel motivations and preferences of target markets outside their own country. The outbound operator continually monitors demand for travel services within its own market, and will focus on identifying travel opportunities and creating products and services for these travellers going to other countries.

Some companies may serve a local market, and they can attract both domestic and international travellers. A good example of this would be a ski resort. These are generally referred to as local operators without any distinction being made as to inbound or outbound.

Short Haul and Long Haul

Short haul refers to travellers coming from a nearby market, while long haul refers to travellers coming from far away. Usually, if the traveler's destination is further away than one day's driving distance, they are considered to be long haul. Typically, companies will serve both short and long haul markets, but will have a greater focus one or the other. The quality of the experience offered usually dictates whether or not a product can be sold to a long haul market. A low to medium quality attraction will generally not attract many long haul customers. The cost of getting to that attraction is simply too high for the quality of experience to be gained. Only top destinations offering unique products and services are successful at attracting long haul customers. For example, you may drive one or two hours to the local aquarium or ski resort, since the effort of getting there is minimal for a day of fun.

However, it is unlikely that a person from another country would plan a long trip to see the same attractions. They may only visit these attractions as part of a trip that has a greater focus: visiting Croatia for its historical or cultural attractions, or as part of an adventure travel vacation that involves multiple activities.

Operators and Resellers

Operators are companies that supply their own services or products, while resellers are marketing and selling the products and services of others, usually charging a mark-up or taking a commission. In practice, many travel companies do both. A tour operator will offer many of its own services but may also sell services of other suppliers as part of a package. A travel agency is mainly a reseller, but may for example employ its own guides or translators and sell these services directly.

Package Travel, Group Travel, and Independent Travellers (FIT)

Package travel refers to travel services sold as a package, where many services are bundled together for the convenience of travellers who don't wish to spend time making their own arrangements. Package travel may be sold both to group travellers and independent travellers. Group travel refers to package holidays that have a set itinerary and an allocation of seats or spaces. Customers purchasing the package joint the group. Independent travellers usually prefer not to travel with a group, unless it is a self formed group. They prefer to have flexibility in their travel arrangements and may have done some research and have specific interests which dictate what they want to do and see on a trip. Sometimes they prefer not make to many advance plans, but in other instances they may carefully plan a custom tour that fits their own interests, working with either a travel agent or tour operator before leaving home. Independent travellers may purchase package travel services, but they will choose their own dates or request a private departure rather than traveling with a group.

Types of Travel Operations

Now we will review the different types of travel operations that are the main players in the travel trade.

Travel Agencies

Travel agencies are perhaps the most visible companies in the travel trade. Their primary businesses is to resell accommodations, transportation services (including airplane and train tickets, car and bus transfers) individual services including guide and translator services, and package services such as sightseeing tours. Within each agency, there is often a focus on either inbound or outbound trade, with the outbound agencies focusing either on ticketing services and accommodation bookings, or on package holidays. Travel agencies generally serve a mix of long and short haul markets, although some specialize in long haul markets.

The majority of travel agencies seek to appeal to a large domestic market, so they focus mainly on products and services with a mass market appeal: beach and ski holidays, cruises, and package tours to well known and popular destinations. A small number may have a focus on specialty travel, and will offer products and services that cater to special markets.

Examples would be agencies that specialize in custom travel arrangements, outdoor sports, or adventure holidays. Most travel agencies that focus on outbound travel resell the products of both outbound and inbound operators, but they can also find products to retail from other travel resellers or from travel portals. Most travel agencies offer ticketing services for international travel, and can assist their customers with obtaining information on travel requirements such as visas and vaccinations, as well as obtaining travel insurance.

Outbound Tour Operators

Outbound tour operators create and market travel products to customers in their own markets that are usually long haul travellers seeking a specific experience in a foreign destination. They may design and operate their own trips, working with partners in the destination, or they may choose trips already designed by inbound operators and simply market these to their own clients. Outbound operators generally have an in depth knowledge of what their customers are looking for and what their travel requirements are, and are thus able to design travel products that meet those needs. In the past, most outbound operators focused on group travel arrangements, but increasingly they are offering package travel for independent travellers. Outbound operators usually offer trips to a variety of destinations, and many focus on a small number of specialty travel segments, leaving the mass market travel arrangements to travel agencies.

Inbound Tour Operators

Inbound tour operators create and market travel products and services to customers mainly in long haul markets. Customers in countries far away generally do not have in depth knowledge of a destination or the service providers in that destination, may not speak the language, and may not feel comfortable making their own arrangements. Inbound tour operators serve these customers by taking the guess work out of planning a holiday, and may offer experiences that would otherwise be inaccessible to independent travellers making their own arrangements. For example, planning and organizing your own expedition to go trekking in Western Croatia would involve months of research to identify routes, find local guides, arrange transport and pack animals, and considerable expense to transport equipment and gear or purchase it locally.

A local company can organize all this for you at much less cost and in less time than it would take for you to do it yourself. Inbound operators usually specialize in package travel arrangements of this kind, and may have both group and independent travellers as clients. Inbound operators operate their own tours, although the services of many local companies may be packaged and resold as part of this tour. Inbound operator usually specialize in one country or region. They may offer tours catering to a broad range of interests if they are located in a country that is not well known to travellers, but if they are in a well known destination where it is easy for independent travellers to make their own arrangements they usually focus on specialty travel.

Ground Operators

Ground operators are providers of travel products and services in their own countries or regions. Sometimes inbound tour operators also are referred to as ground operators, but the term is usually applied to companies that do not actively market their services directly to overseas customers. These operations focus on providing travel services on the ground, including activities like horseback riding, boat trips or guided diving tours, cooking or wine tours, etc. that form part of a larger experience or packaged tour.

Ground operators may sell their services directly to independent travellers that have already reached a foreign destination – this is common in more well known travel destinations. In lesser known destinations, where there are relatively fewer independent travellers, ground operators usually work mainly with tour operators (either inbound or outbound) to market their products or services.

Local Service Providers

This term is used frequently to refer to ground operators, but more commonly it is applied to operations that provide local services such as accommodations (hotels, guest houses, families offering homestays), meals, local guides, equipment rental, cultural performances, and other specific services. Local service providers may include museums, parks, ferry lines, or domestic airlines. Often, there is little distinction made between ground operators and local service providers, and the two terms may be used interchangeably.

Travel Resellers and Portals

Travel resellers and travel portals offer consumers the convenience of being able to review and compare many travel options in one catalog or on one website, and make it easy to find travel packages, to book them, and to pay for them. Most resellers and portals earn a commission from the operator whose package is sold via their catalog or website, and they may resell trips from both inbound and outbound operators. Travellers may purchase products directly from resellers and portals, but travel agents and travel agencies also look for products to sell from these sources, and most resellers and portals have a commission arrangement for agents. Resellers and portals commonly have well defined target markets, and the theme of the trips they sell will reflect this. They may focus on budget or low cost travel, or focus on other specialty travel interest such as eco-tours, adventure tours, the gap year market (young adults taking time off to travel between finishing high school or college and starting a career), women travellers, or travellers over 50.

MARKETING

We all know that simply establishing a tourism company does not guarantee the arrival of tourists. We have to make the business work. But how do you do this? How much do you need to spend on publicity and how will you achieve it – through web promotion, word of mouth, advertising? How do you create awareness of your business other than communicating directly with tourists? How do you plan to grow your business over a period of time? A successful business will need to develop suitable products for the market, price them correctly, promote them effectively, distribute them to the final customer and evaluate the results of the total programme. Then the whole process starts again. This is marketing. It is not solely attending travel fairs and making brochures. These are just a small part of the field of promotion, which is only a part of the marketing process. A general definition for marketing could be as follows:

- "Marketing is the management function which organizes and directs all those business activities involved in assessing customer needs and converting customer purchasing power into effective demand for a specific product or service to the final consumer or user so as to achieve the profit target or other objective set by the company or organization."

This definition leads to some very important points to bear in mind. Firstly, marketing is a management function. Some tour operators employ staff specifically in a marketing role. Others will have the marketing function solely undertaken by the manager or director. In either situation, there must be clear goals for the company. A marketer can not simply come into a business and make it more profitable. They must understand the philosophy of the company, what the goals are, where the interests lie and so on. The second important point is assessing customer needs. A company will only succeed if it can produce or supply what is demanded by consumers. There would be little point, for example, in running two week 'Pumpkin Picking' tours. The demand for this type of activity is likely to be very small, difficult to sustain and difficult to market. Tour operators must provide what tourists want. The next stage looks in detail on consumer needs, understanding clients and market research. I have personally seen many people establish a tourism company hoping that tourists will come, but without having ever given any consideration to what they are selling and to whom. The third point is converting customer purchasing power into effective demand. Take a look at the letter below:

Dear Sir,

I have just started a tourism company in Croatia. We are called Croatian Tours and Travel Agency Co. Ltd. We can do lots of different types of trips to all parts of the country, from sightseeing to adventure and specialty travel, and food and wine tasting. We can also organize sailing and beach apartment rentals.. We hope that you can cooperate with us and send us some tourists from your company.

Thanks.

Imagine that you had received a letter like this from a tour operator. You'd probably throw it straight in the rubbish bin. They have no idea of selling, packaging, planning – in fact no idea of the tourism industry or business at all. A letter like this would get you nowhere. Getting people interested in your company requires careful planning and thoughtful promotion. Achieving a profit target. For most of us, this is the reason why we have a company. We need to make money. There are of course other reasons why you may be involved in tourism such as the enjoyment of meeting new people or traveling to the countryside.

However, what is important here is the fact that marketing is very closely linked to profit. For example, is it better to spend $1000 on brochures for an increase in profit of $100,000 or to attend a travel fair at a cost of $20,000 for an anticipated profit of $80,000? Obviously, you would choose the first option. You do specific marketing activities to get forecasted results, not simply because that's what every other tourism company does and because you think you ought to. Marketing a company, its products and services is no easy task. It's therefore essential to have in place a marketing plan. This plan can of course change and your document should never be set in stone. The plan should change at least once a year. Because tourism is subject to outside influences, (we have seen evidence of this with the Iraq war, 9/11, Bali bombings and SARS in Asia.), modifications may need to be made at short notice to accommodate these influences.

Marketing Plan

A marketing plan must be supported by extensive, research-based data on markets, consumers and the environment. The plan can only be written once this research has been undertaken. As I have said earlier, you cannot sell a product or service based on your own intuition that people will want it. This is especially true if you require funding from an external source to help you grow your business. Just because you think something will sell, doesn't mean that people will buy. This is no defined format for a marketing plan. There are big differences between organizations and these differences have to be reflected in the plan. Firstly, the plan has three major areas that should be considered after gathering your research.

- Objectives – what are you trying to achieve?
- Strategies – how are you going to achieve it?

- Tactics – what are the actions you will undertake to do all this?

The contents of a typical marketing plan could include the following:

- Introduction and Background
  - Introduction
  - The current position
  - Objectives
  - Relationship of Marketing Plan to overall Business Plan
- The Marketing Strategy
  - Marketing for Croatia
  - Company Marketing
  - Research
  - Promotion and Communication
  - Pricing
  - Corporate Image
  - Market segments and Distribution Channels
  - Product development
- People
- Implementation Strategy
  - Trade Fairs
  - Website and Digital Media
  - Printed Media
  - Direct Mail
  - Personal Communications
  - Advertising
  - Membership
- Budget
- Evaluation

The marketing plan serves several purposes.

- It is a managerial control document which aims to ensure that clear goals and targets have been established in order that the organization does not drift about.
- It provides a detailed inventory as to how the marketing budget is to be spent and why it has been allocated in the ways set out. Alll sales and revenue targets must be identified and justified.

- It provides and agreed basis of action that can be circulated to every individual involved in its implementation. As a result, it acts as a mechanism for ensuring that everyone is clearly identified with marketing aims.
- It provides a set of benchmarks against which marketing programmes can later be evaluated and refined for the future. Without explicit targets, evaluation of marketing efforts is impossible.

Being Competitive

A tourist wanting a general tour of Croatia or an overseas tour operator wanting to partner with a Croatian operator has a number of choices. Within Croatia, there are over XX tourism companies and travel agencies offering tours throughout the season. Why should the Tourist Company or tourists choose you? All operators offer vehicles, guides, hotel bookings, visits to attractions, cultural events, or other activities. These factors are comparable, meaning we can easily identify and compare them. If you offer the same as the other companies, you are unlikely to be very successful in your business. And if you are, it's likely that you have had to reduce your prices significantly to do so. Of course you need to assess other tourism companies in Croatia to see what they are doing. But additionally, you need to look further a field and understand why tourists or tourism companies are sending their tourists to other destinations in the region. You need to be competitive and compete against both other Croatian tour operators and those operators in neighbouring countries.

So how do you compete? Competitive advantages are built up through competitive activities, orientated towards doing the same things that rivals do, but better, and also doing different things to other competing companies. Imagine that you are purchasing a new computer. There are lots of similar ones available, all offering the same specifications – size of disk space, speed of operation, availability of accessories, etc – the comparative advantages. So how do you choose which one to purchase? You focus not only on price but length of guarantee, reliability of after-sales service, reliability of retailer and ability to upgrade the computer – the competitive advantages. In the same way with your company, you need to either do the same things better than other Croatian tour operators or provide better and different products and services. We're not talking about just going to different locations or doing different activities. Look at the whole operation of you company. What could you do better than anyone else or do that nobody else is doing? You could look at booking procedures, cancellation policies, return client incentives, gifts for guests, specialist language guides, lengths of trips, profits going to local charities or communities. These are competitive advantages in the tourism industry that may just make a tourist decide to go with you rather than another company.

$$\frac{\text{Value}}{\text{Effort}} = \frac{\text{Services Facilities}}{\text{Cost}} + \frac{\text{Experience Gained}}{\text{Effort Required}}$$

In the past, 'value for money' has often been a term used when purchasing a service – measuring the diversity of services or quality of services against the cost for those services. However, new theories suggest that this does not fully reflect a tourist's way of thinking. The tourism services offered have to be combined with the feelings and sensations obtained from undertaking travel with your company. These then are measured against not only the cost of the trip but also against the efforts the tourist had to go to arrange and undertake the trip and the obstacles or deterrents they faced. If the services were poor, the experience unrewarding, the price high or the trip difficult to organize or undertake then you will not be a competitive business – no matter how wonderful your trip was presented in a brochure. To compete successfully, your business has to offer to the market greater value than your rivals for the same effort on the part of the tourists – or the same value for less effort.

Destination Marketing

In almost all cases, a tourist will decide to come to Croatia before they decide to travel with your company. In the same way, an overseas tour operator will look for a partner in Croatia after they have decided to take clients to Croatia. Therefore, you are not only trying to sell the products and services your company offers but Croatia itself as a tourism destination. Imagine you are attending a travel fair in London. A stand display emblazoned by your company name and a list of the activities you do is unlikely to attract many people, unless your company name includes the words 'Croatia' or 'Croatian'.

The decision making processes of tourists is discussed later in the stage, but at this stage, you need to be aware that marketing the country is likely to bring more success than marketing solely your company. The main thing that any tourist is purchasing when they come here is a Croatian experience, not the services of your guide or the quality of hotels.

This is a decision they make after they have decided to come here. For someone who has never been to Croatia before, whether they are a tourist or a foreign tour operator, they will firstly want to know why they should come here and what the attractions and benefits are over other destinations. This is where competitiveness comes in again. You need to highlight what Croatia has that is better than other neighbouring countries and what is does better or differently than the competing destinations.

Never be complacent and believe that tourists will always want to come to Croatia. Never also believe that everyone knows where Croatia is. Some of you will know from experience that those attendees at travel fairs first ask questions about the country rather than about your company. How sunny is it there? Where is Croatia? Didn't you have a war?

Marketing Research

Marketing research is the design of a plan for the collection of data, the purpose of which is to answer a given question. Such a question could be "Which country's outbound tourists offer the best opportunity for long term sustainable growth?" or "Who is my biggest competition?". Answers to these questions are vital for understanding the market within which your business operates. Research can fall into two areas:

- A descriptive role whereby the aim is to focus on what is happening by concentrating on the collection of factual data to provide a picture of the current situation, or
- An analytical role by shifting the focus to why things are happening in an attempt to explain the situation by seeking out reasons.

In order to develop a marketing plan, it is imperative that information is gathered on the business's performance and the marketplace. Answers are needed for a business to be able to make decisions. Without such information, any decisions being made run the risk of being bad ones which could prove very costly both financially and otherwise to the long term health of the business. Marketing research needs to be undertaken on a regular basis.

Changes within the marketplace, among consumers and within the business will all have an effect on the business. Although information gathered from marketing research will not be perfect, if the research is well planned and executed, it will mean that decisions taken will be more likely to prove successful.

There are various steps in undertaking research. Identify and define the problem – Before beginning the task of gathering information, it is first necessary to identify the problem for which research is required. You do not want to start gathering information only to find later that the information does not answer the questions you have. Investigate available sources – You do not want to start collecting information if that information already exists. You should seek out information which is already available. Travel Research will get you started with places to look for information.

- Determine research plan – Once all available sources of data have been evaluated, a plan is formulated to identify what further information is required and how it should be collected. This will involve generating hypotheses to be tested and methodologies. Methods could be interviews, surveys and observation.

- Data collection – Data should be collected based on the methodology outlined in the research plan.
- Data analysis – Based on the information collected analysis techniques will differ just as to whether the information is quantitative or qualitative.
- Present research results – The information should be tabulated and interpreted so that recommendations can be made regarding the appropriate course of action to take.

When looking for secondary data (data from sources other than your business), sources could include government agencies, trade associations, trade press and magazines, subscription sources, the press, internal company records, international organizations.

A tour operator's need to do marketing research will fall into several areas:

- Consumer satisfaction – If you regularly receive clients, you will need to get feedback on the satisfaction of the services and products you are selling. This form of research would normally be in the form of a questionnaire that would be distributed to clients prior to their departure. The results of this research should help you to make changes to the way you run your operations to improve satisfaction.
- Overseas Operator – To sustain and grow the partnerships you have with foreign operators, you will need to undertake research on their satisfaction with your products and services. It may be that tourists will give feedback to them rather than to you. In which case, again some adjustments may be needed to your operations to ensure that satisfaction levels are maintained. Undertaking research is in itself, a marketing tool. Showing that you actively encourage feedback will impress the clients.
- Industry trends – Whether you just subscribe to industry trade magazines or e-newsletters or purchase

reports on trends within the international tourism industry, it is important that you have some familiarity on what changes are taking place in the popularity of competing destinations, consumer preference for destinations and growing markets for specific activities.

Market Segments and Channels

The Market Segments and Market Channels Presentation in the Learning Tools will walk you through the steps of understanding market segments and channels. The Marketing and Distribution Channel Worksheet that follows it will guide you through the basics of developing a marketing plan.

MAIN MARKETING TOOLS

Trade Fairs

Travel fairs and exhibitions can be a highly-cost effective sales and marketing tool combining all the best characteristics of advertising, promotions, direct mail and selling, either through tour operators and travel agents or, in the case of public shows, directly to consumers. Benefits include direct sales, new product launches, lead generation, penetration of new markets, building and maintaining client/customer relations, market research, database building and networking. Research suggests that more than 80% of visitors to trade fairs are decision makers.

Taking part in a trade fair without first having a clear view of why you are there is an almost certain recipe for failure. Setting objectives is, therefore, an important starting point for any exhibition, giving direction to all aspects of your participation. Setting your objectives will make it possible to measure objectively the result of the exhibition, instead of making such a judgment merely subjective.

At the same time, objectives will help you establish budgetary requirements, motivate your staff and justify your participation next time around. The goals you set for yourself need to be formulated as concretely as possible. They must be realistic, open to evaluation and have a time limit in order to facilitate and provide a firm base for future work. Possible objectives could include; increase in sales, meeting new clients, obtain market intelligence, launch new products, penetrate a new market, change or enhance company image, carry out market testing and study the activities of competitors.

In order to ensure that your objectives are appropriate and attainable, you need to:

- Know what you want to sell or communicate
- Know your target market
- Quantify your objectives in order to set a goal
- Ensure your targets are achievable
- Prioritize your objectives
- Communicate your objectives to your staff

Once you have defined your main goals, the next step is to give careful consideration to which sector of the travel industry you want to direct your sales and marketing efforts towards.

How can you best attract your chosen targets to visit your stand? You could specifically invite companies to the fair, make pre-booked appointments or hold a reception on your stand for selected guests. By staying focused on your target market at all times, you will stand a better-than-average chance of getting your messages across and building new business. For some, having a stand of their own is the most natural way to participate, while others may find it more desirable or cost-effective to share stand space with others.

Sharing with a national airline, a tourism board, a hotel or other tour operator who is not a direct competitor may enhance your presence. Since most tour operators will wish to work directly with overseas operators, it makes sense that attending wholly public fair would not be in your best interests. Your decision on where to exhibit should be made only after careful consideration of the event, the audience it is likely to attract, its timing and location and the cost, not only of exhibiting but also of attending including meals, accommodation and flights. In deciding which fair(s) to participate, you should identify all the possibilities, compile as much information as possible; from organizers (attendance figures, breakdown of visitors, etc), cost implications and comments from other exhibitors. The more information you collect, the easier it will be to cut out those exhibitions that do not match your marketing objectives or your budget. Similarly, timing of the event, the size and importance of their venues and their geographical catchment area will help you reach a decision. Planning is essential to protect your investment in trade fairs, it is the key to getting the best possible return, to ensure smooth and stress free exhibiting, project a cohesive, positive and memorable message and improve your participation the next time around.

Planning for an exhibition should be thorough enough that no surprises crop up during the actual exhibition, the time when all your efforts should be directed towards sales work. One person in the business should be responsible for making all the arrangements. Most fairs will provide you with a manual which should be fully understood. A timetable should be drawn up highlighting key tasks and deadline dates. You should draw up a budget for your participation based on the activities you plan to become involved in. The budget should also be linked to the forecasts for the benefits that you expect to achieve.

The budget could be broken down into six areas:

- Stand space
  - Space rental
  - Design and construction (for space only stands)
  - Displays
  - Furniture
  - Accessories and equipment
  - Electrical installations
  - Connections – water, telephone, fax
  - Plants and Flowers
  - Cleaning and Security Services
  - Audiovisual equipment
  - Insurance
  - Catering
  - Incidentals

- Transport of materials
  - Packing
  - Air Shipment
  - Insurance
  - Customs Fees
  - Storage
  - Handling charges
- Personnel Costs
  - Staff transportation
  - Accommodation
  - Local transportation
  - Meal allowances
  - Interpreters
  - Entertainment
- Promotional Costs
  - Telephone and Mail marketing
  - Brochures and Catalogues printing
  - Post fair distribution of materials
  - Promotional video
  - Press packs
  - Translation of material
  - Promotional give aways
  - Passes for customers
  - Advertising in official fair catalogue
  - National and international magazine advertising
  - Other advertising
  - Sponsorship of fair activities

Your stand at a travel fair should make a strong visual impact and convey at a glance who you are and what you have to offer. For most tour operators, the shell scheme option will provide the best option. It will make it easier to present your products and services, is more cost efficient and minimizes the amount of time you need to spend at the venue during buildup and break down of the exhibition.

A shell scheme is a basic framework or shell erected by the organizers appointed contractor on your behalf. Take only the space you need at a fair. If you take too much, you will be left with the problem of having nothing to fill it with. The location of your stand within the exhibition is important, though with many wellestablished fairs, you may not have much option. Try to ensure that all, you have a stand of the right size, properly equipped, containing the right exhibits and staffed by knowledgeable and well-prepared personnel able to negotiate on behalf of your company. If you have the chance to choose the location for your stand, look for the busiest areas of the hall where traffic flow is likely to be high.

Also, take into account the location of competitors' stands, location of service and access points (entrances, stairways, feature areas, restaurants). The design of the stand should reflect the messages that you wish to give to your clients and potential clients. If you want to get your company better known to all visitors then an open eye-catching display is most appropriate. With graphics, they should visualize clearly what you do, have brief messages and promote benefits and not features.

Ensure that the messages can be read clearly. Remember that if you choose a shell scheme you will still need to decorate it. A shell scheme will normally include a signboard, basic furniture, carpet and electrical connections. It will not do anything to promote your company. If an exhibition organizer does its job properly, it will deliver thousands of potential clients to the exhibition halls. What it will not do and cannot do is persuade those buyers to visit your stand, rather than those of your competitors. That is your job and your organization is the only one that stands to lose out if you do not do it. It is important to inform your target audience that you are exhibiting and about your profile at the show. You will also invite them to the stand and set up specific appointments with them. The key to effective promotion is to match your promotional strategy to your exhibition objectives; to coordinate your activities carefully; to explore all available avenues for promotion before, during and after the event and to heed all deadlines.

In order to promote your attendance before and during the fair, you could consider:

- Advertising in trade magazines and newspapers

- Undertaking direct mail
- Aponsoring fair events or merchandise
- Incentives and small give always
- Advertising in fair catalogue

The number of staff required to man the stand depends upon the size of your stand, the number of leads anticipated and facilities and activities on the stand. As a rule, you should allow one staff member per 4-5 square meters of floor space, this being the space required to allow two people to conduct a conversation comfortably.

On person should be in charge and in attendance at the show all the time. Make sure that the staff on your stand really are friendly, approachable and well informed in the company products and services. Staff training and briefing are essential to exhibition success; training in encouraging visitors on to the stand, how to open and close a conversation, how to qualify visitors and the impact of body language. Also make sure that your staff know what they should be selling and how.

The stand should be manned at all times and should be kept tidy. The essence of sales technique if firstly to arouse interest of the prospects and discover his/her needs or problems. Then steer the conversation towards the way your products or services can solve these. Every person with whom you come into contact then receives individual attention depending on need.

The following sales techniques are important:

- Concentrate on people in your target markets
- Present briefly yourself and your product
- Chart the customer's needs and desires
- Steer the conversation towards the customer's needs and how your product/service satisfies these
- In all cases, make a note of the person's name, company, addressm etc and follow up after the fair, giving additional information and/or making your offer

The visitor information you capture at exhibitions and the way it is recorded, will have a direct effect on the speed and efficiency with which you follow up your leads. Only collecting business cards is not an effective way to compile visitor information, even if you do scribble action points on the back.

There are four steps to an effective follow-up after the fair:

- Prioritize leads just as to urgency
- Follow up leads immediately
- Pursue leads on an ongoing basis
- Track leads to provide some measure of return on investment

When measuring the effectiveness of exhibition participation, there are two areas you need to look at.

Firstly, the extent to which you achieved your specific objectives and secondly the extent to which the exercise proved cost effective.

Look at the value of sales achieved, the number of qualified leads, the number of new contacts made, the level of awareness before and after the show, the number of promotional materials distributed, the media coverage generated, the value of market research undertaken and other benefits.

The following is a suggested timetable of activities that may need to be undertaken when planning participation at a fair:

- 10-12 Months before the fair:
  - Make an initial selection of the itineraries and services that you will be selling
  - Calculate how much space you will require
  - Go over documentation from previous editions of the fair, if you were present at them
  - Draw up an initial budget
  - Get in contact with the fair organizers to let them know that you are interested in participating and request your space pre-registration
  - Examine the fair's rules and regulations
  - Fill out and submit the pre-registration and request information on promotional activities
- 8-10 Months before the fair
  - Draw up a plan and budget for the promotional activities organized prior to the fair
  - Budget for post-fair promotional activities

   - Decide on which information and sales material you will need
   - Analyse your needs for other material and where appropriate, design and develop it
   - Make allowances for trips and book tickets
   - Provide for accommodation and make reservations
- 6-8 Months before the fair
   - Design a support advertising campaign, objectives and timeframe
   - Launch the information campaign aimed at customers and trade media
   - Coordinate promotional activities with the fair organizers
   - Order promotional articles that will be handed out during the fair
   - Anticipate and organize logistics and transport tasks
   - Define the decoration, atmosphere and identity of your stand
- 4-6 Months before the fair
   - Coordinate planned activities with programmes and fair regulations – stand build up, advertising material, promotional material, miscellaneous activities
   - Identify new prospective clients and send them information
   - Order fair organizational services, external services, insurance
   - Design incentives for attracting visitors to the stand
- 2-4 Months before the fair
   - Intensify marketing actions to attract visitors
   - Select and allocate functions to the personnel that will be present on the stand and decide if you need to train staff in sales, train staff in corporate image, conduct practice sessions with products and sales arguments, instruct external personnel,

  - Send information for the fair catalogue
  - Check if periodic payments have been settled with the fair organizers
- 0-2 Months before the fair
  - Check the materials that should be taken to the fair – office materials, sales material, give aways
  - Organize press activities (conferences, invitations)
  - Distribute information on new products, etc to technical magazines and the fair's press office
  - Send out passes and invitations to customers
  - Collect information on the seminars and conferences that are being organized
  - Prepare a form for registering the details provided by visitors that come to your stand
- During stand build up and fair
  - Build up the stand as soon as possible
  - Checklist in hand, make sure that none of the elements, materials or services ordered for the stand are missing
  - Locate the fair organization's offices and services
  - On a daily basis, supervise stand cleaning, stocks of promotional materials
  - Exchange information with other staff on a regular basis
  - Gather competitor information, make notes and compare with equivalent aspects in your own company
- After the fair
  - Supervise stand break down and packing of material and equipment
  - Organize the transport of material, equipment and products
  - Arrange a meeting with all personnel involved in the project to analyse results
  - Launch actions for following-up leads generated at the fair

Brochures and Printed Materials

As we stated earlier, a tour operator's brochure is important because of the intangible nature of the product that is being sold. The brochure should invite people to buy the itineraries it advertises, provide the information necessary to persuade the client to purchase a holiday and create and reinforce the company's image with its clients. Most brochures are designed to an A4 format in Europe and Letter size in the US so the size of your brochure will be important just as to the market you are targeting. Most brochures are printed on glossy coloured paper.

The bigger the brochure, the flimsier the paper it is printed on tends to be, both to keep down production costs and to stop it becoming unmanageably heavy. Pull out price pages are normally printed on cheap coloured paper. Some companies will also have slightly thicker front covers to protect the brochures in transit and on the shelves, and to create a better image.

Although many operators will produce full colour brochures, it is cheaper to choose fewer colours. A full colour brochure could include some pages that are one or two colour (those pages used for terms and conditions, booking information, etc) to cut down costs. Colour is important. Bright colours usually signify cheaper tours. Pale and dark colours signify more expensive tours. Every brochure should contain clear, legible, comprehensive and accurate information to enable the client to exercise and informed judgment in making his choice. Content could include:

- A company's legal identity
- Means of travel
- Destinations or itineraries
- Dates of fixed departures (if you have them)
- Nature of accommodation and meal facilities
- Additional facilities
- Booking conditions
- Insurance details
- Price policy
- Health matters

- Arbitration
- Publication date
- Difficulty ratings
- Maps
- Pictures of attractions, accommodations or previous clients

Of course the content of your brochures may vary just as to whether you are targeting the travel trade or consumers. If you are selling tours in Europe, you may like to familiarize yourself with the EC Package Travel Regulations that outlines how European tour operators must present their information and what brochures must include. The front cover of the brochure is particularly important since it is what the client will see first of all. The cover must therefore be designed to be eye-catching but must simultaneously convey certain crucial messages. It should show the company name and a logo. The choice of picture can make it clear what sort of product is on offer and also for whom the product is aimed at.

The more expensive and exotic the product on offer, the less likely it is to show clients on the cover at all, preferring to concentrate on what they will see at their chosen destination. The main part of the brochure should be clearly structured so that clients can easily identify the information they require. A contents page may be appropriate for brochures with many pages. Coloured borders for pages also help in this regard. General information is usually found at the rear of the brochure.

This would include guidelines for making bookings; information on what is included in the price, insurance and cancellation policies, a booking form, and health and visa requirements. If there are suitable destination marketing materials available that provide much of the destination information, then a company's promotional materials can focus more on their own particular itineraries. The text of a brochure needs careful consideration. Firstly, there should be no grammatical or spelling mistakes. Secondly, the text should present your products in a way that will make them appealing to potential customers.

For Croatian operators, the text should emphasize the the beauty of the nature and uniqueness of the culture, history, cuisine, architecture, etc. as well as the prospects for adventure, good sailing, or outdoor sports. Many brochures will also use "you", "we" and "our" to emphasize the central role of clients and their needs and how 'at home' they will feel even though they are abroad. Photographs have the same purpose of the text, to portray the destination and products in a positive light. The photographs should complement the text and be relevant to it. Obviously the photos should be of a high quality in terms of resolution.

Also, they need to be professional. It would not be appropriate for example to have pictures of clients wearing raincoats standing on a cloudy beach. There should be a good use of colour. Many brochures will use pictures of previous clients enjoying themselves, inviting would-be buyers to imagine themselves in their place. If you use pictures of previous clients be sure that the clients are typical of those you are trying to attract

Websites

A Well designed website will contain much the same information as a well conceptualized brochure. The difference here is that you have much more room for photos, and your use of colour is limited only to the web palette of colours likely to display well on most monitors. You can also make inquiries, bookings, and other interactive functions easy for customers by using web forms, online reservations and payment, etc. Hundreds of websites exist with excellent features.

Search (Google) company websites in your line of business and see which features you think are best, and try to integrate these features into your site planning. Have a professional web developer do your site, and insist that current standards be used in the coding of your website.

Because most search engines give sites using frames poorer rankings, for example, most new websites are now laid out using CSS, which also makes them faster to load. Decide if you will use HTML or XHTML, make sure the site is viewable in the most popular browsers (IE, Firefox, Netscape, and Opera are just a few). Finally, make sure you do a good job of search engine optimization.

PRODUCT DEVELOPMENT

Developing a Product

In designing a tourism product, you want to put together all the information you have collected about your target market and clients. The Product Development and Planning Sheet will help you organize the information. Once you have the facts laid out using the worksheet, developing an itinerary is the next step. Use the template provided (Product Development Planning Part 2) to lay out an itinerary with all the details.A Sample Itinerary is included in the Learning Tools. Studying the itineraries of leading outbound tour operators will give you many ideas about how to improve your own, but this is largely a creative process, and this manual cannot lead you through it step by step. Rather, the feedback you get from clients and outbound tour operators should guide you in continually improving your itineraries. Pricing your product is a process unique to each company.

The Pricing Spreadsheet thatis given as an example is only one way to go about pricing a product. You will have to develop your own spreadsheet or tool that is adapted to your products and services. Just make sure you review all the possible costs associated with each itinerary and ensure you have accounted for them.

Operations and Management

Once you have your products designed, you should ensure that you are set up to operate your tours when they sell, and to manage your business so that your trips run smoothly, the service you give is of good quality, and you have sufficient resources to serve your clients. This manual is not intended to teach you the details of running a small business, but Operations Workflow and Management gives you an illustration of the basic workflow of an outbound tour operator, and some tips on how to organize your operations. If you have a background in small business, it will be easy to adapt this information to setting up a tour company operation. There are some key issues that new tour operators should pay attention to when starting operations. These are listed below.

Key Issues for New Companies:

- Keeping Track - Set up an efficient documentation and filing system before you get much business. It takes too much time to fix it later.
- Safety – client safety should be your absolute first priority. Train all trip staff in first aid (accredited course like Red Cross).
- Liability Insurance – Products sold in the EU must be backed by Errors and Omissions insurance. You should carry liability insurance for this and for Product Liability. Consider whether you need Employers Liability and insurance on your equipment.
- Terms and Conditions – In some cases, clients should sign a document accepting the risks of travel and releasing the tour operator from liability in case of accident and other unplanned events (lost time from delays, trip cancellation due to forces of nature, etc.) Spend a lot of time on your Terms and Conditions document.
- Travellers Insurance – In most cases, require your clients have valid travellers health and accident insurance that also covers emergency evacuation. You should collect at the start of the trip a copy of this and of their passport.
- Service Providers – If possible, have multiple service providers identified for each service that is offered as part of your published trips.
- Hiring staff (esp. guides) – an experienced guide from another company is not always the best solution.
- Staff training - is EVERY YEAR no matter how long the employee has been in the business. Learning new skills is an ongoing process and you should have refresher courses prior to each season.

- The Guide or Trip Leader - is the most important person to the client since they are in contact every day for several days. The client doesn't care about the company director, president, manager. Guides must be able to solve most problems ON THE SPOT, without help from you.
- *Focus on Your Business:* If you are a tour operator, don't try to run a hotel, ticketing agency, and restaurant as part of that business.
- *Ticketing Agent:* A good agent or agency handling your air tickets is worth their weight in gold. If the client can't get to Croatia they are not coming on your trip. Eventually you may need ticketing agents in your major markets.
- *Response Time:* The Most Important factor of getting good business is answering inquiries quickly – and answering the questions the client Asked!
  Excellent = same day, good = 24 to 48 hours. Over 48 hours = lost client in most cases.
- Service Providers often need to be educated about the tourism business.
- Make sure your contract with the service provider lays out rates and terms for the whole season – or you will not be able to respond quickly to requests.
- Some service providers are very difficult to work with. Often if they see you are taking clients t another service provider they will make an effort to change.
- Keep service providers informed about your operations and the markets you serve. Give them client feedback from your trips, so they can also work to improve their services.

Working with Outbound Operators

You are ready to begin contacting outbound operators and agents you have found as part of your marketing research. Don't forget to refer to the specialty travel indexes provided in Travel Research Links in the Tools. Here are some tips on working with outbound operators.

- First Do Homework
  - Before approaching an operator, study their product well.
  - Make sure if you contact them your communication indicates that you understand in general their product type, travel style, and how their itineraries are set up.
  - Make sure you have something of interest to offer them (not already in their catalog), so they will be more disposed to answering your questions.
  - Do not be afraid of asking questions to clarify their requirements. The operator should understand you seek to improve your product offering to them. It is better to ask than to most tour operators expect a certain amount of back and forth before getting the right trip.
- Getting in the Door
  - Sending interesting product descriptions with photos and prices is often effective. Save them time and effort.
  - A familiarization trip is the best way to attract AND repel clients. The outcome will depend on how well you have done your homework and prepared for the visit.
  - Travel fairs are NOT the best place to meet people... it's where people come find you. Try and schedule meetings with your targeted operators before or after the fair – or making a separate trip.
  - Using the right terms is an indication of how easy you will be to work with. Make an effort to learn the terminology of the business.
- Establishing Relationships
  - Signing a contract for one or more trips a season is the first step in the relationship.
  - Offer reliable service
  - Be flexible when you can

  - Offer something new every year that helps them sell their trips.
  - Stick to the terms of the contract you have signed. If you must change something, wait until the contract is up for renewal and give good reasons for the change.
  - Take client feedback seriously, and respond in a positive and appropriate manner. No responses or argumentative ones, and business will go elsewhere.
- Building Relationships
  - Take clients on your trips – especially if they do not use their own trip leaders and do not get to experience the product first hand.
  - Visit clients in their offices when you have a chance, and get to know the staff there.
  - Pass on discounts or cost savings when appropriate.
  - If you sell an itinerary as an exclusive, ensure that you do not offer the same trip to another client.
  - Treat their traveller information as privileged. Never use it for direct marketing or to "steal clients". Word will get around faster than you can imagine.
  - Make it as easy as possible for them to book with you.
- Building Relationships
  - Working well with their trip leaders is an excellent way to build your trip portfolio with any operator. Take trip leaders on mini fam trips if you can keep them in country a few extra days.
  - Always inform the client of any problems as they arise, and steps you are taking to resolve them. If you cannot reach the client, take detailed notes so you can give a good accounting of your actions in case of problems or emergencies.
  - Always take responsibility for any mistakes made by your office or your staff. If you are

honest and bring up problems first, your client will see the incident in a far better light.

- Tips
  - For every itinerary you send, detail what is included in the price and what is excluded.
  - Calculate price breaks just as to pax breaks used by your client.
  - Usually, a trip leader position is offered FOC – this does not mean you pay for their trip leader to travel. It means the cost is already factored in to your pax breaks.
  - If there are changes, always send a new itinerary with a different reference number – in PDF form or by fax. The client should agree in writing and reference this number. This will help avoid any misunderstanding.
- Unpleasant Surprises
  - Serious operators do not ask you to pay airfare.
  - Operators who put continuous downward pressure on prices may not be serious about quality. Selling trips with very low margins does not help your business.
  - Try and check out operators to ensure they are reputable before offering fam trips or giving away detailed information.
  - Be prepared to have any itinerary you publish get copied – and purchased from another cheaper supplier. That's life in the business!
  - Contact lists are gold – keep them secure.
  - Before making big non-refundable deposits on a trip with a new customer, run a credit check.

Continuous Improvement

Finally, as your business develops, you will want to continually improve your product and service. Remember the part on Being Competitive? Using what you know now about competitive products and the simple Gap Analysis Tool of the Learning Tools, you will be able to build a stronger business year by year.

6

Computer Applications

The behavioural scientist—by definition—studies and evaluates the complex interactions of men as individuals, within societies, and within environments. Why then should he be concerned with computers, which belong to the realm of the physical sciences?

The behavioural scientist studies man-machine relations in order to define the role of man in the control and use of the machine and thus to optimize system interactions. In the growth of computer technology, man is assigning increasingly complex tasks to the machine and, in turn, is freeing himself to assume increasingly more complex tasks.

From subjects as basic as perception, learning, and thinking, through analysis of specialized social organizations, man is harnessing the capabilities of the computer as a powerful research tool. The researcher in behavioural science must learn to use this tool or risk being left behind as his discipline advances.

But the computer is more than a research device; it is a production tool. As such, it is being used to automate manufacturing processes, warehousing and office procedures. The applied behavioural scientist must be aware of the effects of this new technology upon industrial management, labour, and the other forces in our society.

As a research tool, the computer may contribute in three principal functions:

- Organization and reduction of statistical data
- Hypothesis seeking, by finding relationships
- Hypothesis testing, through modeling and simulation

Research involves the accumulation of data and their eventual analysis and reduction. As our research capabilities expand, more and more data are accumulated and analysis becomes increasingly complex and time consuming. The statistical techniques are themselves becoming more sophisticated.

If behavioural science remains chained to the desk calculator, it will stagnate. High-speed electronic data processing provides a means for rigorously, analysing masses of data. While analysing and reducing these data, special computer programmes can search for patterns and relationships which, because of the number and quality of variables, might remain obscured and undiscovered. From these patterns, the researcher can develop new and significant hypotheses.

Testing hypotheses can also be facilitated through the use of automatic data processing technology, by using a computer to simulate and study human behaviour. But why study simulation models rather than human beings? The physiological psychologist will immediately recognize the similarity of this question to the older, more common query: "Why do you study rats if you are primarily interested in human behaviour?" And the answer is very much the same: By simulating behaviour on a computer, and studying its operation in detail, we can, by analogy, make inferences about the more complex human activities.

These inferences must then be validated before being applied. By way of illustration, consider the temperature control mechanism of warm blooded animals, or more specifically of man. Normal temperature is 9.6°. The body temperature must remain constant within approximately five degrees.

Yet the temperature of the environment changes from 110° or more in the heat of summer to below freezing in winter. The organism's life depends upon accurate control of heat production and heat loss. As scientists, we are interested in studying the homeostatic mechanisms in temperature control; as computer-oriented researchers, we consider simulating this process. In fact, such a model already exists, for a thermostat operates in a fashion analogous to the hypothalamus. In a low ambient temperature, the body temperature tends to fall. The skin, which has in it receptors for heat and cold, responds to the change.

Messages are sent along nerve fibres to the hypothalamus, and the organism takes action to conserve body heat—action such as shivering and/or the constriction of blood vessels near the skin. Alternately, responding to a high ambient temperature, the message sent to the hypothalamus initiates action to dissipate body heat.

The thermostat works analogously. A desired room temperature is set. A thermometer is the sensing device or receptor. Detecting that the room is too cold, the thermometer creates a message, sent along an electrical conductor that controls and starts the furnace.

When the temperature exceeds the optimal limit, the furnace is stopped. The simulation model, *i.e.*, the thermostat, operates on a feedback principle. The similarity between the operation of the thermostat and the observable control of body heat leads to the conclusion that the human organism uses a similar principle.

The hypothesis is, at the very least, worthy of additional study and testing. In the course of these interactions, the computer specialist learns to design more sophisticated machines, and the behavioural scientist achieves greater understanding of the human organism—the most complex of all machines.

Through the data organization capabilities of the computer, far more complicated relationships can be defined and enormous masses of information processed in terms of those relationships. Thus the computer becomes analogous to organizations such as those comprising another machine, a natural resource, an industry, or a social community. The computer programmed to model an industry, for example, responds to controlled fluctuations in variables such as production, sales, inventory, etc., and provides a basis for generalized conclusions about the parameters and their relationships. The analogy of the organization of the computer itself to that of the human nervous system is even more pertinent to the behavioural scientist. It has been suggested that experience leaves a permanent mark on the brain—possibly by changing the configuration of protein molecules in the brain cells.

The existing memory trace permits recall of the experience. Computer memory is somewhat similar. Information is recorded by magnetizing a certain small area of core memory. The computer can recall this information by checking to determine whether the part is or is not magnetized. During the past few year, much effort has gone into the development of a formal theory of thought and memory. Cybernetics has this basic concept: the brain is a control and communication system which can be described mathematically in the form of logical nets composed of elements and connections.

Although man-made communication nets may become extremely complex, then do not approach the magnitude of complexity existing in the human organism. Certainly, if we were able to describe thought, memory, and other human processes in mathematical terms—John von Neumann has pointed out that self-reproduction is also a mathematical problem—we could achieve a much better understanding of these functions. But the development of a theoretical model is not sufficient in itself. The model must be checked and verified under various operating conditions. For testing, the use of the computer is a necessity. Hand calculation would be infinitely laborious if not outright impossible.

In research, the computer can be used:

- To simulate a system of complex interacting variables, in order to facilitate control of the elements under investigation
- To simulate the environment in which the system must operate, again to permit a study of the system under various environmental conditions
- To record, reduce, and aid in the mathematical analysis of experimental observations

Yet, as versatile as it is, the computer is only a tool. By itself it can accomplish nothing, but in the hands of an imaginative scientist, its potentials are almost limitless. The computer has ushered in the age of self-regulating devices and automatic control. As more extensive use is made of the computer potentialities, man will receive new benefits and face new problems.

Whether the behavioural scientist is interested in pure or applied research, he will be using the electronic computer. In addition, the applied scientist will be concerned with automation and its effects. The trend or direction in which automation is leading us is obvious, for it is simply an extrapolation of our present practices. Just as mechanization has been a continuing process, so one can predict that automation will find ever wider applications throughout the economy. Production, the gross national product, and our standard of living will all continue to rise.

New products that are the result of automated manufacturing techniques will appear on the market. Fewer people will be employed in routine factory and office jobs, but employment will increase in those concerns manufacturing automated equipment. This is the trend. It is obvious, definite and inescapable. Attempts to dismiss it or to counteract it may delay the process, but cannot change it. Automation is on its way. How rapidly it is adopted depends upon how profitable it proves. Many objects—the small table radio for example- are already being manufactured and assembled completely automatically.

Airplanes and missiles are being guided to their destination by an "automatic pilot." Soon it will be possible for a person to start his car, set the dials, lean back and read the newspaper or watch television while an "automatic chauffeur" drives him to the office. Since automation must be economical if it is to be adopted, its greatest benefit may be considered to be the virtual elimination of expensive and unpredictable human labour in the performance of routine jobs. These economic advantages of automation were stated quite precisely and accurately by Frank K. Shallenberger,

President of the Shalco Engineering Corporation of Palo Alto, California, and Professor of Industrial Management at Stanford University: Automation has given us devices which can see better, hear better, and measure better than human operators. They think and move infinitely faster than humans.

They never get tired, they willingly work around the clock, they do not make mistakes, they do not talk back, they are obedient, consistent, and fully predictable. They will not go out on strike, they do not ask annually for higher wages, and they have few personal problems. The country's defence needs have provided another major impetus towards automation.

The nations of the Communist bloc outnumber the Free World in population. To offset their numerical advantage, the free nations of the world must maintain a higher man-hour production rate or risk being overtaken in the Cold War struggle. Our government recognizes this fact, and the country's tax structure and allowable depreciation encourage capital outlay for tools and automated equipment. Besides the many potential advantages of automation, certain deterrents and problem areas must also be recognized.

Because automation means change, management must make the initial difficult decision as to why, where, and how much to automate. New equipment is expensive, and cost is a major consideration. Retooling inevitably means a change in the product design, and this raises questions of consumer acceptance, an intensified sales campaign, etc.

Production problems may arise, because maximum efficiency requires that automated equipment operate continuously. In a seasonal industry, continuous production may result in a large inventory with concomitant storage and cost problems. The impact of the new machinery on the labour force must also be considered, for management neither desires nor can afford to ride roughshod over its employees. The workers must be prepared, so that they accept the change, and trained, so that they can operate and maintain the equipment. Al though these are primarily problem areas for business management, they are also challenges to the industrial psychologist. To make reasonably intelligent decisions, management must have information on the anticipated effects of automation.

More and more, the behavioural scientist is being relied on to provide the necessary data:

- There is a need for market sampling to provide information on how new products, will be received.
- There is a need for improved selection of personnel to fill the newly created technical jobs.
- There is a need for improved techniques of labour-management communication.
- There is a need for improved training methods to develop the new skills required by automation.
- There is a need for improved techniques of retraining in order to equip the semiskilled worker to handle the more technically demanding jobs in the automated plant.

The behavioural scientist must be prepared to meet these needs. Automation thus is providing new impetus for basic research in the social sciences and is expanding the industrial opportunities for the applied scientist. Fortunately, the computer—the same general purpose computer that led to the current industrial revolution and all these new problems-is providing the tool to enable the social scientist to carry on the new research. No discussion of automation is complete without some reference to the problem of technological unemployment.

The phrase "technological unemployment" has a strong emotional connotation, which often distorts objective investigation. Indisputably, automation will displace some people from some jobs. Some people will therefore be unemployed, but this does not mean that there need be any mass technological unemployment.

The harness maker became unemployed when the horse and buggy was replaced by the horseless carriage, yet the over-all effect of the automobile was increased employment. History has shown that in the long run change, invention, and automation result in a higher standard of living and increased employment. "In the long run," however, the individual worker may suffer unless he receives help. Helping the displaced worker is the continual responsibility of government, industry, and organized labour.

These agencies can provide the will and the means to help. The behavioural scientist must provide knowledge about retraining, counseling, and other techniques designed to ease any suffering resulting from the new technology. Finally, one benefit that could result from automation is the shortening of the work week and increased leisure. But leisure is valuable only if it is used constructively. Misused, it can be injurious, and there is evidence that some people are misusing the shorter work week. Increased leisure has been blamed for the increase in crime in recent years. Boredom is said to be responsible for the rise in the number of people requiring psychiatric treatment.

Evidently there is need for a special programme of education designed to teach people to make constructive use of their leisure time and to divert energy to healthful channels of activity. But what is meant by "constructive use of leisure" and "healthful channels of activity"? How is one to decide whether it is healthier to play baseball or watch the game on television? Can the behavioural scientist, the sociologist, psychologist, and educator develop programmes to help? These are some of the challenges of automation, which eventually must be met if automation is to be a true tool of progress

7

Human Resource Management

WORKFORCE PLANNING AND EMPLOYMENT

There are a number of dynamics that increasingly make workforce planning and employment critical components of the organization's strategic plan. The United States economy has transitioned from a manufacturing base to a service base and is in the process of transitioning to a knowledge base. As the economy moves along this continuum, the success of the organization is increasingly based on the quality of its human capital, which is defined as the total current and potential capabilities of the organization's workforce. As this transition occurs, organizational strategies increasingly must be developed to develop the organization's primary resource: people.

The quality of its human capital will allow an organization to differentiate itself in the market place, much as innovative products and services now do. In fact, for many organizations, human capital will become their core competency—the unique capability that distinguishes them from their competitors. To create this competency, an organization must be able to attract the right kinds of people in the right place at the right time. The nature of competition has changed and is global.

Markets and environments are frequently dynamic and volatile, and organizations have been downsized and right-sized to improve cost efficiencies. Globalization requires the organization to understand multiple cultures and how to attract, retain, and motivate persons from those cultures. The dynamics of the environment often require flexibility and adaptation at the lower levels of the organization. All this affects the workforce planning and employment practices. Technology has not only changed the way work is done, it has also changed the knowledge, skills, and abilities needed to do the work. Organizations must plan to either attract those with the right skills to the organization or to develop those skills internally.

The latter requires hiring individuals who have the capacity to learn and to grow. Workforce demographics in the United States are changing. The workforce is aging and contains an increasing percentage of both women and members of minority groups. In addition, workers often come to the organization with deficient skill sets. The organization must plan how to replace the impending retirement of the "Baby Boomers" while developing the skills of those that follow.

The organization must be actively engaged in planning to determine how to react to the dynamics just discussed to develop an internal workforce that is capable of accomplishing the organization's strategic goals. That is the essence of workforce planning and employment.

CONCEPT AND PROCESS OF HUMAN RESOURCE PLANNING

Human resources alignment means integrating decisions about people with decisions about the results an organization is trying to obtain. By integrating human resources management into the agency planning process, emphasizing human resources activities that support broad agency mission goals, and building a strong relationship between HR and management, agencies are able to ensure that the management of human resources contributes to mission accomplishment and that managers are held accountable for their HRM decisions.

This is especially important in light of the Government Performance and Results Act's (GPRA) push to align all agency activities, including HRM, towards achieving defined agency strategic goals and measuring progress towards those goals.

In fiscal year 1999, the U.S. Office of Personnel Management (OPM) embarked on a special study to determine how much progress Federal agencies have made towards aligning HRM with agency strategic goals in support of HRM accountability and agency mission accomplishment. Our key findings and conclusions are summarized as follows. Many more agencies than expected include HR representatives in the agency planning process and integrate human resources management goals, objectives, and strategies into agency strategic plans. However, most agencies are still struggling in this area. Therefore, agency executives and HR leaders need to work together to fully integrate HRM into the planning process so that it will become a fundamental, contributing factor to agency planning and success.

Although some agency HR offices have begun focusing on organizational activities that assist agency decision-making, most are still emphasizing internal HR office efficiency efforts. While internal issues are important to the success of any HR programme, HR offices also need to examine the "big picture" and find ways to impact the success of the agency as a whole. Most agencies are in some way measuring the efficiency and/or effectiveness of the HR function.

These measures, however, are generally output-oriented, focus on internal HR processes and activities, and are used to make improvements to HR-specific policies and procedures. As HR refocuses its activities to broader organizational issues, HRM measures also need to be expanded to gauge the impact HRM has on agency goals and mission. Then, the measurement data can be used to inform agency-level decisions. The relationship between HR and management is becoming more collaborative.

HR executives are beginning to earn a seat at the management table. HR offices are becoming more consultative and involved in day-to-day line management activities. Nevertheless, there is still a long way to go if HR is to become a strategic partner at all levels.

To do so, HR needs to build its own internal competencies to deal with organizational issues, educate itself on agency and programme missions, and find ways to offer creative and innovative solutions to organizationwide issues. Although many National Performance Review initiatives, such as downsizing, reorganizing, streamlining, and delegating HR authorities, were meant to improve HR's ability to focus on organizational issues, they have not taken hold as quickly or thoroughly as hoped.

Therefore, HR is still doing most of the process work, and its ability to focus on alignment has been limited. However, as HR's role in agency planning, activities, and decision-making advances — and it is advancing — so too will the alignment of human resources management with agency mission accomplishment.

Alignment

Strategic human resources management...strategic alignment...alignment with mission accomplishment. These are just a few of the terms being used to describe the new, evolving role of Federal human resources management (HRM). What do these terms really mean?

If you were to ask agency personnelists, managers, or employees, you would probably get a wide range of answers. So, it's important to establish from the beginning what we are really talking about. Human resources management alignment means to integrate decisions about people with decisions about the results an organization is trying to obtain. Our research indicates that agencies that successfully align human resources management with agency mission accomplishment do so by integrating HRM into the agency planning process, emphasizing HR activities that support mission goals, and building strong HR/management relationships.

In addition to being a vital contributor to agency mission accomplishment, HRM alignment is the ultimate level of HRM accountability, as demonstrated in the Hierarchy of Accountability. While HRM accountability must begin with basic legal compliance, it ultimately encompasses all four levels of the pyramid, including demonstrating how HRM supports achievement of the agency strategic goals.

Why Align

Why the sudden emphasis on aligning HRM activities with agency mission accomplishment? Basically, it comes down to demonstrating the value of human resources management to the agency. In the past, one of HR's primary roles has been to ensure compliance with laws, rules, and regulations. Although this is still, and will always be, a necessary function, many recent developments have led to a strong emphasis on results.

The National Performance Review (NPR) took on the task of reinventing government to make it work better, cost less, and get results. NPR mandated many initiatives that changed the focus of HR from just compliance towards results, including downsizing the HR function, delegating HR authorities to line managers, calling for HR to demonstrate its business value, and enhancing customer service. Through these initiatives, management of human resources would become more responsive to mission-related needs because it would take place at the line level, and the HR staff would be able to expend more of its energy on broader organizational issues.

The Government Performance and Results Act (GPRA) of 1993 has also played a large part in focusing agencies on results. The purpose of GPRA is to improve Federal programme effective- ness, accountability, service delivery, decision-making, and internal management, thereby improving confidence in the Federal Government. This is achieved by demonstrating organizational results through strategic planning and performance measures.

Although the primary focus of GPRA is on programmatic functions, agencies are also required to describe how administrative resources, such as HR, are being used to achieve strategic goals. Further, the General Accounting Office (GAO) and the Office of Management and Budget (OMB) have evaluated many of these efforts, and are calling for agencies to improve their discussions of HRM alignment in strategic and annual plans. Therefore, the human resources function is increasingly being aligned to the agency strategic plan, which requires HR to show how it is supporting mission accomplishment. Alignment has already occurred in other key administrative functions. When Congress developed a statutory framework to introduce performance-based management into the Federal Government, it initiated financial, information technology, and procurement reforms through such mandates as the Chief Financial Officer Act and Information Technology Management Reform Act. Human resources management is the administrative missing link to this comprehensive package. The private sector has recognized that it is not just financial and technological capital that provide companies with the competitive edge, but people, or human capital. Without attracting and retaining the right people, in the right jobs, with the right skills and training, an organization cannot succeed.

Therefore, people have been recognized as companies' most important asset. As the Federal Government moves towards a performance-based management approach, we, too, need to realise the importance of our human resources. A huge percentage of agencies' budgets is spent on human resources – salaries, benefits, training, work life programmes, etc. Nowhere else do you make that substantial an investment and not measure the return. Not only do human resources provide the competitive edge, but several recent studies have confirmed that the quality and innovation of HR practices impact business results.

These studies were able to draw a correlation between increased quality of HR practices and increased business success. Among other benefits, HR alignment with mission accomplishment increases HR's ability to anticipate its customers' needs, increases the agency's ability to implement strategic business goals, and provides decision-makers with critical resource allocation information. Finally, HR alignment is a vital process to advance agency accountability. By defining, maintaining, and assessing HRM goals and measures, communicating them throughout the agency, and using the information to make management decisions, agencies are able to ensure that the management of human resources contributes to mission accomplishment and that managers are held accountable for their HRM decisions in support of mission accomplishment.

STRATEGIC PLANNING

AGENCYWIDE PLANNING

To some agencies, strategic planning is a way of life. To others, it's an exercise. To almost all, it's a requirement. As part of GPRA, agencies, unless specifically exempted, follow a continuous, three step strategic planning process: Strategic planning allows agencies to map out where they are, where they want to go, and how they plan to get there.

Some agencies adopted the idea of strategic planning even before GPRA was enacted, whereas others are just beginning to understand its potential benefits. The results of the fiscal year 1999 Merit System Principles Questionnaire (MSPQ), an OPM Governmentwide survey of supervisors and employees, show that agencies are beginning to embrace not only the concept, but also the practice, of strategic planning.

HRM Integration in Agency Strategic Plans

The management of agency human resources is an integral part of how an agency is going to achieve its mission goals. Without people, there is no one to do the work. Therefore, integrating HRM into the agency strategic plan is the first step in aligning it with the mission. Even though GAO and OMB are pushing for improvement of HRM alignment discussions in strategic and annual plans, GPRA's primary focus is still on agency programmes, rather than corporate functions. Therefore, we assumed at the beginning of this study that not many agency strategic plans would have addressed HRM's role in mission accomplishment. We were pleasantly surprised. Out of the 31 strategic plans reviewed, 87 per cent had addressed HRM in some way.

A breakdown of how integration between HRM and the agency plan is achieved, a count of how many strategic plans have integrated HRM in a particular way, and some examples of actual agency approaches. Although some agencies are clearly ahead of the pack, integration of HRM in agency plans is still evolving. When looking at the actual placement of strategic plan HRM discussions, they are generally segregated from the programmatic goals, objectives, and strategies. Considering that an agency's mission cannot be achieved without its people, this is an important point. Could this be an indication that human resources management is not yet recognized as a critical contributor to agency mission accomplishment? In any case, it is clear that though there are some exceptions, as evidenced by some of the examples full HRM integration into agency strategic plans have not yet been realised.

The human resources issues addressed in agency plans provide insight into what aspects of human resources management are most important to agency management. In reviewing the plans, or even just by looking at the examples, it is clear that diversity, recruitment, retention, employee development, and workforce quality are the major areas of interest. Although these could be looked at as process or output programmes, when they are designed and implemented well, they lead to the ultimate result: the right people, with the right skills, in the right positions to carry out the agency mission.

Agency HRM Strategic Measures

Defining practical, meaningful measures that assess the effectiveness of agency human resources management and its support of mission accomplishment is a topic that agencies have been struggling with. It is easy to measure a process — how long does it take to complete an action? It is easy to measure productivity — how many actions were completed in any given time frame?

But how do you measure the outcome of human resources management? How does an agency know if it has the right people, with the right skills, in the right positions to carry out the agency mission? Have any agencies found a way to do this? To help answer these questions, we looked to see if agencies are including HRM measures in their strategic plans, and what types of measures they have identified. Not surprisingly, 71 per cent of the plans did not identify any HRM measures. Moreover, the meaningfulness and practicality of the 29 per cent of agency identified measures could be stronger. About one-third of the 29 per cent contain measures that are not really measures. They are lists of activities or projects that, when completed, will help to reach the goal. In other words, they are strategies labeled as measures. The other two-thirds of that 29 per cent have fairly good measures that are tied to specific mission or support goals and provide seemingly relevant information.

However, even these fairly good measures tend to focus on HR processes (outputs) rather than intended outcomes. For example, some agencies measure the average number of employee training hours to measure workforce skill levels, rather than what skills are actually gained through the training or what skills the workforce actually possesses.

HR Involvement in Agency Strategic Planning

Now that we have seen what types of goals, objectives, strategies, measures, and other forms of HRM integration are present in agency strategic plans, we should look briefly at how these were developed. The legitimacy and ultimate value of these pieces of the plan will depend substantially on where they came from.

Historically, members of the HR community have remarked on the difficulty they have had with top agency management. Rather than being involved in agency planning from the beginning, HR is commonly consulted after decisions have been made in order to help implement any major changes. Considering the invaluable perspective HR has on how decisions will impact agency resources, HR professionals have been frustrated that they are not involved sooner in the planning process.

Therefore, it was surprising when 79 per cent of the agencies we talked to indicated that they do play a role in the overall agency strategic planning process. The roles vary from a peripheral consultant who reviews and comments on preliminary products to an integrated team member who actively helps to identify not only HRM agency strategic goals and objectives, but programmatic goals as well. Two or three of the responding agencies fall in the former category, a handful in the latter, and the rest somewhere in between. Later, we will discuss how some HR officials are able to elevate themselves to agency strategic partner, while most are still struggling to achieve this.

Patent and Trademark Office (PTO): HR's Involvement in Strategic Planning

The PTO's planning process tracks closely. HR, as well as the other administrative functions, is integrally involved in and present during all aspects of planning — the top management discussions, business line planning, and overall ranking and budgetary discussions. The administrative functions serve several purposes: to inform managers what resources are available to them; to determine what resources managers will need; and to discuss the impact programme initiatives will have on the agency.

When it comes to defining actual HRM goals, strategies, and measures, the roles also vary. In general, agencywide HRM-related goals, strategies, and measures are identified by the agency leader or other senior managers with HR collaboration. They decide what is most important to the agency based on the challenges the agency will face in years to come.

Some use a more elaborate collaboration approach that involves agency management, HR officials, and other stakeholders, as is demonstrated in the presented examples from the Department of Commerce's Patent and Trademark Office (PTO) and the Department of Veterans Affairs (VA). Then there are the agencies that use the functional strategic planning approach where the HR office is tasked with coming up with the goals, strategies, and measures itself. In these cases, HR generally uses some type of feedback from customers to identify what is important to the agency and should be included in the plan.

Department of Veterans Affairs Collaborative Approach

The Department of Veterans Affairs (VA) Office of Human Resources Management was integrally involved in the Department's strategic planning process. Although the programme offices were the drivers for the strategic goals, the administrative functions were integrally involved in establishing how resources can be attained, retained, and utilized to support the programmes that deliver services to their customer, the veterans.

The HR staff worked with programme planners and line managers in an iterative and interactive series of meetings that provided HR with information on the Department's current and future business and corresponding human resource needs. The HR staff was able to translate this information into specific objectives with supporting strategies and performance goals that were incorporated into the VA strategic plan. To further refine its priorities, HR held a conference attended by approximately 300 people representing its key stakeholder groups departmentwide including: HR professionals, political appointees, headquarters executives, field line managers, staff offices, unions, and veterans.

A "real time" strategic planning process that included facilitation, formal presentations, and inter-active discussions led to the identification and prioritization of four critical human resources "strategic opportunities" that must be dealt with if VA is to successfully accomplish its mission. Top management at the conference committed to supporting the pursuit of these strategic opportunities, and, subsequently, teams including field and headquarters, line and staff representatives were formed around these opportunities.

Agency Annual Performance Plans

In addition to reviewing strategic plans, we also reviewed 28 agency annual performance plans to see how HRM is addressed. Performance plans are the yearly operational plans defining what the agency will accomplish in that fiscal year that will contribute to the longer-term strategic goals, and how they will measure accomplishment of these performance goals.

Seventy-five per cent of the reviewed plans contain both HRM performance goals and measures. This is not surprising because these operational plans tend to be more process and budgets focused than strategic plans and therefore contain more detail about the resources needed to accomplish the performance goals. Therefore, administrative functions, in general, are represented more fully than in the strategic plan. The development of the performance plan is invariably more functional than overall strategic planning.

At most agencies, each programme and administrative function is responsible for defining its own goals and measures which it then forwards to the planning office for coordination into the annual performance plan. As with the strategic plans, the HRM goals, strategies, and measures identified by HR offices tend to focus more on processes or activities than on overall outcomes. These process measures can be helpful, but because operational goals, strategies, and measures.

HUMAN RESOURCES MANAGEMENT STRATEGIC PLAN

The Health Care Financing Administration (HCFA) has developed a very noteworthy approach to aligning human resources management with mission accomplishment. HCFA's Human Resources Management Group (HRMG), Learning Resources Group (LRG), and Office of Equal Opportunity and Civil Rights (OEOCR) collaborated to develop a draft Human Resources Strategic Plan that goes beyond each of these individual organization's human resources responsibilities and instead addresses the entire sub-component's human resources management responsibilities.

It assigns accountability for specific HRM goals to HRMG, LRG, OEOCR, senior leadership, line managers, employees, the union, and/or other non-HR stakeholders. The HRMG, LRG, and OEOCR worked very closely with the HCFA strategic planning and evaluation office to tie the plan to HCFA's strategic plan. Specifically, the plan includes challenges that HCFA will face in the future, HRM goals that will support HCFA in meeting those challenges, potential performance indicators and strategies for each goal, the roles and responsibilities of HRMG, LRG, OEOCR, managers, employees, and other stakeholders, and finally how to implement and assess its results. help determine achievement of mission goals, they should focus more on whether or not the intended outcome of the activity was achieved.

HR Strategic Plans

Approximately half of the agencies we talked to have developed separate Human Resources strategic plans. These plans generally serve one of two purposes. Either they provide direction for those agencies that have not integrated HRM into the agency strategic plan, or they are used as implementation plans which support agencywide HRM goals, strategies, and measures. These plans are particularly important to those agencies that do not integrate HRM into the agencywide plan because it helps them map out where they want the HR programme to go.

They seem less important to many of the agencies that have thoroughly integrated HRM into the agency plan. For example, the Social Security Administration (SSA) has not developed a specific HR strategic plan because HR's goals and measures are part of the agencywide approach. Then, there are some agencies that integrate HR extensively into the agency plan, but still prefer to have a separate HR operational plan supporting the agencywide plan, as is often done by other corporate functions such as information technology and financial management. Most of these plans focus on internal HR office programme activities, rather than on agencywide accountability for the effective use of human resources in accomplishing the mission.

Therefore, ownership of the plan belongs to the HR office, not the agency. The Health Care Financing Administration (a sub-component of the Department of Health and Human Services) is an interesting exception to this. As with agency strategic plans, the measures identified in HR strategic plans are typically process- oriented and tend to address what steps have been taken to achieve a goal, rather than whether the intended outcome of the goal has been achieved. A little over half of the agencies use management input in developing these plans, generally in the form of previous customer satisfaction surveys. Strategic planning allows agencies to put down on paper where they are, where they want to go, and how they plan to get there. But the best planning in the world does nothing for an agency if it does not act on those plans. Strategic implementation of human resources management means performing activities that support agency mission accomplishment and measuring how well those activities contribute to achieving agency strategic goals.

Strategic HRM Activities

When we talk about HRM activities, we tend to focus on what the HR office, itself, is doing even though we recognize that supervisors would bear the responsibility of HR decisions in an ideal world. After all, NPR advocated deregulation and delegation and the downsizing and out- sourcing of HR office activities so that human resources management could take place at the line level, making it more responsive to mission-related needs.

Additionally, the HR staff would be able to devote more time to broader organizational issues, thereby improving its contribution to mission accomplishment. Unfortunately, deregulation and delegation, as reported in OPM's 1997 special study, Deregulation and Delegation of Human Resources Management Authority in the Federal Government, have not taken hold as quickly or thoroughly as was hoped. HR is still doing most of the HR- related work and is the nerve centre for HRM activities.

That is why the focus of this part is on the HR office and what it does to support mission accomplishment. So what are HR's contributions towards mission accomplishment? Although most line managers we interviewed cannot describe precisely which HR activities support specific agency strategic goals, they recognize that they could not accomplish their mission without HR's help. Ironically, the areas most often mentioned by managers as HR's most valued contributions are also the areas they feel need the most improvement: recruitment and staffing, employee development, and employee relations. They would like to see HR become more involved and innovative in these areas, but they also admit that it would be extremely difficult for them to get their jobs done without the help HR already provides. With this system, HR can immediately identify available deployment candidates for selection as soon as disasters are declared. Additionally, the system allows HR to better identify employee training and promotion needs, match employee expertise with specific disaster site victim needs, and create a selection routine that rotates available employees, thereby avoiding employee burnout.

Clearly, staffing, development, and employee relations are important HR activities that make a difference to agency goal accomplishment. However, there are other areas in which HR offices contribute to and align with mission accomplishment. Agency Reorganizations: Because of all of the downsizing, streamlining, and budget cuts that have been occurring in recent years, many agencies and sub-components have had to redefine their missions and restructure the programme areas that support those missions. Human resources staffs play key roles in some of these redesign efforts. Managers at the Federal Emergency Management Agency and the Department of Labour's Occupational Safety and Health Administration were particularly complimentary of all of the work the HR staffs did to redeploy and retrain the workforce, provide guidance on organizational development issues, and redesign performance standards.

Workforce Planning: In this time of budget cuts, downsizing, and an aging Federal workforce, workforce planning becomes extremely important to increasing agencies' overall ability to achieve their missions. Although few agencies have strong workforce planning systems in place, some are beginning to take steps in this direction. The Department of the Army has an automated civilian forecasting system that uses 15-year workforce data trends to project future employment patterns, up to 7 years. This is part of a developing workforce planning initiative. SSA has developed a methodology to predict the number of actual

Tracking Strategic Progress

Engineers at NASA's Kennedy Space Centre have designed and implemented an excellent strategic management tool: the Goal Performance Evaluation System. This computer system implemented a major performance management change by linking individual employee performance goals all the way up through the Centre and Agency goals. The system tracks the status of performance plans, and allows organizations to track results achieved against their mission. Managers can access the system to see what their units and individual employees are contributing towards the agency strategic goals.

The system functions as a strategic management tool, an employee performance management system, and a Centre-wide communication tool. Kennedy and Johnson Space Centres have piloted the computer system with very positive results. retirements and is developing a workforce transition plan that will identify current and future required skill sets, determine how the workforce can obtain these skills, and set action plan milestones. Additionally, OPM is in the process of developing a workforce planning model that will assist agencies in this area.

Linking Performance Management to Mission Accomplishment: When managers and employees are interviewed, they almost always cite the performance management system as a way they are held accountable for meeting agency goals. So, does this mean performance management systems are aligned with agency strategic goals? In most agencies, the answer is "not yet" — at least not fully. Recently published research has identified over a dozen agencies and agency sub- components that have started to formulate systematic approaches to aligning performance management to strategic goals. Most are starting by linking top management performance plans and contracts to agency goals and rating and rewarding executives based on achievement of those goals. Many of these agencies are planning to cascade the alignment down to the employee level. OPM's 1999 publication, A Measuring Employee Performance: Aligning Employee Performance with Organizational Goals, is a very useful tool to help agencies link employee performance to the goals of the organization and measure employee accomplishments.

A couple of agencies actually mandate the linkage of employee level plans to agency goals, while others are using team-based performance management approaches that include performance targets, informal team assessments, and awards that are linked to mission goals. The National Aeronautics and Space Administration (NASA), as shown in the inset, actually has an automated system that assists in the linkage. Nevertheless, as the General Accounting Office (GAO) concluded in its study, Performance Management: Aligning Employee Performance with Agency Goals at Six Results Act Pilots, aligning performance management systems with organizational missions and goals is still a "work in progress." HR Self-Assessment: A handful of agency and sub-component HR offices are actually assessing how well their programmes align with agency mission accomplishment as part of recently established HR self-assessment programmes.

These assessment programmes focus on the compliance of HR activities with law as well as how effectively HR programmes are achieving their objectives in support of mission accomplishment. Because these assessment programmes are fairly new or are in the process of being revamped, it is too soon to tell the success they will have in measuring HR's impact on organizational mission accomplishment.

HRM Measurement

In the end, HR can only determine its value to the organization by measuring it. Earlier in this report, we saw that most agencies had at least defined HR output measures in agency strategic plans, annual performance plans, and/or HR strategic plans. This is an encouraging trend, but we need to look further at whether these measures are actually being tracked and used for decision- making. The best measures in the world are meaningless if not used. HRM measures in the strategic and annual performance plans are usually tracked by the HR office and forwarded to the planning office for distribution and sharing of the information. A few agencies, such as NASA, SSA, and Education, report actually using the information for decision- making and tracking whether goals are being met. NASA even posts the information on its web page. However, we found that most agencies look at available data without really evaluating how the information can be used to enhance goal attainment.

HR staffs find that measures from HR strategic plans tend to be more useful than those in the agency strategic or annual plans, at least at the functional level. As discussed earlier, HR strategic plan measures tend to focus on internal HR programmes, policies, and processes, and can therefore point to deficiencies in these areas. HR officials can then use this information to make improvements to the problem areas. From an organizational perspective, however, the measures are generally not very helpful in determining achievement of HR goals because they are process rather than outcome oriented. Few agencies have implemented elaborate systems to track HRM goals and measures. Nonetheless, there are quite a few interesting approaches some agencies are using to measure their HRM performance.

Benchmarking is a systematic process of measuring an organization's products, services, and practices against those of a like organization that is a recognized leader in the studied area. Many Federal HR offices are using this practice to identify ways to improve service and align with business results. The most common benchmarking effort Federal HR offices have participated in is the National Academy of Public Administration-Hackett Group HR Benchmarking Study. There are at least 19 Government agencies involved in the benchmarking of 22 HR processes within four areas: administration, risk management, employee development, and decision support. The study also helps to gauge HR alignment through decision support categories such as resource planning, organizational planning, and strategic HR planning. Most participating agencies see the value in the information but have not devised strategies for how to use it.

The Balanced Scorecard in Action

The Veterans Benefits Administration's New York Regional Office implemented a balanced scorecard that uses outcome measures linked to organizational goals at the team, core group, and division-wide levels. The purpose is to determine how successful its operations are and where improvements are needed. This "balanced scorecard" measures five performance areas: customer satisfaction, speed, accuracy, cost-per- claim, and employee development. For each element in the balanced scorecard, teams are awarded points based on how well they are performing, and the scorecard is aligned with individual employee assessments and incentive pay. Veterans' expectations are used to define customer performance targets, and employee measures are derived from climate surveys, team development data, and technical skills inventories.

HR has played an important role in designing the balanced scorecard, including developing measures, peer assessments, and other tools, as well as helping managers understand the approach and how to manage under it. The Balanced Scorecard is a framework many agencies are using to translate strategy into operational terms by measuring a full range of perspectives: financial, customer, internal, and learning and growth. Vice President Gore advocated the use of this type of balanced set of results to evaluate agency performance at the Global Forum on Reinventing Government, January 1999. The scorecard is generally used at the business unit level, as with the Veterans Benefits Administration.

To date, most agencies are in the beginning stages of implementing balanced measurement approaches. Activity Based Costing (ABC) is a method of cost management that determines the true cost, including overhead, for a service or product. Finding the true cost allows agencies to discover cost improvement opportunities, prepare and actualize strategic and operational plans, and improve strategic decision-making. This cost management methodology involves identifying activities, determining activity costs, determining cost drivers, collecting activity data, and calculating the service cost. ABC is being explored by a number of agencies. The Patent and Trademark Office is using ABC agencywide, and the General Services Administration is using it to determine HR costs.

Measuring True Cost and How to Use It

Both the General Services Administration (GSA) and the Department of Commerce's Patent and Trademark Office (PTO) have successfully used Activity Based Costing (ABC) to determine the true cost of human resources management services. The General Services Administration began tracking HR costs due to customer complaints that services were too expensive. The problem was that no one, including HR, knew the actual cost of HR services. By using Activity Based Costing, GSA was able to compute the HR activity costs and make comparisons to other Government and private sector organizations using the Hackett Benchmarking Study data. HR demonstrated to managers that its costs were actually relatively low, and it had the data to prove it.

The Patent and Trademark Office (PTO) has engaged in agencywide Activity Based Costing. All senior managers were trained in the process, and each functional area, including HR, formed teams to identify activities, activity-based drivers, and primary products. PTO has used the information to close out fiscal year 1998 financial activities and to plan the fiscal year 2000 budget. ABC has helped determine the full cost of agency activities, the proper distribution of costs, and has even influenced service rates.

An additional benefit to the system is that it has encouraged strategic thinking. Managers see how much a function, such as HR, costs and starts asking what value that function really adds to the programme. This challenges HR to show its value and return on investment. The Malcolm Baldrige and the President's Quality Award Criteria are each based on a set of core values and concepts that integrate key business requirements into a results-oriented framework. Using the criteria as a framework for management practices and measurement can help agencies to improve performance, facilitate communication and best practice sharing, and serve as a tool for managing performance, planning, training, and assessment. HR measures are 15 per cent of the total Baldrige framework score. Several agencies, most notably the Department of Navy's Inspector General's Office, have successfully used the criteria to assess agency mission programmes.

STRATEGIC RELATIONSHIPS

The lynchpin that holds all of this planning and implementation together is the relationship between HR executives and staffs and agency management. In the past, there was often much contention between the two groups because of HR's role as "gatekeeper," enforcing the laws, rules, and regulations. Now, with the role of the human resources staff shifting towards achieving organizational results, HR and management need to work together to further HRM's ability to have an impact on agency decisions and achievement of goals. So, let's take a look at how well these relationships have been fostered thus far.

Corporate HR and Top Agency Management

The relationship between corporate HR and top agency management varies greatly by agency. A few agencies, like SSA, NASA, Air Force, and GSA, have been able to develop strong working relationships with management in which HR is a full member of the agency decision-making body. Most other agency HR executives have not been so fortunate. They are generally brought into the agency decision-making process during the implementation phase rather than being consulted in the beginning on how decisions may impact agency human resources or vice versa. For some agencies, it has been a hard road. For others, it has been more of a natural transition. In exploring how to elevate HR's role to management partner, agencies where this has been achieved attribute their success to a combination of the following factors: Reporting relationships - In agencies where there is a direct reporting relationship between the head of HR and the head of the agency, HR generally has a more visible role in agency decision-making. Management advocates - In agencies where there is a strong HR advocate in senior management, HR enjoys more involvement in the agency decision-making. Credibility - HR representatives who are formerly programme managers tend to earn more credibility from the other managers.

This type of individual knows, first hand, what the programme concerns are and how HR decisions will impact the programme, and can speak the same programmatic language. The Social Security Administration: How HR Stays at the SSA's HR Office has a good record of contributing substance, creativity, and innovative solutions to dealing with agency issues. For example, when SSA heeded NPR's call to downsize administrative staffs, the HR office devoted substantial time and resourcefulness to redeploying these displaced employees to direct service jobs. For the headquarters employees who did not want to leave the area, HR helped to create a direct service office at headquarters and bring work there.

Not only does this demonstrate HR's ingenuity in turbulent times, but it is a fitting example of how SSA values its employees. Traditionally been part of the culture. Therefore, it is natural for the HR leader to have a voice in agency decisions. Value - In all cases, HR has to bring value to the discussion in order to be considered a member of the management team.

If you have little or nothing to offer, you will not keep your seat at the table. Because HR executives have little control over agency reporting relationships, management advocacy, executive appointments, and agency culture, they need to focus their efforts on providing value to agency business discussions. But what kind of value can HR bring to the agency decision-making table? Other corporate functions have no problem demonstrating their value. The Chief Financial Officer has the money. The Chief Information Officer has the technology. Without money and technology, an organization is severely hindered. But HR has the people, and without the people, the organization has no one to do the work. So why has HR not been able to capitalize on this strength? We were able to identify two reasons. First, HR has not historically had the statistics or data that can excite management and show how HRM influences agency success. Second, HR has focused on internal operations rather than activities that impact the entire agency.

These facts are recognized by the Strategic Human Resources Roundtable, an OPM-sponsored working group of Governmentwide HR Directors that meets periodically to discuss HR's role in GPRA. This group acknowledges that to address these shortcomings, HR needs to ask itself what are the HRM concerns that will gain management's attention, and does HR have the data that can help address those concerns.

The HR Office and Line Management

Now that we have explored the relationship between HR executives and top agency managers, we need to look at how the HR office interacts with its line managers and if there has been any movement towards a more cooperative, consultative relationship. HR's role is changing, but is HR changing with it? As discussed earlier, NPR advocated HR delegating, downsizing, and outsourcing so that it could start concentrating on broader organizational issues rather than transactional processes. This is beginning to occur at the corporate level, but what about the line level?

The problem is that delegation to managers has not taken hold very quickly, but HR offices have already been downsized. Therefore, HR is still expected to do the transactional work it did before, while also focusing on broader organizational issues, and doing all of this with an average of 20 per cent less staff. It is not hard to understand why agency HR offices are struggling to redefine their role to strategic partner. Just how far have they gotten? HR as Consultant: Most agency managers we interviewed acknowledge that their HR office has become more consultative. Rather than telling a manager he/she can or cannot do something, HR professionals are more helpful in finding solutions to HR issues. HR as Contributor to Mission Accomplishment: These same managers also recognize the importance of the HR office to mission accomplishment. There is so much that HR does for managers in terms of recruitment and staffing, employee development, and employee relations that managers would have difficulty doing it on their own. However, HR does have its limitations, particularly the size of the staff in relation to the amount of work it has to do, its knowledge of the mission, and skill gaps resulting from downsizing. HR as Strategic Partner: Few, if any, agency managers feel that their HR office is a true strategic partner.

Few HR offices are included in business planning from the beginning, generally being brought in to implement a decision that has already been made. For HR to become more involved in line-level decision-making, managers would like the office to: C have greater knowledge of the organizational mission, and C get more involved and innovative in broad, organizational HR issues that impact most on the organization, such as recruitment and workforce and succession planning. HR has made some headway, as demonstrated in the following NASA example, but clearly has some distance to go in being involved in line management decision-making. Now let's look at the other side of the coin — how managers are involved in making decisions about HR programmes. Most line HR offices involve managers at least at an informal level, generally through satisfaction surveys or informal discussions. A few have HR/management councils that get together

NASA's Centres Working Together

NASA has 10 field centres, and each of these centres maintains a strong sense of its own identity and purpose and a strong enthusiasm for its mission. At the same time, each centre can identify the linkage to the agency mission. This sense of empowerment appears to help motivate the centre

HR staffs to actively support that identity and purpose. Personnel officers generally participate in deliberations on centre affairs. HR staffs are proactive in their work by making site visits, attending line staff meetings, asking managers for input on HR issues, and briefing managers about changes in HR programmes. Managers are impressed with HR's availability, knowledge, and resourcefulness.

This symbiosis is portrayed well in results from various employee surveys, data trends from the Central Personnel Data File, and third party evaluations of the HR programme. Periodically to discuss human resources issues. This is as close as agencies get to real integration of managers into the HR programme decision-making process. Generally, managers do not feel that they have a large impact on the direction of HR programmes and therefore feel little ownership for them.

Accountability

With the developing relationship between HR and management, both at the top and line levels, along with NPR and GPRA mandates, accountability should become a shared responsibility. Managers are making more and more HRM decisions while the HR staff is becoming more involved in broader organizational issues. This means that both the HR staff and managers are ultimately accountable for effective, legally compliant HRM. Is this shared accountability occurring in Federal agencies? Approximately half of the responding agencies agree that HRM accountability is shared between the HR staff and managers.

Managers are accountable for the business results achieved through good human resources management, the HR staff is accountable for HR compliance, and both are accountable for the overall effectiveness of the agency HRM programme. However, the other half still feels that the ultimate accountability falls on the HR staff. They are the ones responsible if actions are found non-compliant, and little attention is given to whether managers' HRM decisions are an effective use of resources. OPM's HRM Accountability System Development Guide goes into quite a bit of detail on shared accountability and can assist agencies in understanding the concept, determining who is accountable for what, and devising strategies for how to hold them accountable. Strategic alignment of human resources management has come farther than we expected to find when we embarked on this study. There is definitely a trend towards integrating HR into the business planning process, measuring aspects of human resources management and its contribution to the organizational bottom line, and establishing a collaborative working environment between HR and management. Nevertheless, there are several indications that human resources management is not yet recognized as a critical contributor to agency mission accomplishment. HRM alignment is still evolving, and there are several steps agencies can take to help it along. Fully integrate human resources management into the business planning process.

Although many more agencies than expected include HR representatives in the agency planning process and integrate human resources goals, objectives, and strategies into agency strategic plans, most are still struggling in this area. Agency executives need to recognize the value that HR can impart to discussions about agency activities, priorities, and goals. In turn, HR leaders need to understand agency mission needs and be able to contribute substantive, creative solutions to meet these needs. Once these realisations occur, HR will no longer be segregated out as a support function but will become an integral, contributing factor to agency planning and success.

Agency Decision-Making

Because of NPR mandates to downsize, streamline, and improve customer service, HR's recent improvement efforts have focused on the efficiency and effectiveness of traditional HR programmes and processes. These are important endeavors. However, in response to GPRA's call to measure performance and demonstrate value, it is time to start concentrating efforts outside of the traditional realm of HR and on to broader organizational issues. When HR demonstrates that it can have an impact on agency direction, then it will gain credibility with agency executives and earn a seat at the table. To generate that type of impact, HR needs to develop strategies based on actual business needs, which will require involving management in the planning process. In addition, it must address Governmentwide concerns about the workforce capabilities of the future, such as workforce planning, succession planning, training needs assessments, skill gap analyses, etc.

Measure HRM Outcomes

HR's role is evolving. Therefore, HRM measures need to evolve as well. As HR becomes more involved in broader organizational activities, HRM measures should evaluate the impact these activities have on the organization as a whole. At this point, measures typically focus on outputs and processes and are generally internalized to the HR function or office. The data are used mostly to make improvements to HR-specific policies and procedures.

While this kind of measurement is important, measures should also focus on organizational outcomes. Information from these measures should then be used to inform agencywide decisions and find solutions to agencywide concerns. Advance the collaborative working environment between HR and management. To facilitate all of the changes recommended, HR has to have a strong, collaborative working relationship with top agency and line management. Since there is no tradition in most agencies of HR as strategic partner, much depends on personal relationships established by HR officials with top managers and key line managers. Meanwhile, HR and agency management need each other more than ever. Authorities are being delegated to line managers, HR staffs are being downsized, and top agency management is being asked to show how its resources are being used to support mission accomplishment.

HR must be able to make the case that everyone in the agency, from the agency leader down to the HR function, must share accountability for ensuring that the use of human resources not only complies with Federal laws, rules, and regulations, but adds to the success of the agency. This shared accountability is beginning to occur. HR management is beginning to earn a seat at the table. HR line offices are becoming more consultative and involved in day to day management activities. Nevertheless, there is still a long way to go in becoming strategic partners. First, HR needs to build its own internal competencies to deal with organizational issues, change, and strategizing.

Further, it needs to educate itself on agency and programme missions in order to understand what is important to those organizations and be able to offer creative and innovative alternatives and solutions to organizationwide issues. Finally, it must continually assert the absolute criticality of effective HRM to organizational success. This all looks so easy on paper.

Do this, do that, and you will be aligned with the mission and able to demonstrate your contribution towards it. Obviously, it is not that easy. Private sector, public sector, and some Federal entities have been struggling with this issue even before GPRA was enacted — and that works to our advantage. There is a wealth of information out there that can help — hundreds of articles, books, and studies have been written, numerous tools have been created, and many organizations have already tested a number of approaches. We can learn from all of these successes and failures. But the only way to begin is to begin.

To help start you on this path, we have included a rather extensive, though certainly not all-inclusive. In support of its programme to foster development of agency accountability systems, OPM will also offer assistance to individual agencies in developing strategies for strategic alignment and has created a Governmentwide clearinghouse that will provide information on additional real life, successful approaches that agencies are employing.

It is in all of our interests to ensure that Government establishes and maintains a highly skilled workforce that can handle the demands of the 21st century. To achieve this goal, we must all work together. For some reason, people tend to think that the Federal Government has fallen far behind the private sector, and even other public sector entities, when it comes to aligning human resources management with agency mission accomplishment. Although we did not talk directly with private or non-Federal public sector representatives, we conducted a fairly in-depth literature search that tells a somewhat different story.

Private Sector

There are many conflicting views on where the private sector is in regard to HRM alignment. For instance, the Conference Board recently conducted a poll of 155 private sector HR executives, and 63 per cent responded that HR is "never, rarely, or only sometimes" a major player in the companies' strategic process. A Price water house-Coopers poll indicates that although 75 per cent of the responding 70 companies reported that HR's effectiveness is measured by its contribution to business results, only 27 per cent include HR from the beginning of the business planning cycle.

Further, 43 per cent rated HR's planning and policy effectiveness as only average while a mere 6 per cent rated it as excellent. Other private sector surveys and studies over the past few years, however, have found that HR has been integrated into the strategic planning process, HR executives and top company management are strategic planning partners, HR is recognized for the importance of its role in implementing organizational change, and HR is viewed as critical to the success of the business.

Clearly, there are many private sector organizations that exemplify "best-in-class" alignment strategies. They have implemented such alignment approaches as the Balanced Scorecard, Return on Investment, Activity Based Costing, Malcolm Baldrige Award-type criteria, and more. They recognize the importance of their employees to business results, and HR is considered a valued strategic partner. However, even with a number of "best practices" out there, the research agrees that HR alignment, even in the private sector, is still a work in progress.

Non-Federal Public Sector

A recent research, the non-Federal public sector is in much the same boat as the Federal sector. As the Government Performance Project pointed out in its recent study, State governments run into many of the same HR problems as the Federal Government – rigid rules, lack of strategic management decisions, absence of statewide HR data, lack of workforce planning or the ability to plan for the future, etc. State governments have begun making HR reforms, such as reducing job classifications and streamlining hiring procedures. However, as with the Federal Government, States are focusing more on the efficiency and effectiveness of programmes than how they support the bottom line.

That is not to say that local, State, and even foreign governments have not been able to align themselves with mission accomplishment. A few cases can be most instructive for Federal agencies as they ponder this issue. The City of Hampton, Virginia HR staff has played a large role in increasing the performance of government services through improvements to work environment, organizational structure, work design, employee behaviours and organizational systems.

The state of Washington is developing and enhancing HR information systems in support of mission accomplishment, is using personnel data to identify improvement initiatives, and includes the Director of Personnel in the Governor's Cabinet. The Canadian Treasury Board and HR Council of the Federal Government of Canada are developing approaches to measuring HR efficiency, effectiveness, and mission contribution. There are many other examples of how the public sector is moving towards aligning HR with mission accomplishment. Nonetheless, the research indicates that the non-Federal public sector, too, is only in the beginning stages of this transformation.

8

Foreign Investment

THE SELECTIVE PROMOTION

In February of 1984, the National Foreign Investment Commission of Mexico surprised the investment community by announcing that it would apply the Foreign Investment Law of 1973 (FIL) with flexibility and would consider permitting foreign capital investment of up to 100 per cent in a significant number of activities. Actually, Mexico had been expected to increase its restriction of foreign investment in view of the Government's efforts to decrease its economic dependence upon other countries.

For more than a decade, Mexico had limited foreign equity participation to 49 per cent. Since the FIL allows for exceptions, the 49 per cent limitation on foreign ownership is in essence a general principle. The policy, however, had been to enforce strictly the 49 per cent limitation with few exceptions, which prompted the erroneous belief that this policy was in fact the law. The initial reaction of foreign and Mexican investors to the recent shift in policy has been mixed.

Some investors are concerned that businesses that incorporate with 100 per cent foreign equity under the 1984 Guidelines will later be subjected to governmental decrees limiting future activities. These investors would favour fixed statutory rules in the form of a legislative amendment rather than flexible application of the current law. Other investors have assumed a more positive and rational attitude towards the change. They take the position that, even if Mexico were to return to the 51-49 per cent concept, businesses incorporated under the 1984 Guidelines would retain their 100 per cent foreign equity. This position finds support in the fact that businesses that had 100 per cent foreign equity prior to enactment of the FIL in 1973 retained their 100 per cent equity afterwards. Indeed, United States investors currently hold approximately two-thirds of the $11.5 billion in foreign investment in Mexico.

A second question that appears to have been overshadowed by the release of the Guidelines is whether 100 per cent foreign ownership is preferable to 49 per cent foreign ownership with investment incentives. At present, Mexico offers a variety of attractive investment incentives to businesses that incorporate with at least 51 per cent Mexican equity. Consequently, there are distinct advantages to both majority and minority foreign equity. In the final analysis, the needs of the particular enterprise will dictate the decision. Since the Guidelines were announced rather recently, and in view of the state of the world economy, it is too soon to determine their actual impact.

It appears, however, that the pendulum of Mexico's attitude towards foreign investment has finally reached that central balance essential for rational economic development: the selective promotion of industries necessary for positive economic growth. This article provides an overview of the Mexican legislative process and discusses the various restrictions on foreign investment. The current implementation of the 1973 FIL is also examined, including the ramifications of minority and majority foreign ownership.

The substance of the 1984 Guidelines is presented, and the perceptions of bankers, corporations, the Foreign Investment Commission and the foreign investment legal community are explored. Finally, the object analyses the advantages and disadvantages of regulating Mexico's foreign investments through legislative amendments rather than administrative policy, Mexico's changing position on foreign investment and the benefits of 100 per cent foreign ownership under the 1984 Guidelines in view of the investment incentives offered to businesses with 51 per cent Mexican equity.

FOREIGN INVESTMENT LEGISLATION

To a large extent, Mexico's regulations on foreign investment are the result of administrative policy rather than the legislative process. In many cases, these policies have been adopted or changed with little or no publicity, and they frequently have been enforced under laws designed for unrelated purposes.

Consequently, the policies are often difficult to define and must be deduced by their application to specific cases. A prospective foreign investor must examine not only Mexico's foreign investment laws, but also the policies and practices of the executive branch of the federal Government to ascertain if, and to what extent, a business may be established in the country, the conditions under which the business will be received and whether the regulations to which the business will be subject are consistent with its interests. Throughout the past century, foreign investment in Mexico was affected by divergent trends. During the period spanned by the regime of Porfirio Díaz (1876-1911), it was believed that substantial investments in mining, utilities and basic industries would bring Mexico into a position commensurate with that of industrialized countries.

As a result, foreign investment was allowed to such an extent that it dominated the economy. In fact, much of the nationalistic sentiment evoked today in Mexico over foreign investment derives from the prominence attained by foreign enterprises during the lengthy Díaz regime. In the absence of domestic investment sufficient to build a foundation for further development, extensive infusions of foreign capital were necessary, but they inspired a growing fear of increasing foreign influence.

Moreover, Mexico's natural resources and labour were being exploited in the process. By the early 20th century, "the economic penetration of the country by foreign enterprises resulted in almost complete loss of control of the country's destiny to foreigners and foreign interests." Recovery of Mexico's "economic destiny" was one of the primary ideals to emerge during the country's Revolution of 1910-1920 and has remained an essential tenet of every subsequent administration. The Mexican Constitution, promulgated in 1917, placed restraints on foreign economic activities and foreign ownership of land, which indicated the direction that limitations on the role of foreign capital would take in the future.

THE LEGISLATIVE PROCESS

Although Mexico is a federal republic with both federal and state levels of legislative jurisdiction, the overwhelming majority of the statutes affecting its foreign investors are either federal or modeled after federal laws. Federal legislation is enacted by Congress; however, Congress rarely does more than give approval to statutory drafts submitted by the Executive. To become effective, the legislation must be promulgated by the President and published in the Diario Oficial de la Federación.

In addition to indirect control over the legislative process, the President has authority to enact general rules in the form of regulations, which explain and supply detailed precepts for the application of specific laws; to legislate directly in foreign trade; and to exercise other legislative powers pursuant to congressional statutory delegation. Indeed, a significant amount of existing legislation was enacted under the President's "extraordinary legislative power."

In 1938, however, the Constitution was amended to provide that such "authority to legislate could be granted only in connection with a suspension of individual guarantees in times of grave national emergency under article 29." Constitutional guarantees have been suspended only once since that time, in 1944, and, although most of the presidential decrees issued during that period were later repealed, the decree establishing the basis for quantitative restrictions on direct foreign investment remained intact.

RESTRICTIONS ON FOREIGN INVESTMENT

The Emergency Decree of 1944 granted extensive discretionary control over foreign capital to the Ministry of

Foreign Relations and was intended to avert disruption of the economy by temporary investments of flight capital. The decree introduced restraints on the "creation, modification, liquidation and transfer of stock" of Mexican companies that might have foreign shareholders and were organized subsequent to its enactment. While it originally affected few and relatively insignificant activities, the Emergency Decree was nonetheless the precursor of present legal restraints on foreign investment in Mexico.

Two years later, the Interministerial Committee was created to coordinate national and foreign investment. Composed of representatives of the President and several ministries, it was established to make "a systematic and continuing study" of foreign investment in Mexico so that "a proper balance" between foreign and domestic capital could be maintained. The committee, however, "largely ratified the practices already adopted by the Ministry of Foreign Relations under its discretionary powers." Since 1953, the committee has functioned haphazardly, and its significance has depended upon the conduct of the incumbent administration. Nevertheless, the committee's inaction did not deter enforcement of the Emergency Decree, which the Ministry of Foreign Relations in fact expanded beyond its literal provisions. Even though the Emergency Decree applied only to specifically delineated activities, the Ministry instructed notaries and public registry officials that licenses were required for the incorporation or amendment of the articles of any company, regardless of the purpose or nature of the business. At the same time, beginning in the early part of World War II, Mexico's attitude towards foreign capital shifted in an effort to improve the economy.

Between 1940 and 1965, direct foreign investment almost quadrupled, and by 1969, it exceeded two billion dollars. This increase, however, was accompanied by pressure from Mexican industrialists to limit the inflow of foreign capital. Extensive foreign investment was noted to result in decapitalization and to increase the country's balance-of-payments problems. Government economists also were concerned and recommended that "the pattern of investment in assembly and processing operations, characteristic of the 1940's . . . be broken and greater use of domestically produced intermediate materials encouraged to stimulate import substitution." Efforts were increasingly made to displace foreign investment. Joint ventures of Mexican and foreign capital were promoted, as were industrial integration programmes, and foreign participation was excluded from certain industries and severely limited in others.

In 1966 the Ministry adopted another significant policy: to deny licenses for the acquisition of majority interests in existing Mexican companies. The mélange of restricted industries suggests that there was no overall planning or general policy concerning foreign participation in the Mexican economy. Some of the restrictions related to national security and the public welfare, while others seem to have been imposed in response to pressure from ad hoc private groups fearful about foreign competition. Furthermore, although special laws were enacted that expressly limited foreign investment in certain industries, other industries were added to the restricted list "solely on the basis of policy decisions by the Ministry of Foreign Relations, acting either on its own initiative or, more likely, on the initiative of, or at least with the concurrence of, other governmental agencies."

By 1970, the only legal restrictions on the amount of foreign participation in industrial activities were those resulting from the application of the Emergency Decree of 1944 and the exclusion of private participation, both domestic and foreign, in nationalized industries. The Government used other techniques, however, to divest foreigners of control and ownership, including tax incentives and the selective application of import controls. As one author has noted, the administration "seemed to prefer the flexibility in shaping its policies to individual investment projects that was allowed by the absence of a general law on foreign investments," and it adopted "specific statutory restraints in selected industries as it felt the need or desirability [to arise]." The resultant overall attitude towards foreign investment was "one of cautious acceptance," although many perceived it to be excessively protective and nationalistic. Foreign investment was encouraged as a complement to domestic investment, and the Ministry of Commerce and Industrial Promotion increasingly insisted on Mexicanization and industrial integration. Businesses dependent upon imports of raw or intermediate products or materials, or of machinery or equipment learned that procurement of the necessary import licenses might depend on whether they had become Mexicanized.

The Ministry of Commerce and Industrial Promotion supervised not only the issuance of such licenses, but also industrial integration programmes. In return for a guarantee by the Ministry that the necessary licenses would be granted, that imports of competing products would be excluded or that Mexican competitors would need to meet the same conditions, new and existing companies agreed to increase the Mexican content of their products, limit prices and payments abroad, observe quality control standards and divert 51 per cent of their capital stock to Mexicans over a specified period of time. Furthermore, foreign investors learned that the availability of tax concessions depended upon Mexicanization.

As a result, an informal process of clearing investment projects with the Ministry of Commerce and Industrial Promotion developed, as prospective foreign investors sounded out the administration for assurances that their projects would be favourably received. The position of the foreign investor also changed. Tax and other concessions were offered to concerns with majority Mexican ownership under the 1972 Law for the Promotion of New and Necessary Industries, to manufacturing businesses in the border zones and areas outside Mexico City, and to enterprises exporting Mexican manufactured products; but the administration was no longer receptive to the establishment of firms for the final processing or mere assembly of imported parts or intermediate products. Also, enterprises that were heavily dependent on imports were subjected to strong pressure to develop domestic production. The informal process of clearing proposed new investments and important expansions of existing facilities was "virtually institutionalized," and although still not required by law, the Ministry usually insisted that the projects be underwritten with a majority of Mexican capital. Between 1972 and 1976, Mexico extended the controls over foreign investment. Of utmost importance was the Law for the Promotion of Mexican Investment and for the Regulation of Foreign Investment (the Foreign Investment Law or FIL), enacted in 1973. Its purpose was to codify existing laws, regulations and policies, and it established the National Foreign Investment Commission (FIC) to exercise significant discretionary powers created by law, and the National Registry of Foreign Investment (FIR).

THE FOREIGN INVESTMENT LAW AND THE FOREIGN INVESTMENT COMMISSION

Since 1973, the FIL has been the principal source of foreign investment restrictions. It applies to capital investments in Mexican businesses, to investments in the acquisition of Mexican real or personal property, and to other specified transactions, including the pledging of Mexican corporate shares to foreigners and foreign participation in a real property trust. It is restrictive, however, only with regard to direct investment; it does not explicitly regulate indirect investment such as loans. Actually, the FIL set forth only two major changes in the restriction of foreign investment. It limited foreign participation in the management of a corporation to the proportion of foreign capitalization and established the 49-51 per cent concept as a general rule.

This was the first time legislation required majority Mexican participation in a broad spectrum of activities and not in just a single activity. Although the FIL does not explicitly define either foreign investment or foreign investors, it does provide a list of activities and individuals that will be considered as such. It stipulates those economic activities exclusively reserved to the Government, those reserved to Mexican individuals or corporations without foreign participation and those in which foreign participation is specifically limited to less than 49 per cent. It also contains a general provision limiting foreign participation in new businesses whose activities are otherwise not regulated to a maximum of 49 per cent. Furthermore, the FIL requires governmental authorization for investments acquiring more than 25 per cent of the equity or more than 49 per cent of the fixed assets of an existing Mexican company, and for any transaction resulting in the transfer of management to a foreign investor. Unless a foreign investor is interested in establishing a business with more than 49 per cent foreign equity, the business may simply be registered with the FIR.

However, the final decision on whether a foreign investor may hold a majority of foreign capital and control rests with the FIC. Since the 1973 law vested the FIC with broad discretionary powers, the commission could increase the "maximum" 49 per cent foreign equity whenever it deemed the project beneficial to the Mexican economy.

The burden, though, now fell on the foreign investor to show that majority foreign equity and control would "stimulate a balanced and equitable development" and "consolidate the economic independence of the country." The FIC consists of representatives of the President and seven ministries, and meets on a monthly basis.

Pursuant to its statutory powers, it may:

- Increase or reduce the percentage of foreign participation in geographical areas or economic activities when there are no required definite percentages and establish the terms and conditions under which the investment will be received;
- Resolve on specific percentages and conditions for those projects which "may justify special treatment";
- Resolve on projected foreign investment in companies established or to be established in Mexico;
- Resolve on the participation of existing foreign investors in new areas of economic activities or in new product lines; and
- Establish "requirements and criteria" for the application of foreign investment laws and regulations.

Pursuant to the FIL, the FIC issues General Resolutions setting forth standards and requirements for applying the law, although there are no "regulations" *per se*. Applications submitted to the FIC for approval of majority foreign equity are first analysed by a technical committee and then submitted to the FIC for formal acceptance. Invariably, applications undergo a process of negotiation, ranging from 4 to 16 months in duration.

Investment with majority foreign equity has had several disadvantages: the length of time required to obtain approval for either the formation or expansion of a company, and the restricted sources of tax and other investment incentives. In contrast, an investment of 49 per cent or less foreign equity can be organized immediately, may be expanded into different areas or used for new product lines, qualifies automatically for tax and other incentives, and usually will provide easier access to administrative agencies and the various licenses required for imports.

Furthermore, Mexican laws protect minority shareholders, whether Mexican or foreign, against decisions by a majority group of shareholders, and additional protection may be secured by provisions inserted into the bylaws or articles of incorporation. Since the enactment of the 1973 FIL, exceptions to the 49-51 per cent concept have been granted rarely and only under special circumstances. Foreign equity in excess of 49 per cent has tended to be approved in such sectors as tourism, priority industries, advanced technology, capitalization and investments preserving employment, and for priority activities of Mexican corporations with severe economic problems. Furthermore, the overwhelming majority of these exceptions have been contingent upon agreement eventually to Mexicanize.

The FIC bases its decisions on the criteria set forth in the National Industrial Development Plan (NIDP) and the FIL. The foreign investment allowed should always be complementary to the Mexican economy; there should not be substitution of fields covered; the company should be ready to export; it should commit itself to a precise plan to train Mexican personnel; a high percentage of the financing should come from abroad; there should be diversification of the sources of investment; the company should have a significant positive effect on local employment; the project should preserve the cultural and social values of Mexico; it should be located in an underdeveloped geographical area; and it should contribute to the technological development of the country. Two of the most significant criteria considered by the FIC in determining exceptions under the FIL are whether the proposed activity is an industry or is in a geographical area encouraged under the NIDP. Although each presidential administration adopts its own NIDP, the underlying premise remains constant.

The 1983-1988 NIDP incorporates criteria set forth in the FIL. Moreover, the 1983 NIDP contains detailed political and economic policies governing "the Mexican State, the diagnosis of the national problems, the purposes and strategies of solutions in a national and international context, and the bases for implementation of those strategies." Each NIDP, therefore, provides indicators of the attitude and direction to be taken by the incumbent administration towards foreign investment. In February 1983, the Constitution was amended, enabling "the federal government to adopt measures of great scope in economic matters, and reorienting the principles governing the actions of the state and private individuals."

The amendments embody principles consistent with the present administration's philosophy of la Rectoría del Estado (the state as sovereign and the sole conductor of the economy). The amendments identify activities reserved exclusively to the Government, but they also provide for the development of the private sector. In view of the increasing restrictions on the amount of allowable foreign equity in various activities, the formidable effort required to obtain an exception to the 49-51 per cent "rule" and the few exceptions granted, the FIC's announcement in February 1984 that it would consider up to 100 per cent foreign capital investment in a significant number of activities ran completely counter to the expectations of the investment community. Mexico's present policy on foreign investment is in the process of evolution and finds support in the FIL, the NIDP, resolutions of the FIC, and declarations by the Executive Secretary of the FIC and the Secretary of Commerce and Industrial Promotion. It focuses primarily on the selective promotion of new or necessary industries. No longer amenable to the acceptance of foreign investment in an indiscriminate manner, it does, however, encourage activities that will further the economic development of the country.

The primary objective of the 1984 Guidelines for Foreign Investment is the active, systematic and selective promotion of foreign investment in specific activities considered the most important for "a fair and balanced growth of the Mexican economy." That promotion is to focus on those areas which will generate a positive foreign exchange balance, produce competitive exports and import substitution, contribute to national scientific and technological development, advance Mexico's further integration into the international community, involve large investments, and create employment and geographical decentralization of industry. In analysing the basis of foreign investment policy, the FIC acknowledges that, "[a]lthough an adequate Law exists for direct foreign investments, a systematic policy has not always been followed for an effective utilization of its potential for the country's development."

The FIC has found that, in reality, "the effective use of investments to promote national technological development, to efficiently replace imports or generate exports for a positive trade surplus" has been hindered by multinational corporations that "frequently tend to seek benefits through equipment and technologies already obsolete in their own countries, protectively, and obtain excessive gains at the expense of national consumers." Similarly, the FIC concedes that, while past practices have quantitatively limited foreign investment, such practices have not induced a "favourable direction." Instead, foreign investment policy "has been limited to a simple check of investment propositions, set forth in accordance with international production strategies, or marketing of foreign companies' products, not always adequate to local, or national priorities or those of certain sectors." The FIC also recognizes that negotiations regarding foreign investments have been "limited to imposing local integration requirements or filling export quotas," with "[t]he latter in many cases hav[ing] been difficult or impossible to follow." The Guidelines represent the FIC's attempt to correct these deficiencies by adjusting Mexico's policies on foreign investment and its regulation. While foreign investment will remain a "complement" to domestic investment, the "policy will cease to be merely defensive and [will] turn active and systematic, promoting the formation of foreign investment alternatives, just as to needs derived from national development priorities."

The Guidelines list priority activities that may receive up to 100 per cent direct foreign investment. Priority undertakings, as delineated in the Guidelines, include the production of nonelectric equipment and machinery, electric machinery and appliances, electronic equipment and devices, and equipment and material for transportation; metal mechanics; the chemical industry; other manufacturing industries; advanced technology services; and the hotel industry. The Guidelines state, however, that the enumerated activities are of an "indicative character" and that the list may be expanded by the Ministry of Commerce and Industrial Promotion "as a result of specific proposals or through the various groups of the national productive sectors."

Certainly, one of the most important goals of the Guidelines is to encourage national technological development. As the FIC recognizes, however, preference will need to be given to "coinvestment" in order to "guarantee a real transference of technology." Nevertheless, compared to large firms, small and medium-sized foreign companies are to receive "more flexible treatment" since it is presumed that their "investments and transference of technology carry lesser risks of dependency and may be valuable in agricultural and livestock sectors and certain branches of capital equipment and consumers' items." Increases in the percentage of foreign equity in Mexican companies by capitalization of debt, sale of stock or waiver of stock subscription rights of first refusal by Mexican shareholders may be granted for financially troubled industries on the list of national priorities. Alternative measures, however, must first prove unworkable, and the increase of capital must be indispensable to the survival of the company. Furthermore, provision is made for the expansion of existing foreign companies in priority areas where such expansion will lead to the "modernization of the plants, the commitment of greater volumes of exports and increase the level of national integration in the production process." Another significant aspect of the Guidelines is the absence of a requirement to Mexicanize within a specified time period. Although the FIL does not deal with this issue, almost every exceptional allowance of majority foreign equity that was granted before the Guidelines were issued required Mexicanization, usually within 10 years.

The FIC has acknowledged, however, that "the process of Mexicanizing companies in which foreigners participate has in many cases resulted [in] an illusion with undesirable effects on industrial concentration, pricing policies and available investment resources." Some reports announcing the Guidelines have viewed them as an open invitation to any and all foreign investment. The Guidelines very clearly state, however, that only certain activities will be promoted. Although other activities are generally welcome, the requirement of minority foreign equity will continue to apply. The activities promoted under the Guidelines are strategic in nature, in conformity with the goals of the NIDP, and even those activities will be analysed by the FIC in terms of the criteria set forth in both the NIDP and the FIL.

On August 30, 1984, the FIC published five new resolutions pursuant to the Guidelines. Their purposes are twofold: to update the FIC's General Resolutions in accordance with the economic priorities of the NIDP and the Guidelines, and to improve and expedite the application process for majority foreign investments. For example, the resolutions eliminate the need for FIC authorization for certain foreign investment activities in in-bond companies; for the substitution of foreign directors, provided the ratio of domestic and foreign capital is not changed; and, under certain circumstances, for the opening or relocation of specified establishments. Additionally, the resolutions enlarge the powers of the Executive Secretary of the FIC, and he may authorize certain actions without prior FIC approval. The resolutions also include provisions that are expected to decrease significantly the amount of time required to complete an application for majority foreign capitalization.

Pursuant to the resolutions, applications to the FIC are to be negotiated through the Executive Secretary, who is then to submit them to the FIC for its formal acceptance within 30 business days of completion of the file. Announcement of the Guidelines has resulted in much speculation and misunderstanding. Research for this object included interviews that were graciously extended by bankers, corporations, the FIC and foreign investment legal practitioners. Their perceptions of the Guidelines assisted invaluably in the following analysis of Mexico's changing position on foreign investment.

MEXICO'S CHANGING POSITION

Contrary to past practice, the Guidelines were not published in the Diario Oficial, although they were announced in all the major newspapers and distributed in the form of a pamphlet. Because the Diario Oficial is the official repository of all federal legislation, the failure to publish the Guidelines in it signified a definite effort to make clear that the change was one of policy. Even though the FIL allows for exceptions and the 49 per cent limitation on foreign ownership is in essence only a general principle, the fact that the FIC had strictly enforced that limitation with few exceptions for the past 11 years had prompted the erroneous belief that this policy was the law.

When newspapers misleadingly interpreted the change as a new attitude "welcoming" foreign investment, some investors responded with guarded cynicism. Since they had been led to believe that 49 per cent was the legal maximum, some foreign investors would have preferred fixed rules in the form of a legislative revision. Fearful that this policy could just as quickly be replaced by past practices, these investors have been critical and have adopted a wait-and-see attitude. Additionally, foreign investors are concerned that the Government will later issue decrees restricting their future activities.

The perception of both the newspapers and the critics is limited and faulty in many aspects. Businesses incorporated under the 1984 Guidelines would retain their 100 per cent foreign equity even if Mexico were to return to the 49-51 per cent concept. It is extremely unlikely that a future decree could be applied retroactively. It is generally believed that the 1973 FIL cannot be so construed. Moreover, although corporations could not expand by establishing new plants or adding new product lines without Mexicanizing under the FIL, additional protection has been available through the incorporation of an enterprise as a variable capital company since approval of neither the FIC nor the Ministry of Foreign Relations is required to increase or decrease the variable portion of the capital.

Consequently, corporations organized as variable capital companies have been able to expand and avoid pressure to Mexicanize when challenged to do so in the past. Second, Mexico has always "welcomed" foreign investment. It is the manner in which it has structured its foreign investment policies that has led some to believe otherwise. Even after enactment of the FIL in 1973, the amount of foreign investment increased significantly, particularly in the years 1976 and 1980. Also, the Guidelines do not signify an open door "welcome mat."

The Guidelines explicitly state that certain listed activities are being promoted. Certainly, it is not unreasonable for Mexico to refuse to accept indiscriminate foreign investment. A careful examination of Mexican policies and practices over the past century discloses a process that at times has had its divergences, but always with a purpose. An unrestrained open door policy was extended when foreign investment was viewed as beneficial and necessary for industrial growth. When the resultant foreign dominance of the economy became painfully apparent, however, measures were taken to alleviate the detrimental effects. Nonetheless, the character, rather than the magnitude, of foreign investment was affected by the changing regulations. As was uniformly noted by the bankers, lawyers and government officials interviewed, except for outright exclusions, laws really do not affect the magnitude of foreign investment in a country; other circumstances do, including political and economic views, labour rates and export possibilities.

Regardless of the exclusion of foreign investment from certain activities, Mexico generally has been viewed as offering political stability, financial reliability in meeting its debt payments and a safe climate for investment. Those interviewed were asked why, in their opinion, Mexico did not revise the FIL, and two responses predominated. First, the FIL already allows the FIC to grant exceptions when deemed beneficial to the national economy; there is therefore no need for a legislative revision. Second, although Mexico is politically stable, there is a nationalistic sentiment remaining from the periods in which foreign investment was allowed to dominate the economy.

The enactment of a legislative revision would likely create apprehension that Mexico was once again indiscriminately allowing foreign investment to meet a short-term economic problem, and the political cost of such a reaction would be high. As it stands, the Guidelines have not been seen as a threat to Mexican industrialists, but rather as a progressive step towards increased technology. Furthermore, not only is such a revision unnecessary, it is also not in keeping with the goals of the FIC.

The development of a rational economic plan that selectively promotes those industries deemed beneficial to the national economy requires flexibility sufficient to allow continuous reassessment of the country's needs. To lock the administration into further rigidity would preclude the very growth Mexico is striving to achieve. Views differed over whether Mexico will press for Mexicanization in the future. One of' the corporate officials interviewed believes that the Government is likely to promote Mexicanization in specific areas in which it has an interest. An attorney with extensive experience in dealing with the FIC, however, disagrees on the basis that the Government has nothing to gain from Mexicanization at this time. In the past, nationalistic political motives prompted the policy, or the Mexicanization or nationalization was directed to strategic areas of the economy such as oil, mining and petrochemicals. Additionally, as was noted in the preceding part, Mexicanization in itself is no longer viewed by the FIC as a desirable goal. In fact, one of the elements of the new policy will be to examine the effectiveness of Mexicanization operations.

Even if Mexico does later restrict the availability of investment incentives or press for Mexicanization, the fact remains that it is still an excellent investment choice. Almost every state offers a variety of investment incentives in addition to those provided by the federal Government, such as land, physical facilities and access to utilities; labour is still less costly than in most developing countries; and Mexico's marine, land and air transportation services and its geographical position as a neighbour of the United States help make it an attractive location.

There are, of course, advantages to incorporating with majority Mexican capital. An investment of 49 per cent or less foreign equity may be organized immediately by simply registering with the FIR. Although the new resolutions should significantly decrease the length of time required to obtain approval of majority foreign equity by the FIC, common sense suggests that the process will still take considerably longer than incorporating with 49 per cent or less. More important, an investment with majority Mexican capital qualifies automatically for tax and other investment incentives pursuant to the 1972 Law for the Promotion of New and Necessary Industries and other decrees. Although an investor may negotiate for incentives with both the FIC and the government of the state in which it will be operating even if majority foreign capitalization is planned, certain advantageous incentives are available only to companies with majority Mexican equity. Also, a company with majority Mexican equity will probably have easier access to administrative agencies and the various licenses required for imports. Nonetheless, definite benefits may be gained by an investment of 100 per cent foreign equity. One foreign banking official noted that there are both accounting and reporting advantages. In addition, a facility constructed by an investor entirely with foreign capital will have an asset worth more than the original investment after completion. If 51 per cent is later sold to Mexican investors, the company would then be eligible for tax incentives. Majority foreign equity has other positive ramifications. From a lending point of view, the risk may be different. A bank is more likely to extend credit to a subsidiary of a company that is well known or with which the bank has had a prior working relationship.

Experience has proven that a parent company is much more likely to stand behind and support a wholly owned subsidiary, and any creditor is more comfortable lending to a party with which it is familiar, in contrast to a company newly formed with unknown management or shareholders. Last, 100 per cent foreign equity is unavoidable in certain industries. A company that has developed expensive, unique technology will not share that asset with anyone else. Such an attitude does not spring from a fear of Mexicanization; the intangibility of technology precludes nationalization, as was aptly noted by the chief legal adviser of an industrial conglomerate. The particular needs of the enterprise dictate the decision whether to invest with majority foreign equity. For investors in Mexico, the fact that the Guidelines promote specific industries and that the new resolutions should expedite approval by the FIC are obviously factors to be considered.

Regulations, however, do not necessarily affect the economic and political situation of a company, which is usually the main factor taken into account in such a decision. Yet regulations can provide an indication of the governing country's attitude and probable treatment. Mexico has decided that the activities delineated in the Guidelines are the ones that most benefit its economy, and it issued the Guidelines to notify the international community that in these areas it will be most accommodating in meeting the needs of the foreign investor. It is still too soon to detect the impact of the Guidelines, especially when one remembers that there are many other factors that need to be considered in speculating on Mexico's short-term investment growth.

At present, Mexican assets have been frozen as banks wait out the financial crisis and debt restructurings. Even if a company decided to locate in Mexico, the freeze alone could inhibit such a move since most prefer to invest with borrowed money. Also, many plants that had expanded in the early 1980s found themselves idle with the recession and are now trying to orient themselves for exports. Nonetheless, the overwhelming majority of persons interviewed are optimistic in believing that the Guidelines signify an important change in attitude by the Mexican Government. Since 1973, its attitude had been defensive, shaped by an acute awareness of the detrimental effects of unrestrained foreign investment and dominance.

The new attitude of selective promotion of specific industries must be viewed not in terms of the percentage of foreign participation alone but, more importantly, as an identification of the administration's goals for foreign investment, including more sophisticated technology, higher employment, substitution of imports and increased exports. Mexico appears to have finally taken a macroeconomic approach towards foreign investment.

It is an instrument that must be used rationally, for only by selectively promoting those industries beneficial to the nation will Mexico achieve the international standards of competitive technology and exports necessary for continued positive economic growth. Mexico's approach towards foreign investment is in a process of evolution. After veering from completely unrestrained reception to excessively protective and nationalistic restriction of foreign capital, the country appears to have reached an equilibrium. By announcing that it would actively promote foreign investment in specified industries, Mexico has placed the international community on notice of its intention to progress rationally towards further economic growth.

Because its foreign investment regulations are largely the result of policy established by an administrative body with broad discretionary powers, it has been difficult in the past to predict how favourably a prospective enterprise might be received. FIC officials, however, one can now look to the criteria set forth in the NIDP and FIL and to the list of activities to be promoted under the 1984 Guidelines and obtain a clearer indication of the conditions to which a company will be subject and whether they are consistent with its interests. The Guidelines, together with the resolutions of the FIC, signify a changing attitude.

Up to 100 per cent direct foreign investment will be considered in specified activities; increases in the percentage of foreign equity in Mexican companies may also be arranged; and foreign companies in priority industries will be permitted to expand under certain circumstances. Although the FIL had allowed for these exceptions, prior to the announcement of the 1984 Guidelines they had rarely been granted. Foreign investments that are subject to these exceptions, however, will not be approved automatically. They will still need to be analysed by the FIC in terms of the criteria set forth in the NIDP and FIL.

Whether to invest with 100 per cent or 49 per cent foreign capital is a decision dictated by the needs of the particular company; but the availability of a choice makes Mexico an even more attractive country in which to invest. Fear of future restrictions, such as requirements to Mexicanize, is unreasonable in view of the overall profit potential and should not be a determining factor in whether to select Mexico as an investment choice.

Although persons involved in the field are optimistic about this change in attitude, they are also aware that regulations do not substantially affect the magnitude of foreign investment in a country. Other circumstances have much greater significance, and owing to the current recession, it will take time to evaluate with accuracy the impact of these policies on Mexico's shortand long-term economic growth. The development of a rational plan that selectively promotes industries deemed beneficial to the national economy, however, should greatly assist Mexico in achieving competitive international standards.

9

Event Management

INTRODUCTION

There are varied art forms that have been passed down through the ages. One such form of art is that of oil paintings. These have not been just those that are made on canvas, but also the cave paintings, and the wonderful murals. However, in over the last century there has been an escalation in interest in the arts. There are not on more artists, but also the demand and increasing art lovers and connoisseurs. There are a number of companies hosting and organizing events on a regular basis. These range from the small time private events to the large-scale international events.

Yes, the large scales one do happen far rarer, but then the amount of returns they churn out is far beyond expectations. However, in the past there have been events that have also resulted in losses to the hosts and sponsors for varied reasons. But then, all said and done, event management is about organization and execution, and that is precisely where the money lies. Those in the field are paid for their these services. Today, there a number of people, who have entered the field because they realise the potential of the market where demand and supply is concerned.

In fact, the most profitable aspect of this field is the need for creativity. And that is how and where one earns. The management of events calls, largely for coordination, from stage one. The first thing required is to get the orders for the event. This process is also known as pitching for an event. Usually, whether it is for small time events, or then for the larger ones assigned by companies, or then the international concerts; the event manager/company is asked to submit a project report, with the finances involved. On the basis of this is the assignment given to them.

SERVICES

Event management companies and organizations service a variety of areas including corporate events, marketing programmes, and special corporate hospitality events like concerts, award ceremonies, film premieres, launch/release parties, fashion shows, commercial events, private events such as weddings and bar mitzvahs. Clients hire event management companies to handle a specific scope of services for the given event, which at its maximum may include all creative, technical and logistical elements of the event..

EVENT MANAGER

The event manager is the person who plans and executes the event. Event managers and their teams are often behind-the-scenes running the event. Event managers may also be involved in more than just the planning and execution of the event, but also brand building, marketing and communication strategy.

The event manager is an expert at the creative, technical and logistical elements that help an event succeed. This includes event design, audio-visual production, scriptwriting, logistics, budgeting, negotiation and, of course, client service. It is a multi-dimensional profession. The event manager may become involved at the early initiation stages of the event. If the event manager has budget responsibilities at this early stage they may be termed an event or production executive.

The early stages include:

- Brief clarification
- Budget drafting
- Cash flow management
- Client Service
- Health and Safety
- Procurement

- Scheduling
- Site design
- Site surveying
- Supply chain identification
- Technical design

An event manager who becomes involved closer to the event will often have a more limited brief. The key disciplines closer to the event are:

- Detailed scheduling
- Health and Safety including crowd management,
- Light
- Logistics
- Rigging
- Security
- Sound
- Video

AS AN INDUSTRY

Event Management is a multi-million dollar industry, growing rapidly, with mega shows and events hosted regularly. Surprisingly, there is no formalized research conducted to assess the growth of this industry.

The industry includes fields such as the MICE, exhibitions, conferences and seminars as well as live music and sporting events. The logistics side of the industry is paid less than the sales/sponsorship side, though some may say that these are two different industries.

TECHNOLOGY

Event management software companies provide event planners with software tools to handle many common activities such as delegate registration, hotel booking, travel booking or allocation of exhibition floorspace.

EDUCATION

There are an increasing number of universities which offer Graduate Degree/Diploma in Event Management, especially in the UK where they have been quick to catch on to the new interest and many are now offering certificate, diploma, degree and masters degree coursework. In the Netherlands - Rotterdam - EuroCollege University of Professional Education offers Hospitality and Events Management. In India National Academy of Event Management and Development - NAEMD offers Diploma and Post Graduate Diploma in Event Management, National Institute of Event Management - NIEM, Event Management Development Institute - EMDI and Amity University also offer courses on event management.

In addition to these academic courses, there are many associations and societies that provide courses on the various aspects of the industry. Study includes organizational skills, technical knowledge, P.R., marketing, advertising, catering, logistics, decor, glamor identity, human relations, study of law and licenses, risk management, budgeting, study of allied industries like television, other media and several other areas.

Career opportunities are in the following Industries :

- Event Management
- Event Management Consultancy
- Hotel, travel and hospitality Industries
- Advertising Agencies
- Public Relations Firms
- Corporations
- News Media
- Non-profit organization
- Integrated Marketing and Communications
- Event Budgeting and Accounting

MARKETING

Event management is considered one of the strategic marketing and communication tools by companies of all sizes. From product launches to press conferences, companies create promotional events to help them communicate with clients and potential clients.

They might target their audience by using the news media, hoping to generate media coverage which will reach thousands or millions of people. They can also invite their audience to their events and reach them at the actual event.

TYPES OF EVENTS

Event management deals with creation of successful events. There is a galore of different kind of events for which an event manager has to do different kind of arrangements just as to the different types of requirement the event demands. There are these sports events which may be at inter school level or intra school level or in colleges or even at state levels. Sports events are not one day events, it needs extensive planning right from the day it starts till the finale. On a larger level, national and international sports events are planned by a bug group of event mangers working together. Corporate event management is another field which includes in-house events as well as larger ones for promotion of products or services. Such fields become meeting point of corporate people of same field. There are musical events, where in audience has to be taken care of along with issues like ticketing and managing availability of seats etc. accommodation of the artist and co workers is another deal. Exhibition and trade fairs also require a great deal of management. Arrangement of stalls, food system and drinking water system etc. plus the sponsors and guests and audience also need a lot of attention. Another marvelous event in India which needs great planning and perfection is the grand Indian wedding. The complexities are dealt nicely with a event management company.

Grand events include prospects like weather, security, celebrities and companies etc. Generally big budgets are involved in them. On other hand, small events like little shows for children, small office parties need to need the purpose and target audience. Other diverse events which are organized and are taken care of by event management companies are cause related events, entertainment events, concerts or live performances, brand and product launches, marketing events, meetings, seminars, workshops, conferences, governmental, social and cultural events and more.

EVENT MANAGEMENT INDUSTRY IN INDIA

The economy of India is growing by leaps and bounds and there are various ever-growing industries that are contributing to increasing the nation's coffers. One such industry is that of event management. This industry has come a long way in the last five years or so and today is no less than a multi-crore industry, as a whole.

And the size of the companies varies from the rather small ones that manage small events such as birthdays and weddings, to the larger players, who organize national and international events. During the early part of the 1900s the industry had spent up to Rs. 20 Crores, per annum on events. And in the last couple of years, all the event companies are spending to the tune of approximately Rs. 1,800 Crores, per annum. The event management industry in India involves the requirement of various skills that have caused it grow the way it is in recent past.

These skills include:

- Advertising
- Budgeting
- Catering
- Decor
- Glamour identity
- Human relations
- Local and national, as well as international events
- Logistics
- Marketing
- Organizational skills
- Public relations
- Risk management
- Study of all allied media
- Technical knowledge
- Understanding of laws and licenses

FINANCE IN EVENT MANAGEMENT

The most important factor in terms of finance during planning of an event is budgeting. Allocation of money in proper terms for various purposes is necessary for enhancing quality of events. A good event manager will always know the summary of extended expenditure along with proposals for how to meet them. Whatever may be the scale of event, working within the limitations is required. The constraints involved are important enough and cannot be neglected. Playing with money is not so easy. Budget format is one which is followed by many companies.

They build up budgets by placing figures and involving marketing factors. Aggregates are placed in the format and final budget system is obtained. The head office has one member as the head or the financial head who is the main person involved in formation of a budget. Supervision and the execution of process with allocation of money is ensure simultaneously while preparation of the budget. It is checked whether or not the work done requires money within the figures. Margin has to maintained while preparation of the budget. And this percentage of margin is usually referred to as the buffer margin.

This helps to one to remain under the limit. The budget gives us the facts and figures which are gained by the company with regards to the expenses. The amount of money which is received by the sponsors is also determined by this budgeting process. It is required that any person from the event managing company chooses to provide budget to a potential sponsor only. Hence, budgeting for any event is like preparing a list of things you need to but before going out and buying the things from the market. Budgeting thus helps a lot in planning the overall features of an event.

ROLE OF EVENT MANAGER

Making arrangement for an important day becomes utterly manageable with the help of a good event manager. Choosing a good event managing company is the first step of course. An event planner has the ability to work under stressful conditions. They are trained to meet deadlines and complete work with a tint of fineness. Working in circumstances where it is needed to deal with a lot of people together and handle too many things simultaneously. This busy schedule requires working on weekends too. Even many of the events take place at the end of the week. Selecting guest list, entertainment modes, venues and content everything goes smoothly and in a planned manner with the aid of an event planner. They look after every minute detail in the whole planning of event right from the budgeting, confirmation of dates and schedule, choosing an agency for booking suitable venue and taking enough care about the layout of the venue in terms of parking facility, accommodation, decorations, table and chair arrangement, stage if necessary, the security facility, catering and the quality of food, lighting arrangement and other technical system, management in case of emergency and mush more. Minor things also make a big difference like transportation facility for the members and priorities to be provided as per the guest.

Working for an event planner is always a collaborative process. He or she has to work with a lot people and thus has to be well trained in team work apart from being skilled in technical aspects. An event manager possesses the quality of understanding the needs of the client. Knowing the taste, requirement and preferences along with the monetary condition helps good planning by event manager. Management of time is best known to an event planner.

IMPORTANCE OF EVENT CORRELATION AND AUTOMATION

From the time of their inception, computer systems were designed to serve the needs of businesses. Therefore, it was necessary to know if they were operational. The critical need of the business function that was performed governed how quickly this information had to be obtained. Early computers were installed to perform batch number-crunching tasks for such business functions as payroll and accounts receivable, in less time and with more efficiency than humans could perform them.

Each day, the results of the batch processing were examined. If problems occurred, they were resolved and the batch jobs were executed again. As their capabilities expanded, computers began to be used for functions such as order entry and inventory. These mission-critical applications needed to be online and operational during business hours required immediate responses. Companies questioned the reliability of computers and did not want to risk losing customers because of computer problems. Paper forms and manual backup procedures provided insurance to companies that they could still perform their primary business in the event of a computer failure. Since these batch and online applications were vital to the business of the company, it became more important to ascertain in a timely fashion whether they were available and working properly.

Software was enhanced to provide information and errors, which were displayed on one or more consoles. Computer operators watched the consoles, ignored the informational messages, and responded to the errors. Tools became available to automatically reply to messages that always required the same response. With the many advances in technology, computers grew more sophisticated and were applied to more business functions. Personal computers and distributed systems flourished, adding to the complexity of the IT environment.

Due to the increased reliability of the machines and software, it became impractical to run a business manually. Companies surrendered their paper forms and manual backup procedures to become completely dependent upon the functioning of the computer systems. Managing the systems, now critical to the survival of a business, became the responsibility of separate staffs within an IT organization. Each team used its own set of tools to do the necessary monitoring of its own resources. Each viewed its own set of error messages and responded to them.

Many received phone calls directly from users who experienced problems. To increase the productivity of the support staffs and to offload some of their problem support responsibilities, help desks were formed. Help desks served as central contact points for users to report problems with their computers or applications. They provided initial problem determination and resolution services. The support staffs did not need to watch their tools for error messages, since software was installed to aggregate the messages at a central location.

The help desk or an operations center monitored messages from various monitoring tools and notified the appropriate support staff when problems surfaced. Today, changes in technology provide still more challenges. The widespread use of the Internet to perform mission-critical applications necessitates 24 × 7 availability of systems.

Organizations need to know immediately when there are failures, and recovery must be almost instantaneous. On-demand and grid computing allow businesses to run applications wherever cycles are available to ensure they can meet the demands of their customers. However, this increases the complexity of monitoring the applications, since it is now insufficient to know the status of one system without knowing how it relates to others. Operators cannot be expected to understand these relationships and account for them in handling problems, particularly in complex environments.

There are several problems with the traditional approach to managing systems:

- *Missed problems:* Operators can overlook real problems while sifting through screens of informational messages. Users may call to report problems before they are noticed and acted upon by the operator.
- *False alarms:* Messages can seem to indicate real problems, when in fact they are not. Sometimes additional data may be needed to validate the condition and, in distributed environments, that information may come from a different system than the one reporting the problem.
- *Inconsistency:* Various operators can respond differently to the same type of events.
- *Duplication of effort:* Multiple error messages may be produced for a single problem, possibly resulting in more than one support person handling the same problem.
- *Improper problem assignment:* Manually routing problems to the support staffs sometimes results in support personnel being assigning problems that are not their responsibility.

- *Problems that cannot be diagnosed:* Sometimes when an intermittent problem condition clears before someone has had the chance to respond to it, the diagnostic data required to determine the cause of the problem disappears.

Event correlation and automation address these issues by:

- Eliminating information messages from view to easily identify real problems
- Validating problems
- Responding consistently to events
- Suppressing extraneous indications of a problem
- Automatically assigning problems to support staffs
- Collecting diagnostic data

Event correlation and automation are the next logical steps in the evolution of event handling. They are critical to successfully managing today's ever-changing, fast-paced IT environments with the reduced staffs with which companies are forced to operate.

TERMINOLOGY

Before we discuss the best ways to implement event correlation and automation, we need to establish the meaning of the terms we use. While several systems management terms are generally used to describe event management, these terms are sometimes used in different ways by different authors. In this part, we provide definitions of the terms as they are used throughout this redbook.

EVENT

Since event management and correlation center around the processing of events, it is important to clearly define what is meant by an event. In the context of this redbook, an event is a piece of data that provides information about one or more system resources.

Events can be triggered by incidents or problems affecting a system resource. Similarly, changes to the status or configuration of a resource, regardless of whether they are intentional, can generate events. Events may also be used as reminders to take action manually or as notification that an action has occurred.

EVENT MANAGEMENT

The way in which an organization deals with events is known as event management. It may include the organization's objectives for managing events, assigned roles and responsibilities, ownership of tools and processes, critical success factors, standards, and event-handling procedures.

The linkages between the various departments within the organization required to handle events and the flow of this information between them is the focus of event management. Tools are mentioned in reference to how they fit into the flow of event information through the organization and to which standards should be applied to that flow.

Since events are used to report problems, event management is sometimes considered a sub-discipline of problem management. However, it can really be considered a discipline of its own, for it interfaces directly with several other systems management disciplines. For example, system upgrades and new installations can result in new event types that must be handled. Maintaining systems both through regularly scheduled and emergency maintenance can result in temporary outages that trigger events.

This clearly indicates a relationship between event management and change management. In small organizations, it may be possible to handle events through informal means. However, as organizations grow both in size of the IT support staffs and the number of resources they manage, it becomes more crucial to have a formal, documented event management process. Formalizing the process ensures consistent responses to events, eliminates duplication of effort, and simplifies the configuration and maintenance of the tools used for event management.

EVENT PROCESSING

While event management focuses on the high-level flow of events through an organization, event processing deals with tools. Specifically, the term event processing is used to indicate the actions taken upon events automatically by systems management software tools. Event processing includes such actions as changing the status or severity of an event, dropping the event, generating problem tickets and notifications, and performing recovery actions.

AUTOMATION AND AUTOMATED ACTIONS

Automation is a type of actions that can be performed when processing events. It refers to the process of taking actions on system resources without human intervention in response to an event. The actual actions executed are referred to as automated actions.

Automated actions may include recovery commands performed on a failing resource to restore its service and failover processes to bring up backup resources. Changing the status or severity of an event, closing it, and similar functions are not considered automated actions. That is because they are performed on the event itself rather than on one or more system resources referred to or affected by the event.

THEORIES AND ISSUES

This part presents the concepts and issues associated with event processing. Additional terminology is introduced as needed.

EVENT FLOW

An event cannot provide value to an organization in managing its system resources unless the event is acted upon, either manually by a support person or automatically by software. The path an event takes from its source to the software or person who takes action on it is known as the event flow.

The event flow begins at the point of generation of the event, known as the event source. The source of an event may be the failing system itself, as in the case of a router that sends information about its health to an event processor. An agent that runs on the system to monitor for and report error conditions is another type of event source. A proxy systems that monitor devices other than itself, such as Simple Network Management Protocol manager that periodically checks the status of TCP/IP devices, and reports a failure if it receives no response, is also considered an event source. Event processors are devices that run software capable of recognizing and acting upon events.

The functionality of the event processors can vary widely. Some are capable of merely forwarding or discarding events. Others can perform more sophisticated functions such as reformatting the event, correlating it with other events received, displaying it on a console, and initiating recovery actions. Most event processors have the capability to forward events to other event processors.

This functionality is useful in consolidating events from various sources at a central site for management by a help desk or operations center. The hierarchy of event processors used to handle events can be referred to as the event processing hierarchy. The first receiver of the event is the entry point into the hierarchy, and the collection of all the entry points is called the entry tier of the hierarchy. Similarly, all second receivers of events can be collectively referred to as the second tier in the hierarchy and so forth.

We refer to the top level of the hierarchy as the enterprise tier, because it typically consolidates events from sources across an entire enterprise. Operators typically view events of significance from a console, which provides a graphical user interface through which the operator can take action on events. Consoles can be proprietary, requiring special software for accessing the console. Or they can adhere to open standards, such as Web-based consoles that can be accessed from properly configured Web browsers. The collection of event sources, processors, and consoles is sometimes referred to as the event management infrastructure.

FILTERING AND FORWARDING

Many devices generate informational messages that are not indicative of problems. Sending these messages as events through the event processing hierarchy is undesirable. The reason is because processing power and bandwidth are needed to handle them and they clutter the operator consoles, possibly masking true problems. The process of suppressing these messages is called event filtering or filtering. There are several ways to perform event filtering.

Events can be prevented from ever entering the event processing hierarchy. This is referred to as filtering at the source. Event processors can discard or drop the unnecessary events. Likewise, consoles can be configured to hide them from view. The event filtering methods that are available are product specific. Some SNMP devices, for example, can be configured to send all or none of their messages to an event processor or to block messages within specific categories such as security or configuration. Other devices allow blocking to be configured by message type. When an event is allowed to enter the event processing hierarchy, it is said to be forwarded. Events can be forwarded from event sources to event processors and between event processors.

DUPLICATE DETECTION AND THROTTLING

Events that are deemed necessary must be forwarded to at least one event processor to ensure that they are handled by either manual or automated means. However, sometimes the event source generates the desired message more than once when a problem occurs. Usually, only one event is required for action.

The process of determining which events are identical is referred to as duplicate detection. The time frame in which a condition is responded to may vary, depending upon the nature of the problem being reporting. Often, it should be addressed immediately when the first indication of a problem occurs.

This is especially true in situations where a device or process is down. Subsequent events can then be discarded. Other times, a problem does not need to be investigated until it occurs several times. For example, a high CPU condition may not be a problem if a single process, such as a backup, uses many cycles for a minute or two. However, if the condition happens several times within a certain time interval, there most likely is a problem. In this case, the problem should be addressed after the necessary number of occurrences. Unless diagnostic data, such as the raw CPU busy values, is required from subsequent events, they can be dropped. The process of reporting events after a certain number of occurrences is known as throttling.

CORRELATION

When multiple events are generated as a result of the same initial problem or provide information about the same system resource, there may be a relationship between the events. The process of defining this relationship in an event processor and implementing actions to deal with the related events is known as event correlation.

Correlated events may reference the same affected resource or different resources. They may generated by the same event source or handled by the same event processor.

Problem and Clearing Event Correlation

This part presents an example of events that are generated from the same event source and deal with the same system resource. An agent monitoring a system detects that a service has failed and sends an event to an event processor. The event describes an error condition, called a problem event.

When the service is later restored, the agent sends another event to inform the event processor the service is again running and the error condition has cleared. This event is known as a clearing event. The relationship between the problem and clearing event can be depicted graphically.

The correlation sequence is described as follows:

- Problem is reported when received.
- Event is closed when a recovery event is received
- Taking this example further, assume that multiple agents are on the system. One reads the system log, extracts error messages, and sends them as events. The second agent actively monitors system resources and

generates events when it detects error conditions. A service running on the system writes an error message to the system log when it dies. The first agent reads the log, extracts the error messages, and sends it as an event to the event processor. The second agent, configured to monitor the status of the service, detects that is has stopped and sends an event as well. When the service is restored, the agent writes a message to the system log, which is sent as an event, and the monitor detects the recovery and sends its own event. The event processor receives both problem events, but only needs to report the service failure once. The events can be correlated and one of them dropped. Likewise, only one of the clearing events is required.

This scenario is different from duplicate detection. The events being correlated both report service down, but they are from different event sources and most likely have different formats.

Duplicate detection implies that the events are of the same format and are usually, though not always, from the same event source. If the monitoring agent in this example detects a down service, and repeatedly sends events reporting that the service is down, these events can be handled with duplicate detection.

Event Escalation

Sometimes multiple events are sent to indicate a worsening error condition for a system resource. For example, an agent monitoring a file system may send a warning message to indicate the file system is greater than 90% full, a second, more severe event when greater than 95% full, and a critical event greater than 98% full.

In this case, the event processor does not need to report the file system error multiple times. It can merely increase the severity of the initial event to indicate that the problem has become more critical and needs to be responded to more quickly. The same escalation logic applies. This type of correlation sequence assumes that severities are clearly defined and the allowable time to respond to events of those severities has been communicated within the organization.

Root Cause Correlation

A problem may sometimes trigger other problems, and each problem may be reported by events. The event reporting the initial problem is referred to as a root cause, or primary event. Those that report the subsequent problems are called symptom or secondary events. At this point, it is important to note the difference between a root cause event and the root cause of a problem.

The former is the event that provides information about the first of a series of related, reported problems. The latter is what caused the problem condition to happen. Root cause events and root causes of problems may be closely related. For example, a root cause event reporting a faulty NIC card may be correlated with secondary events such as "Interface Down" from an SNMP manager or "Application unreachable" from a transaction monitoring agent. The root cause of the problem is the broken card.

However, sometimes the two are not as closely associated. Consider an event that reports a Filesystem Full condition. The full file system may cause a process or service to die, producing a secondary event. The Filesystem Full event is the root cause event, but it is not the root cause of the problem. A looping application that is repeatedly logging information into the file system may be the root cause of the problem. When situations such as these are encountered, you must set up monitoring to check for the root cause of the problem and produce an event for it.

That event then becomes the root cause event in the sequence. In our example, a monitor that detects and reports looping application logging may be implemented. The resulting event can then be correlated with the others and becomes the root cause event. Because of this ambiguity in terms, we prefer to use the term primary event rather than root cause event. The action taken in response to a root cause event may automatically resolve the secondary problems.

Sometimes, though, a symptom event may require a separate action, depending upon the nature of the problem it reports. Examples of each scenario follow.

Symptom Events not Requiring Action

Assume that an agent on a UNIX® system is monitoring file systems for adequate space and critical processes for availability. One of the key processes is required to run at all times and is set up to automatically respawn if it fails. The process depends upon adequate free space in the file system where it stores its temporary data files and cannot execute without it.

The file system upon which the process depends fills up, and the agent detects the condition and sends an event. The process dies, and the operating system unsuccessfully attempts to restart it repeatedly. The agent detects the failure and generates a second event to report it. There are essentially two problems here. The primary problem is the full file system, and the process failure is the secondary problem. When appropriate action is taken on the first event to free space within the file system, the process successfully respawns automatically.

Symptom Events Requiring Action

Now suppose that an application stores its data in a local database. An agent runs on the application server to monitor the availability of both the application and the database. A database table fills and cannot be extended, causing the application to hang. The agent detects both conditions and sends events to report them. The full database table is the primary problem, and the hanging application is the secondary problem. A database administrator corrects the primary problem. However, the application is hung and cannot recover itself. It must be recycled.

The correlation sequence is as follows:

- The Filesystem Full event is reported if received.
- The Process Down event is reported as dependent upon the file system being resolved.

- The Filesystem Full event is closed when the Filesystem Recovered clearing event is received.
- The Process Down event is cleared when the Service Recovered clearing event is received.

An important implication of this scenario must be addressed. Handling the secondary event depends upon the resolution of the primary event. Until the database is repaired, any attempts to restart the application fail. Implementation of correlation sequences of this sort can challenging.

Cross-platform Correlation

In the previous application and database correlation scenario, the correlated events refer to different types of system resources. We refer to this as cross-platform correlation. Some examples of platforms include operating systems, databases, middleware, applications, and hardware. Often, cross-platform correlation sequences result in symptom events that require action. This is because the support person handling the first resource type does not usually have administrative responsibility for the second type. Also, many systems are not sophisticated enough to recognize the system resources affected by a failure and to automatically recover them when the failure is resolved. For these reasons, cross-platform correlation sequences provide an excellent opportunity for automated recovery actions.

Cross-host Correlation

In distributed processing environments, there are countless situations in which conditions on one system affect the proper functioning of another system. Web applications, for example, often rely on a series of Web, application, and database servers to run a transaction. If a database is inaccessible, the transaction fails.

Likewise, servers may share data through message queuing software, requiring the creation of the queue by one server before it is accessed from another. When problems arise in scenarios such as these, events can be generated by multiple hosts to report a problem. It may be necessary to correlate these events to determine which require action. The process of correlating events from different systems is known as cross-host correlation. The database can easily reside on a different server than the application accessing it. The event processor takes the same actions on each event as described previously. However, it has the additional burden of checking the relationship between hosts before determining if the events correlate.

Cross-host correlation is particularly useful in clustered and failover environments. For clusters, some conditions may not represent problems unless they are reported by all systems in the cluster. As long as one system is successfully running an application, for example, no action is required. In this case, the event processor needs to know which systems constitute the cluster and track which systems report the error. In failover scenarios, an error condition may require action if it is reported by either host.

Consider, for example, paired firewalls. If the primary firewall fails and the secondary takes over, each may report the switch, and cross-host correlation may be used to report failure of the primary. However, a hard failure of the primary may mean that the failover event is sent only by the secondary. This event should indicate the failure of the primary firewall as the condition that requires action. Again, the event processor needs to know the relationship between the firewalls before correlating failover events.

Topology-based Correlation

When such networking resources as routers fail, they may cause a large number of other systems to become inaccessible. In these situations, events may be reported that refer to several unreachable system resources. The events may be reported by SNMP managers that receive no answer to their status queries or by systems that can no longer reach resources with which they normally communicate. Correlating these events requires knowledge of the network topology, and therefore are referred to as topology-based correlation. This type of correlation, while similar to cross-host correlation, differs in that the systems have a hierarchical, rather than a peer, relationship. The placement of the systems within the network determines the hierarchy. The failure of one networking component affects the resources downstream from it. Clearly, the event reporting the failing networking resource is the primary, or root, cause event and needs to be handled. Often, the secondary events refer to unreachable resources that become accessible once the networking resource is restored to service. In this case, these events may be unnecessary. Sometimes, however, a downstream resource may need to be recycled to resynchronize it with its peer resources. Secondary events dealing with these resources require corrective action. Since SNMP managers typically discover network topology and understand the relationships between devices, they are often used to implement topology-based correlation.

Timing Considerations

An important consideration in performing event correlation is the timing of the events. It is not always the case that the primary event is received first. Network delays may prevent the primary event from arriving until after the secondary is received. Likewise, in situations where monitoring agents are scheduled to check periodically for certain conditions, the monitor that checks for the secondary problem may run first and produce that event before the root cause condition is checked.

To properly perform event correlation in this scenario, configure the event processor to wait a certain amount of time to ensure that the primary condition does not exist before reporting that action is required for the secondary event. The interval chosen must be long enough to allow the associated events to be received, but short enough to minimize the delay in reporting the problem.

EVENT SYNCHRONIZATION

When events are forwarded through multiple tiers of the event management hierarchy, it is likely that different actions are performed on the event by different event processors.

These actions may include correlating, dropping, or closing events. Problems can arise when one event processor reports that an event is in a certain state and another reports that it is in a different state. For example, assume that the problem reported by an event is resolved, and the event is closed at the central event processor but not at the event processors in the lower tiers in the hierarchy. The problem recurs, and a new event is generated.

The lower-level event processor shows an outstanding event already reporting the condition and discards the event. The new problem is never reported or resolved. To ensure that this situation does not happen, status changes made to events at one event processor can be propagated to the others through which the event has passed. This process is known as event synchronization. Implementing event synchronization can be challenging, particularly in complex environments with several tiers of event processors. Also, environments designed for high availability need some way to synchronize events between their primary and backup event processors.

NOTIFICATION

Notification is the process of informing support personnel that an event has occurred. It is typically used to supplement use of the event processor's primary console, not to replace it. Notification is useful in situations when the assigned person does not have access to the primary console, such after hours, or when software licensing or system resource constraints prevent its use. It can also be helpful in escalating events that are not handled in a timely manner.

Paging, e-mail, and pop-up windows are the most common means of notification. Usually, these functions exist outside the event processor's software and must be implemented using an interface. Sometimes that interface is built into the event processor. Often, the event processor provides the ability to execute scripts or BAT files that can be used to trigger the notification software. This is one of the simplest ways to interface with the notification system. It is difficult to track the various types of notifications listed previously, and the methods are often unreliable. In environments where accountability is important, more robust means may be necessary to ensure that support personnel are informed about events requiring their action.

TROUBLE TICKETING

Problems experienced by users can be tracked using trouble tickets. The tickets can be opened manually by the help desk or operations center in response to a user's phone call or automatically by an event processor. Trouble ticketing is one of the actions that some event processors can take upon receipt of an event. It refers to the process of forwarding the event to a trouble-ticketing system in a format that system can understand. This can typically be implemented by executing a script or sending an e-mail to the trouble-ticketing system's interface or application programming interface. The trouble-ticketing system itself can be considered a special type of event processor. It can open trouble tickets for problem events and close them when their corresponding clearing events are received.

As such, it needs to be synchronized with the other event processors in the event management hierarchy. The actions of opening and closing trouble tickets are also referred to as trouble ticketing. In environments where accountability is important, robust trouble-ticketing systems may provide the tracking functions needed to ensure that problems are resolved by the right people in a timely manner.

ESCALATION

The severity of events based on the receipt of related events. This escalation is handled by the event source, which sends increasingly more critical events as a problem worsens. There are a few kinds of event escalation that require consideration.

Escalation to Ensure Problems are Addressed

An event is useless in managing IT resources if no action is taken to resolve the problem reported. A way to ensure that an event is handled is for an event processor to escalate its severity if it has not been acknowledged or closed within an acceptable time frame. Timers can be set in some event processors to automatically increase the severity of an event if it remains in an unacknowledged state. The higher severity event is generally highlighted in some fashion to draw greater attention to it on the operator console on which it is displayed. The operators viewing the events may inform management that the problem has not been handled, or this notification may be automated.

In addition to serving as a means of ensuring that events are not missed, escalation is useful in situations where the IT department must meet service-level agreements. The timers may be set to values that force escalation of events, indicating to the support staff that the event needs to be handled quickly or SLAs may be violated. For escalation to be implemented, the allowable time frames to respond to events of particular severities and the chain of people to inform when the events are not handled must be clearly defined.

Business Impact Escalation

Events can also be escalated based upon business impact. Problems that affect a larger number of users should be resolved more quickly than those that impact only a few users. Likewise, failures of key business applications should be addressed faster than those of less important applications.

There are several ways to escalate events based upon their business significance:

- *Device type:* An event may be escalated when it is issued for a certain device type. Router failures, for example, may affect large numbers of users because they are critical components in communication paths in the network. A server outage may affect only a handful of users who regularly access it as part of their daily jobs. When deploying this type of escalation, the event processor checks to see the type of device that failed and sets the severity of the event accordingly. In our example, events for router failures may be escalated to a higher severity while events of servers remain unchanged.

- *Device priority:* Some organizations perform asset classifications in which they evaluate the risk to the business of losing various systems. A switch supporting 50 users may be more critical than a switch used by five users. In this escalation type, the event processor checks the risk assigned to the device referenced in an event and increases the severity of those with a higher rating.
- *Other:* It is also possible to perform escalation based on which resources a system fails, assigning different priorities to the various applications and services that run on a machine. Another hybrid approach combines device type and priority to determine event severity. For example, routers may take higher priority than servers. The routers are further categorized by core routers for the backbone network and distributed routers for the user rings, with the core routers receiving heavier weighting in determining event severity. An organization should look at its support structure, network architecture, server functions, and SLAs to determine the best approach to use in handling event escalation.

MAINTENANCE MODE

When administrative functions performed on a system disrupt its normal processing, the system is said to be in maintenance mode. Applying fixes, upgrading software, and reconfiguring system components are all examples of activities that can put a system into maintenance mode. Unless an administrator stops the monitoring agents on the machine, events continue to flow while the system is maintained.

These events may relate to components that are affected by the maintenance or to other system resources. In the former case, the events do not represent real problems, but in the latter case, they may. From an event management point of view, the difficulty is how to handle systems that are in maintenance mode. Often, it is awkward to reconfigure the monitoring agents to temporarily ignore only the resources affected by the maintenance. Shutting down monitoring completely may suppress the detection and reporting of a real problem that has nothing to do with the maintenance. Both of these approaches rely on the intervention of the administrator to stop and restart the monitoring, which may not happen, particularly during late night maintenance windows. Another problem is that maintenance may cause a chain reaction of events generated by other devices.

A server that is in maintenance mode may only affect a few machines with which it has contact during normal operations. A network device may affect large portions of the network when maintained, causing a flood of events to occur. How to predict the effect of the maintenance, and how to handle it are issues that need to be addressed.

AUTOMATION

You can perform four basic types of automated actions upon receipt of an event:

- *Problem verification:* It is not always possible to filter events that are not indicative of real problems. For example, an SNMP manager that queries a device for its status may not receive an answer due to network congestion rather than the failure of the device. In this case, the manager believes the device is down. Further processing is required to determine whether the device is really operational. This processing can be automated.
- *Recovery:* Some failure conditions lend themselves to automated recovery. For example, if a service or process dies, it can generally be restarted using a simple BAT file or script.
- *Diagnostics:* If diagnostic information is typically obtained by the support person to resolve a certain type of problem, that information can be gathered automatically when the failure occurs and merely accessed when needed. This can help to reduce the

mean-time to repair for the problem. It is also particularly useful in cases where the diagnostic data, such as the list of processes running during periods of high CPU usage, may disappear before a support person has time to respond to the event.

- *Repetitive command sequences:* When operators frequently enter the same series of commands, automation can be built to perform those commands. The automated action can be triggered by an event indicating that it is time to run the command sequence. Environments where operators are informed by events to initiate the command sequences, such as starting or shutting down applications, lend themselves well to this type of automation.

Some events traverse different tiers of the event processing hierarchy. In these cases, you must decide at which place to initiate the automation. The capabilities of the tools to perform the necessary automated actions, security required initiating them, and bandwidth constraints are some considerations to remember when deciding from which event processor to launch the automation.

CONTROL AND BUDGETING

CONTROL SYSTEM

A control system is a device or set of devices to manage, command, direct or regulate the behaviour of other devices or systems. There are two common classes of control systems, with many variations and combinations: logic or sequential controls, and feedback or linear controls. There is also fuzzy logic, which attempts to combine some of the design simplicity of logic with the utility of linear control.

Some devices or systems are inherently not controllable. The term "control system" may be applied to the essentially manual controls that allow an operator to, for example, close and open a hydraulic press, where the logic requires that it cannot be moved unless safety guards are in place. An automatic sequential control system may trigger a series of mechanical actuators in the correct sequence to perform a task.

For example various electric and pneumatic transducers may fold and glue a cardboard box, fill it with product and then seal it in an automatic packaging machine. In the case of linear feedback systems, a control loop, including sensors, control algorithms and actuators, is arranged in such a fashion as to try to regulate a variable at a setpoint or reference value. An example of this may increase the fuel supply to a furnace when a measured temperature drops.

PID controllers are common and effective in cases such as this. Control systems that include some sensing of the results they are trying to achieve are making use of feedback and so can, to some extent, adapt to varying circumstances. Open-loop control systems do not directly make use of feedback, but run only in pre-arranged ways. Pure logic control systems were historically implemented by electricians with networks of relays, and designed with a notation called ladder logic. Today, most such systems are constructed with programmable logic devices or microcontrollers.

Logic controllers may respond to switches, light sensors, pressure switches etc and cause the machinery to perform some operation. Logic systems are used to sequence mechanical operations in many applications. Examples include elevators, washing machines and other systems with interrelated stop-go operations. Logic systems are quite easy to design, and can handle very complex operations. Some aspects of logic system design make use of Boolean logic. For example, a thermostat is a simple negative-feedback control: when the temperature goes below a set point, the heater is switched on.

Another example could be a pressure switch on an air compressor: when the pressure drops below the threshold, the pump is powered. Refrigerators and vacuum pumps contain similar mechanisms operating in reverse, but still providing negative feedback to correct errors. Simple on–off feedback control systems like these are cheap and effective. In some cases, like the simple compressor example, they may represent a good design choice. In most applications of on–off feedback control, some consideration needs to be given to other costs, such as wear and tear of control valves and maybe other start-up costs when power is reapplied each time the MV drops. Therefore, practical on–off control systems are designed to include hysteresis, usually in the form of a deadband, a region around the setpoint value in which no control action occurs. The width of deadband may be adjustable or programmable. Linear control systems use linear negative feedback to produce a control signal mathematically based on other variables, with a view to maintaining the controlled process within an acceptable operating range.

The output from a linear control system into the controlled process may be in the form of a directly variable signal, such as a valve that may be 0 or 100% open or anywhere in between. Sometimes this is not feasible and so, after calculating the current required corrective signal, a linear control system may repeatedly switch an actuator, such as a pump, motor or heater, fully on and then fully off again, regulating the duty cycle using pulse-width modulation. When controlling the temperature of an industrial furnace, it is usually better to control the opening of the fuel valve in proportion to the current needs of the furnace. This helps avoid thermal shocks and applies heat more effectively.

Proportional negative-feedback systems are based on the difference between the required set point and measured value of the controlled variable. This difference is called the error. Power is applied in direct proportion to the current measured error, in the correct sense so as to tend to reduce the error. The amount of corrective action that is applied for a given error is set by the gain or sensitivity of the control system. At low gains, only a small corrective action is applied when errors are detected: the system may be safe and stable, but may be sluggish in response to changing conditions; errors will remain uncorrected for relatively long periods of time: it is over-damped.

If the proportional gain is increased, such systems become more responsive and errors are dealt with more quickly. There is an optimal value for the gain setting when the overall system is said to be critically damped. Increases in loop gain beyond this point will lead to oscillations in the MV; such a system is under-damped. In the furnace example, suppose the temperature is increasing towards a set point at which, say, 50% of the available power will be required for steady-state. At low temperatures, 100% of available power is applied. When the MV is within, say 10° of the SP the heat input begins to be reduced by the proportional controller.. At the setpoint the controller will be applying 50% power as required, but stray stored heat within the heater sub-system and in the walls of the furnace will keep the measured temperature rising beyond what is required. At 10° above SP, we reach the top of the proportional band and no power is applied, but the temperature may continue to rise even further before beginning to fall back.

Eventually as the MV falls back into the PB, heat is applied again, but now the heater and the furnace walls are too cool and the temperature falls too low before its fall is arrested, so that the oscillations continue. The temperature oscillations that an under-damped furnace control system produces are unacceptable for many reasons, including the waste of fuel and time, as well as the likelihood of seriously overheating both the furnace and its contents. Suppose that the gain of the control system is reduced drastically and it is restarted. As the temperature approaches, say 30° below SP, the heat input begins to be reduced, the rate of heating of the furnace has time to slow and, as the heat is still further reduced, it eventually is brought up to set point, just as 50% power input is reached and the furnace is operating as required.

There was some wasted time while the furnace crept to its final temperature using only 52% then 51% of available power, but at least no harm was done. By carefully increasing the gain this over-damped and sluggish behaviour can be improved until the system is critically damped for this SP temperature. Doing this is known as 'tuning' the control system. A well-tuned proportional furnace temperature control system will usually be more effective than on-off control, but will still respond slower than the furnace could under skillful manual control. Apart from sluggish performance to avoid oscillations, another problem with proportional-only control is that power application is always in direct proportion to the error. In the example, we assumed that the set temperature could be maintained with 50% power. What happens if the furnace is required in a different application where a higher set temperature will require 80% power to maintain it? If the gain was finally set to a 50° PB, then 80% power will not be applied unless the furnace is 15° below setpoint, so for this other application the operators will have to remember always to set the setpoint temperature 15° higher than actually needed.

This 15° figure is not completely constant either: it will depend on the surrounding ambient temperature, as well as other factors that affect heat loss from or absorption within the furnace. To resolve these two problems, many feedback control schemes include mathematical extensions to improve performance. The most common extensions lead to proportional-integral-derivative control, or PID control. The derivative part is concerned with the rate-of-change of the error with time: If the measured variable approaches the setpoint rapidly, then the actuator is backed off early to allow it to coast to the required level; conversely if the measured value begins to move rapidly away from the setpoint, extra effort is applied—in proportion to that rapidity—to try to maintain it. Derivative action makes a control system behave much more intelligently.

On systems like the temperature of a furnace, or perhaps the motion-control of a heavy item like a gun or camera on a moving vehicle, the derivative action of a well-tuned PID controller can allow it to reach and maintain a setpoint better than most skilled human operators could. If derivative action is over-applied, it can lead to oscillations too. An example would be a MV that increased rapidly towards SP, then halted early and seemed to "shy away" from the setpoint before rising towards it again. The integral term magnifies the effect of long-term steady-state errors, applying ever-increasing effort until they reduce to zero. In the example of the furnace working at various temperatures, if the heat being applied does not bring the furnace up to setpoint, for whatever reason, integral action increasingly moves the proportional band relative to the setpoint until the time-integral of the MV error is reduced to zero and the setpoint is achieved. Another common technique is to filter the MV or error signal. Such a filter can reduce the response of the system to undesirable frequencies, to help eliminate instability or oscillations.

Some feedback systems will oscillate at just one frequency. By filtering out that frequency, one can use very "stiff" feedback and the system can be very responsive without shaking itself apart. The most complex linear control systems developed to date are in oil refineries. The chemical reaction paths and control systems are normally designed together using specialized computer-aided-design software. Feedback systems can be combined in many ways. One example is cascade control in which one control loop applies control algorithms to a measured variable against a setpoint, but then actually outputs a setpoint to another controller, rather than affecting power input directly. Usually if a system has several measurements to be controlled, feedback systems will be present for each of them. Fuzzy logic is an attempt to get the easy design of logic controllers and yet control continuously-varying systems.

Basically, a measurement in a fuzzy logic system can be partly true, that is if yes is 1 and no is 0, a fuzzy measurement can be between 0 and 1. The rules of the system are written in natural language and translated into fuzzy logic. For example, the design for a furnace would start with: "If the temperature is too high, reduce the fuel to the furnace. If the temperature is too low, increase the fuel to the furnace." Measurements from the real world are converted to values between 0 and 1 by seeing where they fall on a triangle. Usually the tip of the triangle is the maximum possible value which translates to "1." The fuzzy calculations make a value between zero and one. That number is used to select a value on a line whose slope and height converts the fuzzy value to a real-world output number. The number then controls real machinery. If the triangles are defined correctly and rules are right the result can be a good control system. When a robust fuzzy design is reduced into a single, quick calculation, it begins to resemble a conventional feedback loop solution and it might appear that the fuzzy design was unnecessary.

However, the fuzzy logic paradigm may provide scalability for large control systems where conventional methods become unwieldy or costly to derive. Fuzzy electronics is an electronic technology that uses fuzzy logic instead of the two-value logic more commonly used in digital electronics. Since modern small microcontrollers are so cheap, it's very common to implement control systems, including feedback loops, with computers, often in an embedded system.

The feedback controls are simulated by having the computer make periodic measurements and then calculating from this stream of measurements. Computers emulate logic devices by making measurements of switch inputs, calculating a logic function from these measurements and then sending the results out to electronically-controlled switches. Logic systems and feedback controllers are usually implemented with programmable logic controllers which are devices available from electrical supply houses. They include a little computer and a simplified system for programming. Most often they are programmed with personal computers. Logic controllers have also been constructed from relays, hydraulic and pneumatic devices, and electronics using both transistors and vacuum tubes.

METHODS OF CONTROL

Quantitative Methods

Quantitative methods use data and various quantitative tools to monitor and control production output. Two common quantitative tools are budgets and audits. By far the most widely recognized quantitative tool is the chart. Charts used as control tools normally contrast time and performance. The visual impact of a chart often provides the quickest method of relating data. A difference in numbers is much more noticeable when displayed graphically. Most charts are versions of either the Gantt chart or the Programme Evaluation and Review Technique .

Budgets

By far the best known control device is the budget. Budgets and control are, in fact, synonymous. An organization's budget is an expression in financial terms of a plan for meeting the organization's goals for a specific period. A budget is an instrument of planning, management, and control. We use budgets in two ways. First, we use them as established facts that must be factored into our operational planning. Second, we use them to prepare narrative descriptions and financial information that our chain of command uses in its annual request and management of its funds. At present, the Department of the Navy uses two major budget systems. These are zero-based budgeting and the planning, programming, and budgeting system.

Audits

Internal auditing provides an independent review and appraisal of accounting, financial, and other nontactical operations. As a management tool, the audit measures and evaluates the effectiveness of management controls. The Naval Audit Service provides an independent audit of programmes, activities, systems, and procedures. It also provides an independent audit of other operations involving the use of funds and resources and the accomplishment of management goals.

Nonquantitative Methods

Nonquantitative methods refer to total or overall control of performance rather than specific processes. These methods use tools such as inspections, reports, direct supervision, and performance evaluation/counseling to accomplish goals.

CONTROL MANAGEMENT

Control is one of the managerial functions like planning, organizing, staffing and directing. It is an important function because it helps to check the errors and to take the corrective action so that deviation from standards are minimized and stated goals of the organization are achieved in desired manner.

A modern concepts, control is a foreseeing action whereas earlier concept of control was used only when errors were detected. Control in management means setting standards, measuring actual performance and taking corrective action. Thus, control comprises these three main activities.

THE ELEMENTS OF CONTROL

The four basic elements in a control system:

1. The characteristic or condition to be controlled,
2. The sensor,
3. The comparator , and
4. The activator – occur in the same sequence and maintain a consistent relationship to each other in every system.

The first element is the characteristic or condition of the operating system which is to be measured. We select a specific characteristic because a correlation exists between it and how the system is performing.

The characteristic may be the output of the system during any stage of processing or it may be a condition that has resulted from the output of the system. For example, it may be the heat energy produced by the furnace or the temperature in the room which has changed because of the heat generated by the furnace. In an elementary school system, the hours a teacher works or the gain in knowledge demonstrated by the students on a national examination are examples of characteristics that may be selected for measurement, or control. The second element of control, the sensor, is a means for measuring the characteristic or condition.

The control subsystem must be designed to include a sensory device or method of measurement. In a home heating system this device would be the thermostat, and in a quality-control system this measurement might be performed by a visual inspection of the product. The third element of control, the comparator, determines the need for correction by comparing what is occurring with what has been planned. Some deviation from plan is usual and expected, but when variations are beyond those considered acceptable, corrective action is required.

It is often possible to identify trends in performance and to take action before an unacceptable variation from the norm occurs. This sort of preventative action indicates that good control is being achieved. The fourth element of control, the activator, is the corrective action taken to return the system to expected output.

The actual person, device, or method used to direct corrective inputs into the operating system may take a variety of forms. It may be a hydraulic controller positioned by a solenoid or electric motor in response to an electronic error signal, an employee directed to rework the parts that failed to pass quality inspection, or a school principal who decides to buy additional books to provide for an increased number of students.

As long as a plan is performed within allowable limits, corrective action is not necessary; this seldom occurs in practice, however. Information is the medium of control, because the flow of sensory data and later the flow of corrective information allow a characteristic or condition of the system to be controlled. To illustrate how information flow facilitates control, let us review the elements of control in the context of information.

PROCESS OF CONTROLLING

- Setting performance standards.
- Measurement of actual performance.
- Comparing actual performance with standards.
- Analysing deviations.
- Correcting deviations.

TYPES OF CONTROL

Control may be grouped just as to three general classifications:

- The nature of the information flow designed into the

system,

- The kind of components included in the design, and
- The relationship of control to the decision process.

Open- and Closed-Loop Control

A street-lighting system controlled by a timing device is an example of an open-loop system. At a certain time each evening, a mechanical device closes the circuit and energy flows through the electric lines to light the lamps. Note, however, that the timing mechanism is an independent unit and is not measuring the objective function of the lighting system.

If the lights should be needed on a dark, stormy day the timing device would not recognize this need and therefore would not activate energy inputs. Corrective properties may sometimes be built into the controller but this would not close the loop. In another instance, the sensing, comparison, or adjustment may be made through action taken by an individual who is not part of the system. For example, the lights may be turned on by someone who happens to pass by and recognizes the need for additional light. If control is exercised as a result of the operation rather than because of outside or predetermined arrangements, it is a closed-loop system. The home thermostat is the classic example of a control device in a closed-loop system.

When the room temperature drops below the desired point, the control mechanism closes the circuit to start the furnace and the temperature rises. The furnace-activating circuit is turned off as the temperature reaches the preselected level. The significant difference between this type of system and an open-loop system is that the control device is an element of the system it serves and measures the performance of the system. In other words, all four control elements are integral to the specific system.

An essential part of a closed-loop system is feedback; that is, the output of the system is measured continually through the item controlled, and the input is modified to reduce any difference or error towards zero. Many of the patterns of information flow in organizations are found to have the nature of closed loops, which use feedback. The reason for such a condition is apparent when one recognizes that any system, if it is to achieve a predetermined goal, must have available to it at all times an indication of its degree of attainment. In general, every goal-seeking system employs feedback.

Man and Machine Control

The elements of control are easy to identify in machine systems. For example, the characteristic to be controlled might be some variable like speed or temperature, and the sensing device could be a speedometer or a thermometer. An expectation of precision exists because the characteristic is quantifiable and the standard and the normal variation to be expected can be described in exact terms.

In automatic machine systems, inputs of information are used in a process of continual adjustment to achieve output specifications. When even a small variation from the standard occurs, the correction process begins. The automatic system is highly structured, designed to accept certain kinds of input and produce specific output, and programmed to regulate the transformation of inputs within a narrow range of variation. For an illustration of mechanical control, as the load on a steam engine increases and the engine starts to slow down, the regulator reacts by opening a valve that releases additional inputs of steam energy. This new input returns the engine to the desired number of revolutions per minute.

This type of mechanical control is crude in comparison to the more sophisticated electronic control systems in everyday use. Consider the complex missile-guidance systems that measure the actual course just as to predetermined mathematical calculations and make almost instantaneous corrections to direct the missile to its target. Machine systems can be complex because of the sophisticated technology, whereas control of people is complex because the elements of control are difficult to determine.

In human control systems, the relationship between objectives and associated characteristics is often vague; the measurement of the characteristic may be extremely subjective; the expected standard is difficult to define; and the amount of new inputs required is impossible to quantify. To illustrate, let us refer once more to a formalized social system in which deviant behaviour is controlled through a process of observed violation of the existing law, court hearings and trials, incarceration when the accused is found guilty, and release from custody after rehabilitation of the prisoner has occurred. The speed limit established for freeway driving is one standard of performance that is quantifiable, but even in this instance, the degree of permissible variation and the amount of the actual variation are often a subject of disagreement between the patrolman and the suspected violator.

The complexity of our society is reflected in many of our laws and regulations, which establish the general standards for economic, political, and social operations. A citizen may not know or understand the law and consequently would not know whether or not he was guilty of a violation. Most organized systems are some combination of man and machine; some elements of control may be performed by machine whereas others are accomplished by man. In addition, some standards may be precisely structured whereas others may be little more than general guidelines with wide variations expected in output.

Man must act as the controller when measurement is subjective and judgment is required. Machines such as computers are incapable of making exceptions from the specified control criteria regardless of how much a particular case might warrant special consideration. A pilot acts in conjunction with computers and automatic pilots to fly large jets. In the event of unexpected weather changes, or possible collision with another plane, he must intercede and assume direct control.

COMPARISON BETWEEN ORGANIZATIONAL AND OPERATIONAL CONTROL

The concept of organizational control is implicit in the bureaucratic theory of Max Weber. Associated with this theory are such concepts as "span of control", "closeness of supervision", and "hierarchical authority". Weber's view tends to include all levels or types of organizational control as being the same. More recently, writers have tended to differentiate the control process between that which emphasizes the nature of the organizational or systems design and that which deals with daily operations. To illustrate the difference, we "evaluate" the performance of a system to see how effective and efficient the design proved to be or to discover why it failed. In contrast, we operate and "control" the system with respect to the daily inputs of material, information, and energy.

In both instances, the elements of feedback are present, but organizational control tends to review and evaluate the nature and arrangement of components in the system, whereas operational control tends to adjust the daily inputs. The direction for organizational control comes from the goals and strategic plans of the organization. General plans are translated into specific performance measures such as share of the market, earnings, return on investment, and budgets. The process of organizational control is to review and evaluate the performance of the system against these established norms. Rewards for meeting or exceeding standards may range from special recognition to salary increases or promotions. On the other hand, a failure to meet expectations may signal the need to reorganize or redesign. In organizational control, the approach used in the programme of review and evaluation depends on the reason for the evaluation — that is, is it because the system is not effective?

Is the system failing to achieve an expected standard of efficiency? Is the evaluation being conducted because of a breakdown or failure in operations? Is it merely a periodic audit-and-review process? When a system has failed or is in great difficulty, special diagnostic techniques may be required to isolate the trouble areas and to identify the causes of the difficulty. It is appropriate to investigate areas that have been troublesome before or areas where some measure of performance can be quickly identified. For example, if an organization's output backlog builds rapidly, it is logical to check first to see if the problem is due to such readily obtainable measures as increased demand or to a drop in available man hours. When a more detailed analysis is necessary, a systematic procedure should be followed. In contrast to organizational control, operational control serves to regulate the day-to-day output relative to schedules, specifications, and costs. Is the output of product or service the proper quality and is it available as scheduled? Are inventories of raw materials, goods-in-process, and finished products being purchased and produced in the desired quantities?

Are the costs associated with the transformation process in line with cost estimates? Is the information needed in the transformation process available in the right form and at the right time? Is the energy resource being utilized efficiently? The most difficult task of management concerns monitoring the behaviour of individuals, comparing performance to some standard, and providing rewards or punishment as indicated. Sometimes this control over people relates entirely to their output. For example, a manager might not be concerned with the behaviour of a salesman as long as sales were as high as expected. In other instances, close supervision of the salesman might be appropriate if achieving customer satisfaction were one of the sales organization's main objectives. The larger the unit, the more likely that the control characteristic will be related to some output goal.

It also follows that if it is difficult or impossible to identify the actual output of individuals, it is better to measure the performance of the entire group. This means that individuals' levels of motivation and the measurement of their performance become subjective judgments made by the supervisor. Controlling output also suggests the difficulty of controlling individuals' performance and relating this to the total system's objectives.

DIFFICULTIES OF CONTROL

The perfect plan could be outlined if every possible variation of input could be anticipated and if the system would operate as predicted. This kind of planning is neither realistic, economical, nor feasible for most business systems. If it were feasible, planning requirements would be so complex that the system would be out of date before it could be operated. Therefore, we design control into systems. This requires more thought in the systems design but allows more flexibility of operations and makes it possible to operate a system using unpredictable components and undetermined input. Still, the design and effective operation of control are not without problems.

The objective of the system is to perform some specified function. The purpose of organizational control is to see that the specified function is achieved; the objective of operational control is to ensure that variations in daily output are maintained within prescribed limits. It is one thing to design a system that contains all of the elements of control, and quite another to make it operate true to the best objectives of design. Operating "in control" or "with plan" does not guarantee optimum performance. For example, the plan may not make the best use of the inputs of materials, energy, or information — in other words, the system may not be designed to operate efficiently. Some of the more typical problems relating to control include the difficulty of measurement, the problem of timing information flow, and the setting of proper standards.

Measurement of Output

When objectives are not limited to quantitative output, the measurement of system effectiveness is difficult to make and subsequently perplexing to evaluate. Many of the characteristics pertaining to output do not lend themselves to quantitative measurement. This is true particularly when inputs of human energy cannot be related directly to output. The same situation applies to machines and other equipment associated with human involvement, when output is not in specific units. In evaluating man-machine or human-oriented systems, psychological and sociological factors obviously do not easily translate into quantifiable terms. For example, how does mental fatigue affect the quality or quantity of output?

And, if it does, is mental fatigue a function of the lack of a challenging assignment or the fear of a potential injury? Subjective inputs may be transferred into numerical data, but there is always the danger of an incorrect appraisal and transfer, and the danger that the analyst may assume undue confidence in such data after they have been quantified. Let us suppose, for example, that the decisions made by an executive are rated from 1 to 10, 10 being the perfect decision. After determining the ranking for each decision, adding these, and dividing by the total number of decisions made, the average ranking would indicate a particular executive's score in his decision-making role.

On the basis of this score, judgments — which could be quite erroneous — might be made about his decision-making effectiveness. One executive with a ranking of 6.75 might be considered more effective than another who had a ranking of 6.25, and yet the two managers may have made decisions under different circumstances and conditions. External factors over which neither executive had any control may have influenced the difference in "effectiveness". Quantifying human behaviour, despite its extreme difficulty, subjectivity, and imprecision in relation to measuring physical characteristics is the most prevalent and important measurement made in large systems. The behaviour of individuals ultimately dictates the success or failure of every man-made system.

Information Flow

Another problem of control relates to the improper timing of information introduced into the feedback channel. Improper timing can occur in both computerized and human control systems, either by mistakes in measurement or in judgment. The more rapid the system's response to an error signal, the more likely it is that the system could overadjust; yet the need for prompt action is important because any delay in providing corrective input could also be crucial. A system generating feedback inconsistent with current need will tend to fluctuate and will not adjust in the desired manner. The most serious problem in information flow arises when the delay in feedback is exactly one-half cycle, for then the corrective action is superimposed on a variation from norm which, at that moment, is in the same direction as that of the correction. This causes the system to overcorrect, and then if the reverse adjustment is made out of cycle, to correct too much in the other direction, and so on until the system fluctuates out of control. If, at Point A, the trend below standard is recognized and new inputs are added, but not until Point B, the system will overreact and go beyond the allowable limits. Again, if this is recognized at Point C, but inputs are not withdrawn until Point D, it will cause the system to drop below the lower limit of allowable variation.

One solution to this problem rests in anticipation, which involves measuring not only the change but also the rate of change. The correction is outlined as a factor of the type and rate of the error. The difficulty also might be overcome by reducing the time lag between the measurement of the output and the adjustment to input. If a trend can be indicated, a time lead can be introduced to compensate for the time lag, bringing about consistency between the need for correction and the type and magnitude of the indicated action. It is usually more effective for an organization to maintain continuous measurement of its performance and to make small adjustments in operations constantly.

MIS REPORTING

Reports form an integral part of any organization. Each employee maintains a report of the tasks that have been conducted during the course of the day or the week. This helps discern the productivity of an employee, of a department and the organization as a whole. Reports are dominant base that help in taking some critical decisions about the progress in the future. However, things become a puzzled maze if reports are not properly named and stored and are inaccessible when required. With Management Information System or MIS Reporting, we provide you with a centralized report management application to save all the required repots in a common place. Our team will analyse and understand the reporting needs of the professionals in your organization. Spreadsheets are created accordingly encompassing all the required details. The format is created in such an easy to use format to help inculcate the habit of everyday reporting. If all the reports in your organization are managed well, it can help you with TIBCO decisions. Furthermore, with globalization, most of the companies are providing services round the clock. It is not always that people from both the shifts are able to meet and discuss their progress. It is however essential to know the details of the task done by the person in the previous shift for you to carry on further with the tasks of the day to avoid replication. This is where MIS Reporting is helpful. Binary's MIS Reporting services will help you centralize the report system removing the haze and creating clarity. Being in the industry for so may years have helped us understand various industries and their requirements. We aim to help you make your business and processes more efficient and effective by avoiding unwanted problems.

BUDGET

A budget is generally a list of all planned expenses and revenues. It is a plan for saving and spending. A budget is an important concept in microeconomics, which uses a budget line to illustrate the trade-offs between two or more goods. In other terms, a budget is an organizational plan stated in monetary terms.

In summary, the purpose of budgeting is to:

1. Provide a forecast of revenues and expenditures *i.e.* construct a model of how our business might perform financially speaking if certain strategies, events and plans are carried out.
2. Enable the actual financial operation of the business to be measured against the forecast.

Event Management Budget

A budget is a fundamental tool for an event director to predict with reasonable accuracy whether the event will result in a profit, a loss or will break-even. A budget can also be used as a pricing tool.

Business Start-up Budget

The process of calculating the costs of starting a small business begins with a list of all necessary purchases including tangible assets and services, working capital, sources and collateral. The budget should contain a narrative explaining how you decided on the amount of this reserve and a description of the expected financial results of business activities. The assets should be valued with each and every cost. All other expenses are like labour factory overhead all freshmen expenses are also included into business budgeting

Corporate Budget

The budget of a company is often compiled annually, but may not be. A finished budget, usually requiring considerable effort, is a plan for the short-term future, typically one year. While traditionally the Finance department compiles the company's budget, modern software allows hundreds or even thousands of people in various departments to list their expected revenues and expenses in the final budget.

If the actual figures delivered through the budget period come close to the budget, this suggests that the managers understand their business and have been successfully driving it in the intended direction. On the other hand, if the figures diverge wildly from the budget, this sends an 'out of control' signal, and the share price could suffer as a result.

Bibliography

Alan, A.: *Tourism in China,* New Delhi: Manas Publications, 2004.

Ankomah, P.: *Education Tourism: A Strategy to Sustainable Tourism Development,* Philippines: Oxford University Press, 2006.

Charles, K.: *Progress in Tourism and Hospitality,* New Delhi: Oxford University Press, 2001.

Colin, Michael: *The Geography of Tourism and Recreation: Environment, Place, and Space,* Guwahati: United Publishers, 1998.

Jafari, Jafar: *Encyclopedia of Tourism,* Guwahati: United Publishers, 1998.

Jafari, Javed.: *Towards a Framework for Tourism Education,* Princeton: Princeton University Press, 1998.

John, C.: *Global Alliances in Tourism and Hospitality Management,* New York: Prentice Hall, 2007.

Kasper, C.: *Tourism Marketing and Management Handbook,* New York: Prentice Hall, 1997.

Ketyer, E.: *Tourism Education in Formal Education,* New Delhi: Oxford University Press, 1998.

Lavery, P.: *Tourism Marketing and Management Handbook,* New York, Prentice Hall, 2002.

Moscardo, G.: *The Journal of Tourism Studies,* New Delhi: Penguin Books, 2000.

Payne, K.: *Tourism and Hospitality Research,* Guwahati: United Publishers, 1998.

Picard, Michel: *Tourism, Ethnicity, and The State in Asian and Pacific Societies,* New York: Prentice Hall, 1997.

Tao, H.: *The Development and Construction of Tourism Personnel*, London: Yale University Press, 2003.

Tarun, Nikunj: *Tourism Administration*, New Delhi: Manas Publications, 2004.

Tribe, J.: *The Tourism Curriculum*, London: Yale University Press, 1998.

Vroom, J. A.: *Tourism Education: A Model Program*, New Delhi: Manas Publications, 2004.

Vukonic, B.: *Tourism as a Field of Research*, New Delhi: Oxford University Press, 2005.

Walsh, M. E.: *Tourism Management*, New Delhi: Government of India Press, 2007.

Watson, J.: *Developing Tourism Managers*, New Delhi: Government of India Press, 2005.

Index